Sitti Djalia Turabin

LGBTQ Activism in the Philippines – Unauthorized

Malik Dos Santos

ISBN: 9781779696052
Imprint: Telephasic Workshop
Copyright © 2024 Malik Dos Santos.
All Rights Reserved.

Contents

The Stonewall Riots: A Turning Point in LGBTQ Activism

The Stonewall Riots, which erupted in the early hours of June 28, 1969, at the Stonewall Inn in New York City, marked a watershed moment in the history of LGBTQ activism. This event is widely regarded as the catalyst for the modern LGBTQ rights movement, igniting a fierce push for equality and justice that reverberated not only across the United States but also around the globe. The riots were not merely a reaction to a specific police raid; they represented the culmination of years of systemic oppression, discrimination, and violence faced by LGBTQ individuals.

1.1.1 Background of the Riots

To fully understand the significance of the Stonewall Riots, it is essential to explore the socio-political climate of the time. During the 1960s, homosexuality was classified as a mental illness, and LGBTQ individuals were subjected to criminalization and stigmatization. Police raids on gay bars were common, and patrons were often arrested for minor infractions, such as failing to adhere to gender norms in their clothing.

The Stonewall Inn, a popular gathering place for the LGBTQ community, was one of the few establishments that welcomed gay patrons. However, on that fateful night in June, the New York City Police Department (NYPD) conducted a raid on the bar, leading to an unexpected uprising. The patrons, fueled by years of pent-up frustration and anger, fought back against the police, marking the beginning of a series of protests that lasted for several days.

1.1.2 The Role of Marsha P. Johnson and Sylvia Rivera

Two key figures emerged from the chaos of the Stonewall Riots: Marsha P. Johnson and Sylvia Rivera. Johnson, a Black transgender activist, and Rivera, a Venezuelan-American transgender activist, played crucial roles in the riots and the subsequent movement. Their bravery and leadership not only helped to galvanize the crowd but also highlighted the intersectionality of race, gender, and sexuality within the LGBTQ struggle.

Johnson famously declared, "I got my civil rights," as she led the charge against the police. Rivera, who faced her own struggles as a transgender woman, emphasized the importance of including the voices of marginalized groups within the LGBTQ community. Their activism underscored the necessity of intersectionality in the fight for LGBTQ rights, a principle that continues to resonate today.

1.1.3 Impact on LGBTQ Activism in the Philippines

The Stonewall Riots had a profound impact on LGBTQ activism worldwide, including in the Philippines. The events at Stonewall inspired Filipino activists to mobilize and organize, leading to the formation of various LGBTQ organizations in the years that followed. The influence of global LGBTQ movements, particularly the visibility gained from the Stonewall Riots, provided Filipino activists with a framework for advocating for their rights within a local context.

In the Philippines, where colonial legacies and cultural attitudes often marginalized LGBTQ individuals, the Stonewall Riots served as a beacon of hope. Activists began to draw parallels between their struggles and those faced by LGBTQ individuals in the United States, fostering a sense of solidarity and shared purpose. This newfound inspiration led to the establishment of Pride events and advocacy campaigns aimed at combating discrimination and promoting equality.

1.1.4 Other Historical Moments in LGBTQ Activism

The Stonewall Riots were not an isolated event; they were part of a broader tapestry of LGBTQ activism that included significant historical moments. Prior to Stonewall, events such as the Mattachine Society's formation in 1950 and the Daughters of Bilitis' establishment in 1955 laid the groundwork for organized LGBTQ advocacy. These organizations focused on education, legal reform, and community support, paving the way for the activism that would surge following the riots.

In the decades following Stonewall, LGBTQ activists continued to build upon the momentum generated by the riots. The first Pride marches, held in New York City in 1970 to commemorate the anniversary of Stonewall, became an annual tradition and a symbol of resistance. The impact of Stonewall can also be seen in the establishment of various LGBTQ rights organizations, the push for legal reforms, and the growing visibility of LGBTQ individuals in media and politics.

In conclusion, the Stonewall Riots were not just a pivotal moment in LGBTQ history; they were a turning point that transformed the landscape of activism. The legacy of Stonewall continues to inspire generations of activists, reminding us that the fight for equality is ongoing and that every voice matters in the struggle for justice.

The Stonewall Riots: A Turning Point in LGBTQ Activism

The Stonewall Riots, which erupted in the early hours of June 28, 1969, at the Stonewall Inn in New York City, are widely regarded as a pivotal moment in the history of LGBTQ activism. This uprising against police brutality and systemic discrimination marked the beginning of a new era in the fight for LGBTQ rights, transforming the landscape of activism and community organizing.

1.1.1 Background of the Riots

To understand the significance of the Stonewall Riots, it is essential to consider the socio-political climate of the 1960s. During this period, homosexuality was criminalized in many states, and LGBTQ individuals faced widespread discrimination, stigma, and violence. The police regularly raided gay bars, arresting patrons for public indecency, and enforcing societal norms that marginalized sexual and gender minorities.

The Stonewall Inn, a gay bar located in Greenwich Village, served as a sanctuary for the LGBTQ community. However, on that fateful night, police raided the establishment, leading to a confrontation between law enforcement and patrons. The initial resistance by the bar's patrons quickly escalated into a full-blown riot, with community members fighting back against the police, sparking several nights of protests and demonstrations.

1.1.2 The Role of Marsha P. Johnson and Sylvia Rivera

Among the iconic figures of the Stonewall Riots were Marsha P. Johnson and Sylvia Rivera, two trans women of color whose involvement in the uprising exemplified the intersectionality of the LGBTQ movement. Johnson, a Black transgender activist, famously declared, "I got my civil rights," as she threw a brick during the riots. Rivera, a Latina transgender activist, played a crucial role in mobilizing the community and advocating for the rights of marginalized groups within the LGBTQ spectrum.

Their contributions highlight the importance of recognizing diverse voices within the movement, as the struggles of trans women of color often intersect with broader issues of race, gender, and sexuality. Johnson and Rivera later co-founded the Street Transvestite Action Revolutionaries (STAR), which provided support and advocacy for homeless transgender and gender-nonconforming individuals.

1.1.3 Impact on LGBTQ Activism in the Philippines

The reverberations of the Stonewall Riots extended far beyond the borders of the United States, influencing LGBTQ activism globally, including in the Philippines. The emergence of Pride marches, advocacy organizations, and a more organized movement for LGBTQ rights can be traced back to the spirit of resistance ignited by Stonewall.

In the Philippines, the first Pride March took place in 1994, drawing inspiration from the Stonewall legacy. Activists began to organize around issues such as anti-discrimination laws, same-sex marriage, and LGBTQ visibility. The riots served as a catalyst for Filipino activists to assert their rights and demand equality, fostering a sense of solidarity and community among LGBTQ individuals.

1.1.4 Other Historical Moments in LGBTQ Activism

While the Stonewall Riots are often cited as the catalyst for the modern LGBTQ rights movement, they were not an isolated event. The riots were part of a broader historical context that included earlier efforts for LGBTQ rights, such as the Mattachine Society and the Daughters of Bilitis, which laid the groundwork for activism. These organizations focused on education, social acceptance, and legal reform, setting the stage for the explosive growth of the movement in the years following Stonewall.

Moreover, the AIDS crisis of the 1980s further galvanized the LGBTQ community, leading to the formation of organizations like ACT UP (AIDS Coalition to Unleash Power), which demanded government action and healthcare access for those affected by the epidemic. This period of activism was marked by a sense of urgency and the necessity for intersectional approaches to advocacy, recognizing the diverse experiences within the LGBTQ community.

1.1.5 Conclusion

In conclusion, the Stonewall Riots represented a turning point in LGBTQ activism, igniting a movement that transcended borders and cultures. The bravery of individuals like Marsha P. Johnson and Sylvia Rivera, combined with the collective resistance of the LGBTQ community, forged a path toward greater visibility, acceptance, and rights. As the Philippines and other nations continue to grapple with issues of equality and justice, the legacy of Stonewall serves as a powerful reminder of the ongoing struggle for LGBTQ rights and the importance of solidarity within the movement.

$$\text{Impact of Stonewall} = \text{Increased Activism} + \text{Community Solidarity} + \text{Global Influence} \tag{1}$$

ERROR. thisXsection() returned an empty string with textbook depth = 3.
ERROR. thisXsection() returned an empty string with textbook depth = 3.
ERROR. thisXsection() returned an empty string with textbook depth = 3.

The Role of Marsha P. Johnson and Sylvia Rivera

Marsha P. Johnson and Sylvia Rivera were pivotal figures in the LGBTQ rights movement, particularly during the tumultuous period surrounding the Stonewall Riots of 1969. As trans women of color, they faced not only the challenges of societal discrimination but also the intersectional struggles of race, gender identity, and sexual orientation. Their activism laid the groundwork for future movements and highlighted the need for inclusivity within the LGBTQ community.

Background and Early Activism

Marsha P. Johnson, born in 1945 in New Jersey, was a Black transgender woman who became a prominent figure in the Stonewall Riots. Johnson's activism began in the early 1960s when she moved to New York City. She was known for her vibrant personality and her commitment to advocating for marginalized communities. Alongside her, Sylvia Rivera, a Venezuelan-American transgender activist born in 1951, emerged as a powerful voice for the rights of trans individuals and LGBTQ people, particularly those from impoverished backgrounds.

The Stonewall Riots

The Stonewall Riots, which took place in June 1969, were a response to a police raid at the Stonewall Inn, a gay bar in Greenwich Village. This event marked a significant turning point in LGBTQ activism, sparking a series of protests and the formation of various advocacy groups. Johnson and Rivera were among the first to resist police brutality during the raid, with Johnson famously declaring, "I got my black cat in the fight." Their bravery during this pivotal moment galvanized the LGBTQ community and brought visibility to the struggles faced by trans individuals.

Founding of Street Transvestite Action Revolutionaries (STAR)

In 1970, Johnson and Rivera co-founded the Street Transvestite Action Revolutionaries (STAR), an organization dedicated to supporting homeless transgender and gender non-conforming individuals. STAR provided shelter, food, and advocacy for those who were often overlooked by mainstream LGBTQ organizations. This initiative underscored the importance of intersectionality in activism, as both women recognized the unique challenges faced by trans people, particularly those of color and those living in poverty.

Advocacy for Trans Rights

Johnson and Rivera's activism extended beyond the confines of the Stonewall Riots. They were vocal advocates for trans rights at a time when the broader LGBTQ movement often marginalized trans individuals. Their efforts included organizing rallies, speaking out against discrimination, and pushing for legislative changes that would protect the rights of transgender people. They emphasized that the fight for LGBTQ rights must include all identities, not just those that fit within the traditional binary framework.

Legacy and Impact on LGBTQ Activism

The contributions of Marsha P. Johnson and Sylvia Rivera continue to resonate within the LGBTQ community. Their work laid the foundation for future generations of activists who strive for equality and justice. Johnson's tragic death in 1992 and Rivera's passing in 2002 highlighted the ongoing violence faced by trans individuals, particularly those of color. In recent years, their legacies have been honored through various memorials, documentaries, and initiatives aimed at elevating the voices of marginalized communities within the LGBTQ movement.

Conclusion

In conclusion, Marsha P. Johnson and Sylvia Rivera were not only key figures in the Stonewall Riots but also foundational leaders in the ongoing struggle for LGBTQ rights. Their commitment to inclusivity and their relentless fight against discrimination serve as a reminder that true activism must address the diverse needs of all individuals within the community. As we reflect on their contributions, it is crucial to recognize the importance of intersectionality in activism and the need for continued advocacy for the rights of trans individuals and other marginalized groups.

$$\text{Activism}_{\text{inclusive}} = \sum_{\text{identities}} \text{Rights}_{\text{individuals}} \tag{2}$$

This equation symbolizes the necessity of including all identities in the fight for rights, echoing the principles championed by Johnson and Rivera.

Impact on LGBTQ Activism in the Philippines

The Stonewall Riots, which took place in June 1969, are often heralded as a pivotal moment in the global LGBTQ rights movement. The events at the Stonewall Inn in

New York City not only galvanized activists in the United States but also sent ripples across the globe, including the Philippines. The impact of these riots on LGBTQ activism in the Philippines can be analyzed through various lenses, including the mobilization of community organizations, the emergence of pride events, and the influence on local advocacy strategies.

Mobilization of Community Organizations

In the aftermath of the Stonewall Riots, LGBTQ individuals worldwide began to organize more effectively. In the Philippines, the late 20th century saw the emergence of several LGBTQ organizations that sought to address issues of discrimination, violence, and social stigma. The first significant organization, *The Society of Transsexual Women of the Philippines* (STRAP), was founded in 2003, inspired by the global LGBTQ movement's call for rights and recognition. This organization, along with others, aimed to provide a support network for transgender individuals and advocate for their rights.

The activism inspired by Stonewall led to the establishment of the *Pinoy LGBT* organization, which served as a platform for addressing the unique challenges faced by LGBTQ Filipinos. These organizations were crucial in mobilizing individuals to participate in advocacy efforts, such as lobbying for anti-discrimination laws and raising awareness about LGBTQ issues in the Philippines.

Emergence of Pride Events

The influence of the Stonewall Riots also manifested in the celebration of pride events in the Philippines. The first Pride March in Manila took place in 1994, commemorating the spirit of resistance and solidarity seen during the Stonewall Riots. This annual event has grown exponentially, attracting thousands of participants from diverse backgrounds, and serves as a powerful symbol of the LGBTQ community's resilience and demand for equality.

Pride events in the Philippines are not just celebrations; they are also platforms for political expression. They highlight the ongoing struggles for rights, such as the passage of the Anti-Discrimination Bill, which aims to protect LGBTQ individuals from discrimination in various sectors, including employment, education, and healthcare. The visibility generated by these events has been instrumental in fostering a sense of community and solidarity among LGBTQ individuals, while also educating the broader public about LGBTQ issues.

Influence on Local Advocacy Strategies

The legacy of the Stonewall Riots has influenced the strategies employed by LGBTQ activists in the Philippines. Inspired by the direct action tactics used during the riots, Filipino activists have adopted similar approaches to draw attention to their cause. For example, protests against discriminatory policies and practices have become more common, with activists employing creative forms of expression, such as art, performance, and social media campaigns, to amplify their message.

Moreover, the concept of intersectionality has gained traction within Filipino LGBTQ activism, emphasizing the importance of understanding how various forms of discrimination—such as those based on gender, class, and ethnicity—interact with sexual orientation and gender identity. This broader approach has allowed activists to create more inclusive spaces and address the diverse needs of the LGBTQ community, particularly marginalized groups such as transgender individuals and LGBTQ people of color.

Challenges and Ongoing Struggles

Despite the progress made since the Stonewall Riots, LGBTQ activists in the Philippines continue to face significant challenges. The deeply rooted cultural and religious conservatism in the country often leads to resistance against LGBTQ rights. Activists encounter threats of violence, harassment, and discrimination, which can hinder their ability to organize and advocate effectively.

Moreover, the lack of comprehensive legal protections for LGBTQ individuals poses a significant barrier to achieving equality. While there have been some advancements, such as local ordinances prohibiting discrimination in certain cities, the national government has yet to pass a comprehensive anti-discrimination law. This ongoing struggle for legal recognition and protection highlights the need for continued advocacy and mobilization within the LGBTQ community.

Conclusion

The impact of the Stonewall Riots on LGBTQ activism in the Philippines is profound and multifaceted. From the mobilization of community organizations and the emergence of pride events to the evolution of local advocacy strategies, the legacy of Stonewall continues to inspire and empower Filipino activists. However, the journey toward equality is far from over, as challenges persist. The spirit of resistance and the call for justice that ignited during the Stonewall Riots remain relevant, driving the ongoing fight for LGBTQ rights in the Philippines today.

Other Historical Moments in LGBTQ Activism

LGBTQ activism has a rich history marked by significant events that have shaped the movement and influenced societal attitudes toward sexual orientation and gender identity. This section highlights key historical moments that, while perhaps less well-known than the Stonewall Riots, have played a crucial role in the evolution of LGBTQ rights and activism globally and in the Philippines.

The Formation of the Mattachine Society (1950)

One of the earliest LGBTQ rights organizations in the United States, the Mattachine Society, was founded in 1950 by Harry Hay and a group of gay activists in Los Angeles. This organization aimed to promote unity among gay men and challenge the societal stigma surrounding homosexuality. The Mattachine Society utilized a strategy of education and advocacy, emphasizing the need for acceptance and understanding. Their work laid the groundwork for future LGBTQ organizations and provided a model for collective action.

The Establishment of the Gay Liberation Front (1969)

Following the Stonewall Riots, the Gay Liberation Front (GLF) emerged as a radical group advocating for LGBTQ rights. Formed in New York City in 1969, the GLF sought to dismantle the societal and institutional structures that perpetuated discrimination against LGBTQ individuals. The GLF's activism was characterized by direct action, protests, and a focus on intersectionality, recognizing the interconnectedness of various social justice issues. Their slogan, "Gay is Good," encapsulated a newfound pride and determination among LGBTQ individuals to fight for their rights.

The AIDS Crisis and Activism (1980s-1990s)

The emergence of the AIDS epidemic in the 1980s profoundly impacted the LGBTQ community and catalyzed a new wave of activism. Organizations such as ACT UP (AIDS Coalition to Unleash Power) were established to demand government action, healthcare access, and research funding for AIDS treatment. The slogan "Silence = Death" became a rallying cry for activists, highlighting the urgent need for awareness and action. This period also saw the rise of LGBTQ leaders like Larry Kramer, who advocated fiercely for the rights of those affected by the epidemic, emphasizing the importance of community solidarity.

The First Pride March (1970)

In 1970, the first Pride marches took place in New York City, commemorating the one-year anniversary of the Stonewall Riots. This event marked a significant shift in LGBTQ visibility and activism, as thousands took to the streets to demand equality and celebrate their identities. Pride marches quickly spread to other cities and countries, evolving into an annual celebration of LGBTQ culture and rights. The significance of Pride lies not only in its celebration of diversity but also in its role as a platform for activism, raising awareness of ongoing struggles faced by the LGBTQ community.

The Philippines: The First LGBTQ Pride March (1994)

In the Philippines, the first LGBTQ Pride March took place in 1994 in Quezon City, organized by the group ProGay (Promotion of Gays' Rights Advocates). This event marked a pivotal moment in Filipino LGBTQ activism, as it provided a space for individuals to express their identities and advocate for their rights publicly. The march was met with both support and opposition, reflecting the complex landscape of LGBTQ rights in the country. Since then, Pride events have grown in size and visibility, becoming a crucial aspect of LGBTQ activism in the Philippines.

The Decriminalization of Homosexuality in Various Countries

Throughout the late 20th and early 21st centuries, numerous countries have taken significant steps toward decriminalizing homosexuality. For instance, in 2003, the United States Supreme Court's decision in *Lawrence v. Texas* invalidated sodomy laws, affirming the rights of LGBTQ individuals to engage in consensual sexual activity. Similarly, India's Supreme Court decriminalized homosexuality in 2018, a landmark decision that was celebrated by activists and allies worldwide. These legal victories represent not only a shift in policy but also a broader societal acceptance of LGBTQ individuals.

The Fight for Marriage Equality

The quest for marriage equality has been a defining issue in LGBTQ activism. In 2015, the U.S. Supreme Court's ruling in *Obergefell v. Hodges* legalized same-sex marriage nationwide, marking a historic victory for LGBTQ rights. This decision was the culmination of decades of advocacy, legal battles, and grassroots organizing. The fight for marriage equality has inspired similar movements in other countries, leading to the legalization of same-sex marriage in various nations, including Canada, the Netherlands, and Argentina. However, the struggle for equality continues, as many countries still deny LGBTQ individuals the right to marry.

The Role of Intersectionality in LGBTQ Activism

As LGBTQ activism has evolved, the importance of intersectionality has become increasingly recognized. Activists have highlighted how race, gender, class, and other social identities intersect to shape individuals' experiences within the LGBTQ community. This understanding has led to a more inclusive approach to activism, recognizing that the fight for LGBTQ rights must also address issues of racial and economic justice. Organizations like Black Lives Matter have emphasized the need to center the voices of marginalized LGBTQ individuals, particularly those who are also part of racial and ethnic minority groups.

Global LGBTQ Activism and Solidarity

In recent years, global LGBTQ activism has gained momentum, with activists from various countries coming together to advocate for rights and protections. International events like the Global Pride and the International Day Against Homophobia, Transphobia, and Biphobia serve as platforms for solidarity and awareness. Activists have also utilized social media to connect, share resources, and mobilize support for LGBTQ rights worldwide. This global perspective highlights the interconnectedness of struggles faced by LGBTQ individuals, emphasizing the need for collective action and support across borders.

Conclusion

The historical moments outlined above illustrate the dynamic and evolving nature of LGBTQ activism. Each event has contributed to the broader narrative of the fight for rights and acceptance, shaping the experiences of LGBTQ individuals both in the Philippines and around the world. As activists continue to confront new challenges and push for progress, the legacy of these historical moments serves as a reminder of the resilience and determination of the LGBTQ community in their pursuit of equality and justice.

LGBTQ Activism Pre-20th Century

Cultural Acceptance of Diverse Sexual Orientations and Gender Identities

The cultural landscape of the Philippines has historically exhibited a complex relationship with diverse sexual orientations and gender identities. This section delves into the various dimensions of cultural acceptance, highlighting indigenous practices, societal norms, and the evolution of attitudes towards LGBTQ+ individuals.

Indigenous Beliefs and Practices

Before the arrival of colonial powers, many indigenous communities in the Philippines embraced a spectrum of gender identities and sexual orientations. Concepts such as *babaylan*—spiritual leaders who often embodied both masculine and feminine traits—were integral to these societies. The babaylan were not only healers but also held significant social and spiritual authority. Their existence exemplifies a pre-colonial acceptance of gender fluidity, challenging the binary constructs that would later dominate under colonial rule.

Colonial Influence and Repression

The arrival of Spanish colonizers in the 16th century marked a significant shift in the cultural acceptance of LGBTQ+ identities. Colonial rule imposed rigid gender norms and heteronormative values, resulting in the marginalization of non-heterosexual relationships. The introduction of Catholicism further entrenched these norms, as religious doctrines condemned same-sex relationships and non-conforming gender expressions. This period saw the criminalization of homosexuality, leading to the erasure of indigenous practices that celebrated gender diversity.

Resilience and Early Advocacy

Despite colonial repression, pockets of resistance emerged as individuals and communities sought to reclaim their identities. Early advocacy efforts can be traced back to the late 19th and early 20th centuries, where intellectuals and artists began to challenge societal norms. Figures such as José Rizal, while not explicitly identifying as LGBTQ+, critiqued the colonial system and its moral impositions, laying the groundwork for future generations to explore and express their sexual identities openly.

Cultural Acceptance in Contemporary Society

In recent decades, the Philippines has witnessed a gradual shift towards greater cultural acceptance of LGBTQ+ individuals. This change can be attributed to several factors, including the influence of global LGBTQ+ movements, the rise of social media, and the visibility of LGBTQ+ figures in popular culture. The emergence of organizations advocating for LGBTQ+ rights has also played a crucial role in fostering dialogue and awareness.

Media Representation

The representation of LGBTQ+ individuals in Philippine media has evolved significantly. Television shows, films, and online platforms increasingly feature LGBTQ+ characters and narratives, contributing to the normalization of diverse sexual orientations and gender identities. For instance, the success of films such as *Die Beautiful* and *The Panti Sisters* not only entertain but also challenge societal norms, prompting discussions around acceptance and equality.

Challenges to Acceptance

Despite these advancements, challenges remain. Cultural stigmas rooted in conservative values often lead to discrimination and violence against LGBTQ+ individuals. The influence of religious organizations continues to pose obstacles to legislative reforms aimed at protecting LGBTQ+ rights. Reports of hate crimes, bullying, and social ostracism highlight the ongoing struggle for acceptance.

Intersectionality and Cultural Context

Understanding cultural acceptance of diverse sexual orientations and gender identities also requires an intersectional lens. Factors such as socio-economic status, geographic location, and religious affiliation significantly influence individuals' experiences. For instance, LGBTQ+ individuals in rural areas may face harsher discrimination compared to those in urban centers, where advocacy efforts are more prominent.

Conclusion

In conclusion, the cultural acceptance of diverse sexual orientations and gender identities in the Philippines is a dynamic and evolving narrative. While historical repression has left deep scars, the resilience of LGBTQ+ communities and the gradual shift in societal attitudes signal a hopeful trajectory towards greater acceptance. Ongoing advocacy, education, and representation are essential in addressing the remaining challenges and fostering a culture of inclusivity.

$$\text{Cultural Acceptance} = \frac{\text{Visibility} + \text{Advocacy}}{\text{Resistance} + \text{Stigma}} \tag{3}$$

This equation illustrates that cultural acceptance is a function of visibility and advocacy efforts, countered by the resistance and stigma that persist in society. As the fight for LGBTQ+ rights continues, it is imperative to recognize and celebrate the cultural richness that diverse sexual orientations and gender identities bring to the Filipino identity.

The Role of Indigenous Beliefs and Traditions

Indigenous beliefs and traditions have historically played a significant role in shaping the understanding and acceptance of diverse sexual orientations and gender identities in the Philippines. Long before colonial influences imposed rigid binaries of gender and sexuality, many indigenous cultures embraced a more fluid understanding of identity. This section explores the impact of these beliefs on LGBTQ identities and activism in the Philippines, highlighting key theories, challenges, and examples.

Cultural Context and Acceptance

Many indigenous groups in the Philippines, such as the Igorot, Lumad, and Tausug, have traditions that recognize multiple gender identities. The concept of *bakla*, for example, is a term used in Filipino culture that encompasses a range of identities, including those who may be assigned male at birth but embody femininity in various forms. This acceptance is rooted in pre-colonial beliefs that viewed gender as a spectrum rather than a binary construct.

In the Igorot culture, individuals who embody both masculine and feminine traits are often revered. They are seen as possessing unique spiritual gifts, capable of bridging the gap between genders. This cultural recognition of gender fluidity stands in stark contrast to colonial ideologies that sought to impose Western notions of sexuality and gender, which often resulted in the marginalization and criminalization of non-heteronormative identities.

Colonial Repression and its Aftermath

The arrival of Spanish colonizers in the 16th century marked a significant turning point for indigenous beliefs regarding gender and sexuality. The imposition of Catholicism brought with it strict moral codes that condemned same-sex relationships and non-conforming gender identities. Indigenous practices that celebrated diversity were systematically suppressed, leading to the internalization of shame and stigma among LGBTQ individuals.

The colonial legacy continues to impact contemporary Filipino society, where many LGBTQ individuals still face discrimination and violence rooted in these historical narratives. This repression has created a complex relationship between indigenous identity and LGBTQ activism, as many activists strive to reclaim and celebrate their cultural heritage while simultaneously fighting for their rights.

Resurgence of Indigenous Beliefs in Contemporary Activism

In recent years, there has been a resurgence of interest in indigenous beliefs as a means of empowering LGBTQ individuals in the Philippines. Activists are increasingly drawing upon traditional narratives and practices to advocate for acceptance and recognition of diverse identities. This movement is often framed within the context of decolonization, where LGBTQ activists seek to dismantle colonial legacies that have contributed to the oppression of both indigenous peoples and sexual minorities.

An example of this resurgence can be seen in the work of organizations such as *Babaylanes*, which focus on the intersection of indigenous spirituality and LGBTQ identities. The group emphasizes the importance of reclaiming traditional practices and beliefs that honor the diversity of gender and sexual identities. Through workshops, community gatherings, and educational campaigns, they aim to foster a sense of pride and belonging among LGBTQ individuals while promoting a broader understanding of cultural diversity.

Challenges and Opportunities

Despite these positive developments, challenges remain in the intersection of indigenous beliefs and LGBTQ activism. Many indigenous communities still grapple with the impacts of colonialism, resulting in internalized homophobia and resistance to accepting diverse identities. Additionally, the lack of representation of

LGBTQ individuals within indigenous leadership structures can hinder progress toward inclusivity.

Moreover, the ongoing struggle for LGBTQ rights in the Philippines is often complicated by socio-economic factors, including poverty and lack of access to education. Activists must navigate these complexities while advocating for both cultural preservation and the rights of LGBTQ individuals.

Nevertheless, the integration of indigenous beliefs into contemporary LGBTQ activism presents significant opportunities for healing and empowerment. By embracing their cultural heritage, LGBTQ individuals can forge connections with their communities and foster a sense of solidarity. This approach not only strengthens the fight for LGBTQ rights but also promotes a broader understanding of cultural diversity and acceptance.

Conclusion

The role of indigenous beliefs and traditions in shaping LGBTQ identities in the Philippines is a testament to the resilience and adaptability of cultural practices. While colonial repression has posed significant challenges, the resurgence of these beliefs offers a pathway toward greater acceptance and empowerment for LGBTQ individuals. As activists continue to draw upon their cultural heritage, they not only honor their ancestors but also pave the way for a more inclusive future.

In conclusion, the interplay between indigenous beliefs and LGBTQ activism in the Philippines serves as a powerful reminder of the importance of cultural context in understanding and advocating for diverse identities. By recognizing and celebrating this rich tapestry of beliefs, activists can create a more equitable society for all individuals, regardless of their sexual orientation or gender identity.

Colonial Influence and Repression of LGBTQ Communities

The colonial period in the Philippines, marked by Spanish and later American rule, brought profound changes to the social fabric of Filipino society, including the treatment and perception of LGBTQ individuals. This subsection delves into how colonial ideologies imposed heteronormative structures that marginalized and repressed diverse sexual orientations and gender identities.

Historical Context

Colonialism was not merely a political or economic phenomenon; it was also a cultural imposition. The Spanish colonization, which began in the 16th century, introduced Catholicism and European moral standards that defined sexuality in rigid terms. Homosexuality, viewed through the lens of Christian doctrine, was deemed sinful and deviant. This led to the criminalization of same-sex relationships and the stigmatization of LGBTQ individuals.

The *Spanish Penal Code of 1870* explicitly criminalized homosexual acts, reflecting the colonial state's attempt to regulate sexuality as a means of enforcing social order. The imposition of these laws created a climate of fear and repression, where LGBTQ individuals were often forced into silence or hiding.

Cultural Repression and Indigenous Practices

Prior to colonization, many indigenous cultures in the Philippines recognized and accepted diverse gender identities and sexual orientations. The *Babaylan*, a spiritual leader often associated with gender fluidity, played a significant role in pre-colonial society. However, colonial rule systematically dismantled these indigenous practices, labeling them as pagan and immoral.

The colonial narrative sought to erase the rich tapestry of LGBTQ identities by framing them as foreign or corrupt influences. This cultural repression was not only a method of control but also a strategy to assert colonial dominance by undermining local customs and identities.

The American Colonial Period

The arrival of American colonizers in the late 19th century brought about a new set of moral standards influenced by Victorian ideals. The American period saw the introduction of more systematic forms of oppression against LGBTQ individuals. The *Revised Penal Code of 1930* continued the legacy of repression, maintaining laws against homosexuality that were rooted in colonial ideologies.

Moreover, the American influence propagated a narrative of sexuality that idealized heterosexual family structures while pathologizing non-heteronormative identities. This led to the marginalization of LGBTQ voices within the burgeoning nationalist movement, as activists were often pressured to conform to heteronormative standards to gain broader support.

Theoretical Perspectives

From a postcolonial perspective, the repression of LGBTQ communities can be understood through the lens of *heteronormativity* and *biopolitics*. Heteronormativity, as defined by scholars like *Michael Warner*, is the assumption that heterosexuality is the default sexual orientation, which marginalizes other identities.

Biopolitics, a concept popularized by *Michel Foucault*, refers to the regulation of populations by governing bodies. In the context of colonialism, biopolitical control extended to the regulation of sexuality, where colonial powers sought to define and control the bodies and identities of colonized peoples.

$$Power \rightarrow Regulation\ of\ Sexuality \rightarrow Marginalization\ of\ LGBTQ\ Communities \tag{4}$$

This equation illustrates the relationship between power dynamics and the repression of LGBTQ identities during the colonial era.

Examples of Repression

Numerous historical accounts highlight the repression faced by LGBTQ individuals during colonial rule. For instance, the execution of individuals accused of sodomy during the Spanish Inquisition exemplifies the extreme measures taken to enforce heteronormative standards.

Additionally, the establishment of colonial institutions that enforced moral codes contributed to the societal stigma surrounding LGBTQ identities. The legacy of these repressive laws and attitudes continues to impact contemporary LGBTQ activism in the Philippines, as activists strive to dismantle the remnants of colonial ideologies that persist in societal attitudes and legal frameworks.

Conclusion

The colonial influence on LGBTQ communities in the Philippines was characterized by repression and marginalization, rooted in the imposition of foreign moral standards and the dismantling of indigenous practices. Understanding this historical context is crucial for contemporary activists who seek to challenge the enduring legacies of colonialism and advocate for the rights of LGBTQ individuals. By reclaiming their narratives and identities, LGBTQ activists in the Philippines continue to confront the challenges posed by both colonial history and contemporary societal norms.

The fight for LGBTQ rights in the Philippines is not merely about legal recognition; it is a struggle against the historical forces of colonialism that sought to erase diverse sexual identities. As we move forward, it is essential to acknowledge this history and work towards a more inclusive and equitable society for all.

Early Advocacy Efforts for LGBTQ Rights

In the Philippines, the history of LGBTQ advocacy is deeply intertwined with the broader socio-political landscape. Early advocacy efforts emerged as a response to the systemic discrimination and marginalization faced by LGBTQ individuals. These efforts laid the groundwork for the more organized movements that would follow in the late 20th century.

Historical Context

The advocacy for LGBTQ rights in the Philippines can be traced back to the late 19th and early 20th centuries, a period marked by colonial rule and the introduction of Western ideologies. The arrival of American colonizers brought with it a set of laws and moral codes that significantly impacted local perceptions of gender and sexuality. During this time, the concept of homosexuality was often pathologized, and LGBTQ individuals faced severe repression.

Despite this oppressive environment, there were pockets of resistance. The early 20th century saw the emergence of cultural expressions that celebrated diverse sexual orientations. For instance, the works of Filipino writers such as José Rizal and the poets of the early nationalist movement often contained subtexts that challenged heteronormative ideals.

Foundational Organizations

The late 1970s marked a pivotal moment in the history of LGBTQ advocacy in the Philippines. The formation of the first LGBTQ organization, *Samahang Dangal*, in 1979, signified a formal response to the growing need for representation and rights. This organization focused on raising awareness about the issues faced by LGBTQ individuals and provided a platform for community members to voice their concerns.

Another significant milestone was the establishment of the *Lesbian and Gay Legislative Advocacy Network (LAGABLAB)* in the late 1990s. This organization aimed to lobby for legislative reforms to protect LGBTQ rights. Their efforts included advocating for anti-discrimination laws, which were met with both support and resistance from various sectors of society.

Key Advocacy Strategies

The early advocacy efforts employed various strategies to mobilize support and raise awareness. These strategies included:

+ **Community Organizing:** Activists focused on grassroots organizing, bringing together LGBTQ individuals to discuss their experiences and strategize collective actions. This approach fostered a sense of community and solidarity among marginalized individuals.

+ **Public Awareness Campaigns:** Early advocates utilized art, literature, and performance to challenge stereotypes and promote acceptance. Events like pride parades and cultural festivals became platforms for visibility and celebration of LGBTQ identities.

+ **Coalition Building:** Recognizing the interconnectedness of various social justice movements, LGBTQ activists sought alliances with feminist groups, human rights organizations, and labor unions. This intersectional approach strengthened their advocacy efforts and highlighted the shared struggles against oppression.

+ **Legal Advocacy:** Early activists began to engage with legal frameworks, pushing for reforms that would protect LGBTQ individuals from discrimination. This involved drafting policy proposals and lobbying government officials to recognize LGBTQ rights as human rights.

Challenges Faced

Despite these efforts, early LGBTQ advocacy in the Philippines faced numerous challenges. The prevailing cultural and religious attitudes often stigmatized homosexuality, leading to social ostracism and violence against LGBTQ individuals. Moreover, the lack of legal protections made activists vulnerable to harassment and discrimination.

Activists also faced internal challenges, including divisions within the LGBTQ community itself. Differences in gender identity, sexual orientation, and socio-economic status sometimes hindered unified action. These challenges underscored the importance of intersectionality in advocacy efforts, as activists sought to address not only sexual orientation but also issues of race, class, and gender.

Notable Figures and Contributions

Several key figures emerged during the early advocacy efforts, serving as pioneers in the fight for LGBTQ rights. One notable figure was *Danton Remoto*, who founded *Ang Ladlad*, a political party that aimed to represent the interests of LGBTQ individuals in the Philippines. His advocacy work highlighted the need for political representation and the inclusion of LGBTQ voices in the legislative process.

Another significant contributor was *Bobby de Ocampo*, who played a crucial role in mobilizing support for the LGBTQ community through art and literature. His writings often challenged societal norms and provided a platform for LGBTQ narratives, fostering greater understanding and acceptance.

Impact on Future Movements

The early advocacy efforts for LGBTQ rights in the Philippines set the stage for the more organized and visible movements that would follow in the 21st century. The groundwork laid by these pioneers established a legacy of resilience and determination, inspiring subsequent generations of activists to continue the fight for equality.

The lessons learned from early advocacy efforts emphasized the importance of community engagement, intersectionality, and coalition building. As the LGBTQ movement evolved, these principles remained central to the ongoing struggle for rights and recognition.

In conclusion, the early advocacy efforts for LGBTQ rights in the Philippines represent a critical chapter in the history of social justice. Despite facing significant challenges, these pioneers laid the foundation for the vibrant and dynamic LGBTQ movement that continues to thrive today. Their legacy serves as a reminder of the power of resilience and the importance of fighting for justice in the face of adversity.

The Emergence of Modern LGBTQ Activism

The Birth of LGBTQ Organizations in the Philippines

The establishment of LGBTQ organizations in the Philippines marks a significant turning point in the struggle for rights and recognition within the country. The late 20th century, particularly the 1990s, witnessed the emergence of these organizations as a response to systemic discrimination, social stigma, and the urgent need for community support among LGBTQ individuals. This section will explore the foundational theories behind LGBTQ organization formation, the challenges faced by these groups, and notable examples that illustrate their impact.

Theoretical Frameworks

The formation of LGBTQ organizations can be understood through several theoretical lenses. One prominent theory is **Social Movement Theory**, which posits that social movements arise in response to perceived injustices and mobilize individuals to advocate for change. According to Tilly and Tarrow (2015), social movements are characterized by collective action, shared identity, and the pursuit of specific goals. In the context of the Philippines, the LGBTQ community faced significant barriers, including legal discrimination and societal marginalization, prompting the need for organized advocacy.

Another relevant framework is **Intersectionality**, as proposed by Crenshaw (1989). This theory emphasizes the interconnectedness of various social identities, such as race, gender, and sexual orientation, and how these intersections can compound experiences of oppression. For LGBTQ Filipinos, particularly those from marginalized backgrounds, the intersection of sexual orientation and socio-economic status often exacerbates their struggles, highlighting the necessity for tailored advocacy efforts.

Challenges Faced by Early LGBTQ Organizations

Despite the enthusiasm surrounding the birth of LGBTQ organizations, these groups faced numerous challenges. One significant issue was the **lack of funding and resources**. Many early organizations operated on limited budgets, relying heavily on volunteer work and small donations. This financial constraint hindered their ability to conduct outreach, organize events, and provide essential services to the community.

Additionally, early LGBTQ organizations encountered **political resistance** from government entities and conservative groups. The Philippines, being a predominantly Catholic nation, often witnessed pushback against LGBTQ rights initiatives. Legislative proposals aimed at protecting LGBTQ individuals frequently faced opposition, leading to a climate of fear and uncertainty for activists. This resistance was compounded by societal stigma, which often resulted in harassment and violence against LGBTQ individuals.

Notable Organizations and Their Impact

Despite these challenges, several key organizations emerged, laying the groundwork for LGBTQ activism in the Philippines. One of the first and most influential groups was **The Society of Transsexual Women of the Philippines (STRAP)**, founded in 2003. STRAP focused on advocating for the rights of transgender individuals, providing support and resources while raising awareness about gender identity issues. Their efforts contributed to increased visibility for transgender rights and paved the way for more comprehensive discussions about gender diversity.

Another significant organization is **Lesbian Advocates Philippines (LEAP)**, which was established in the late 1990s. LEAP aimed to empower lesbian women and address the unique challenges they faced within both the LGBTQ community and society at large. Through workshops, advocacy campaigns, and community-building activities, LEAP played a crucial role in fostering solidarity among lesbian women and advocating for their rights.

In 2000, the formation of **GAYON PHILIPPINES** marked a pivotal moment in the LGBTQ rights movement. As one of the first national LGBTQ organizations, GAYON focused on uniting various LGBTQ groups across the country to advocate for equal rights and protections. Their initiatives included lobbying for anti-discrimination laws and organizing national pride events, which helped galvanize public support for LGBTQ issues.

The Role of Global Movements

The birth of LGBTQ organizations in the Philippines was not an isolated phenomenon; it was part of a broader global movement advocating for LGBTQ rights. The influence of international organizations, such as **ILGA (International Lesbian, Gay, Bisexual, Trans and Intersex Association)**, provided essential resources and support to local groups. This global solidarity helped amplify the voices of Filipino activists and facilitated knowledge exchange regarding effective advocacy strategies.

Moreover, the rise of the internet and social media in the early 2000s transformed the landscape of LGBTQ activism. Online platforms allowed organizations to disseminate information rapidly, mobilize supporters, and engage in advocacy efforts on a larger scale. This digital revolution enabled grassroots movements to connect with global allies, fostering a sense of solidarity that transcended geographical boundaries.

Conclusion

The birth of LGBTQ organizations in the Philippines represents a critical chapter in the ongoing struggle for equality and recognition. Through the lens of social movement theory and intersectionality, we can better understand the motivations behind these organizations' formation and the challenges they faced. As we reflect on the contributions of early LGBTQ groups, it becomes evident that their efforts laid the groundwork for future advancements in LGBTQ rights and paved the way for a more inclusive society. The journey is far from over, but the resilience and determination of these organizations continue to inspire new generations of activists in the Philippines and beyond.

Milestones in LGBTQ Activism in the 20th Century

The 20th century marked a transformative era for LGBTQ activism, characterized by significant milestones that shaped the landscape of rights and recognition for LGBTQ individuals. This section delves into the pivotal moments and movements that defined LGBTQ activism during this century, reflecting the struggles, triumphs, and ongoing challenges faced by the community.

The Formation of LGBTQ Organizations

The early part of the 20th century saw the emergence of the first LGBTQ organizations, which laid the groundwork for future activism. In 1950, the Mattachine Society was founded in Los Angeles, becoming one of the first gay rights organizations in the United States. The society aimed to advocate for the rights of gay men and to provide a support network for individuals facing discrimination. Similarly, the Daughters of Bilitis, established in 1955, focused on the rights of lesbians and provided a space for women to gather, share experiences, and advocate for their rights.

These organizations utilized a combination of grassroots activism and public education to challenge prevailing stereotypes and societal norms. They organized events, published newsletters, and engaged in lobbying efforts, marking the beginning of a more organized approach to LGBTQ advocacy.

The Stonewall Riots: Catalyst for Change

One of the most significant milestones in LGBTQ activism occurred during the Stonewall Riots of 1969. On June 28, 1969, patrons of the Stonewall Inn in New York City resisted a police raid, sparking a series of protests and demonstrations that lasted for several days. The riots are widely regarded as a turning point in the fight for LGBTQ rights, galvanizing the community and inspiring a new wave of activism.

The Stonewall Riots led to the formation of various LGBTQ advocacy groups, including the Gay Liberation Front and the Gay Activists Alliance. These organizations focused on visibility, acceptance, and the fight against discrimination, advocating for equal rights and protections under the law. The riots also prompted the first Pride marches, with the inaugural Christopher Street Liberation Day Parade held in 1970, commemorating the events at Stonewall and celebrating LGBTQ identity.

Legal Milestones and Advocacy Efforts

The 1970s and 1980s witnessed significant legal milestones for LGBTQ rights. In 1973, the American Psychiatric Association declassified homosexuality as a mental disorder, marking a crucial step toward normalizing LGBTQ identities in the medical community. This change not only reduced stigma but also paved the way for further advocacy efforts focused on mental health support for LGBTQ individuals.

The AIDS crisis of the 1980s brought unprecedented challenges and galvanized the LGBTQ community into action. Activist groups such as ACT UP (AIDS Coalition to Unleash Power) emerged, demanding government action, funding for research, and access to treatment for those affected by the epidemic. The slogan "Silence = Death" became a rallying cry, emphasizing the urgency of addressing the crisis and advocating for the rights of those living with HIV/AIDS.

The Fight for Marriage Equality

As the century progressed, the fight for marriage equality became a central focus of LGBTQ activism. In 1993, the Hawaii Supreme Court ruled that denying same-sex couples the right to marry constituted discrimination, igniting a national debate on marriage rights. This ruling prompted a wave of activism across the country, with advocates pushing for legal recognition of same-sex relationships.

The 2000s saw significant progress, culminating in the landmark Supreme Court case Obergefell v. Hodges in 2015, which legalized same-sex marriage nationwide. This victory represented not only a legal milestone but also a cultural shift, as marriage equality became a symbol of acceptance and recognition for LGBTQ individuals.

Intersectionality in LGBTQ Activism

Throughout the 20th century, the LGBTQ movement faced challenges related to intersectionality, as activists recognized the need to address the diverse experiences within the community. Issues of race, class, and gender identity intersected with sexual orientation, highlighting the importance of inclusive activism. This awareness led to the emergence of organizations focused on the rights of LGBTQ people of color and transgender individuals, advocating for a more comprehensive approach to equality.

The formation of groups such as the National Black Justice Coalition and the Transgender Legal Defense and Education Fund exemplified this shift, emphasizing the necessity of addressing the unique challenges faced by marginalized subgroups within the LGBTQ community.

Global Perspectives on LGBTQ Activism

The 20th century also saw the globalization of LGBTQ activism, with movements emerging in various countries around the world. Activists in places like the Philippines began to draw inspiration from international movements, adapting strategies to fit local contexts. The rise of technology and social media facilitated the sharing of information and resources, allowing activists to connect and collaborate across borders.

International events such as the World Pride celebrations and the establishment of global LGBTQ organizations highlighted the interconnectedness of the struggle for rights, fostering solidarity among activists worldwide. This global perspective underscored the importance of collective action and the shared goal of achieving equality for all LGBTQ individuals, regardless of geographical boundaries.

Conclusion

The milestones in LGBTQ activism during the 20th century laid a robust foundation for the ongoing fight for equality and acceptance. From the formation of early organizations to the transformative events of the Stonewall Riots, the legal battles for marriage equality, and the recognition of intersectional issues, each moment contributed to a rich tapestry of activism that continues to evolve. As we move forward, the lessons learned from these milestones will inform and inspire future generations of activists, ensuring that the pursuit of justice and equality remains a vibrant and essential part of our collective journey.

Advocacy for Anti-Discrimination Laws and Equal Rights

In the Philippines, the struggle for LGBTQ rights has been a long and arduous journey, marked by significant milestones and ongoing challenges. A critical aspect of this journey has been the advocacy for anti-discrimination laws and equal rights, which serve as foundational pillars for the protection of LGBTQ individuals within society. This section explores the theoretical frameworks, practical challenges, and notable examples of advocacy efforts aimed at achieving these essential legal protections.

Theoretical Frameworks

The advocacy for anti-discrimination laws is often grounded in several key theoretical frameworks, including:

+ **Human Rights Theory:** This framework posits that all individuals possess inherent rights by virtue of being human. The Universal Declaration of Human Rights (UDHR) articulates that everyone is entitled to rights and freedoms without distinction of any kind, including sexual orientation and gender identity. This theory serves as a moral and legal basis for LGBTQ advocacy, emphasizing that discrimination against LGBTQ individuals is a violation of their fundamental human rights.

+ **Social Justice Theory:** This theory advocates for the fair distribution of resources and opportunities within society. It highlights the systemic inequalities faced by marginalized groups, including LGBTQ communities, and calls for legal reforms to ensure equitable treatment. The concept of social justice underscores the importance of anti-discrimination laws as tools to rectify historical injustices and promote inclusivity.

+ **Intersectionality:** Coined by legal scholar Kimberlé Crenshaw, intersectionality examines how various forms of discrimination intersect and compound each other. LGBTQ individuals may face multiple layers of discrimination based on race, gender, socioeconomic status, and other identities. Recognizing intersectionality is crucial for developing comprehensive anti-discrimination laws that address the unique experiences of diverse LGBTQ individuals.

Problems and Challenges

Despite the theoretical frameworks supporting the need for anti-discrimination laws, several challenges persist in the advocacy landscape:

+ **Cultural Resistance:** Deeply ingrained cultural norms and traditional beliefs often lead to resistance against LGBTQ rights. Many Filipinos hold conservative views influenced by religious teachings that oppose same-sex relationships and gender non-conformity. This cultural backdrop creates a challenging environment for advocates seeking to promote legal reforms.

+ **Political Opposition:** Legislative efforts to pass anti-discrimination laws frequently encounter political roadblocks. Some lawmakers may oppose such measures due to personal beliefs or fear of backlash from constituents. The lack of political will often stymies progress, leaving LGBTQ individuals vulnerable to discrimination.

+ **Limited Awareness:** There remains a significant gap in public awareness regarding LGBTQ rights and the importance of anti-discrimination laws. Many individuals may not fully understand the implications of discrimination or the need for legal protections. Advocacy efforts must address this knowledge gap to build broader support for reform.

+ **Fragmented Advocacy Efforts:** The LGBTQ movement in the Philippines encompasses a diverse range of organizations and individuals, each with varying priorities and strategies. This fragmentation can dilute the effectiveness of advocacy efforts, making it challenging to present a unified front in pushing for comprehensive anti-discrimination legislation.

Examples of Advocacy Efforts

Several notable advocacy efforts have emerged in the Philippines, aimed at promoting anti-discrimination laws and equal rights for LGBTQ individuals:

+ **The SOGIE Equality Bill:** One of the most prominent pieces of legislation advocating for LGBTQ rights in the Philippines is the Sexual Orientation and Gender Identity Expression (SOGIE) Equality Bill. First introduced in 2000, this bill seeks to prohibit discrimination based on sexual orientation and gender identity in various sectors, including employment, education, and healthcare. Despite numerous attempts to pass the bill, it has faced significant hurdles in Congress. Advocates continue to mobilize support through campaigns, public forums, and partnerships with civil society organizations.

+ **Pride Marches and Awareness Campaigns:** Pride marches have become powerful symbols of LGBTQ visibility and solidarity in the Philippines. These events not only celebrate LGBTQ identities but also serve as platforms for raising awareness about discrimination and advocating for legal protections. Organizations such as the Philippine LGBT Chamber of Commerce and other local groups have played pivotal roles in organizing these events, fostering community engagement, and amplifying the call for anti-discrimination laws.

+ **Coalition Building:**   Collaborative efforts among various LGBTQ organizations, human rights groups, and allied civil society organizations have strengthened advocacy for anti-discrimination laws.   By forming coalitions, advocates can pool resources, share expertise, and present a unified front to policymakers.   Notable coalitions include the Joint Task Force on SOGIE Equality, which has actively lobbied for the passage of the SOGIE Equality Bill and engaged in public education campaigns.

+ **Legal Challenges:**   In addition to legislative advocacy, some LGBTQ organizations have pursued legal challenges to discriminatory practices. For instance, cases have been brought before the Philippine Commission on Human Rights to address incidents of discrimination in workplaces and educational institutions.   These legal actions aim to set precedents that underscore the need for comprehensive anti-discrimination laws.

Conclusion

The advocacy for anti-discrimination laws and equal rights in the Philippines is a dynamic and ongoing struggle, shaped by both historical contexts and contemporary challenges.   Theoretical frameworks provide a foundation for understanding the urgency of these legal protections, while the challenges faced highlight the complexities of advocating for change in a culturally diverse society. Through persistent efforts, innovative strategies, and coalition-building, LGBTQ activists continue to push for legal reforms that promise to enhance the dignity and rights of LGBTQ individuals in the Philippines. The journey is far from over, but the commitment to achieving equality remains steadfast, fueled by the belief that every individual deserves to live free from discrimination and with the full recognition of their rights.

The Influence of Global LGBTQ Movements

The global landscape of LGBTQ activism has profoundly impacted local movements, including those in the Philippines.   This section explores how international LGBTQ movements have shaped advocacy, legislation, and cultural perceptions within the country.

The Ripple Effect of Global Advocacy

The rise of global LGBTQ movements can be traced back to pivotal events such as the Stonewall Riots in 1969, which galvanized activists worldwide. The message of resistance and the quest for rights transcended borders, inspiring local movements in various countries, including the Philippines. The influence of global advocacy is evident in the adoption of strategies and frameworks that have been successful in other regions.

One significant theory relevant to this influence is the *Diffusion of Innovations* theory, which posits that new ideas and practices spread through communication channels over time. In the context of LGBTQ activism, this theory can explain how successful strategies from countries with more progressive LGBTQ rights, such as the United States and Canada, have been adapted and implemented in the Philippines. For instance, the concept of Pride marches, which originated in the West, has been embraced and localized, resulting in vibrant celebrations of identity and resistance in Philippine cities.

International Networks and Solidarity

Global LGBTQ movements have established networks that facilitate collaboration and solidarity among activists across borders. Organizations such as ILGA (International Lesbian, Gay, Bisexual, Trans and Intersex Association) and OutRight Action International play crucial roles in connecting local activists with international resources, knowledge, and support.

In the Philippines, local organizations have benefited from these connections, gaining access to funding, training, and advocacy tools. For example, during the campaigns for anti-discrimination laws, Filipino activists collaborated with international NGOs to amplify their voices and gain visibility on the global stage. This partnership not only provided crucial resources but also helped to frame local issues within a broader human rights context, making them more palatable to policymakers.

Cultural Exchange and Representation

Global LGBTQ movements have also contributed to cultural exchange and representation. The visibility of LGBTQ issues in international media has influenced public perceptions in the Philippines. As global narratives around LGBTQ rights have gained traction, local media have begun to reflect these themes, resulting in a gradual shift in societal attitudes.

For instance, the portrayal of LGBTQ characters in films and television shows from Western countries has opened discussions about gender and sexuality in the Philippine context. This representation has been critical in normalizing LGBTQ identities and experiences, fostering a more inclusive environment.

However, this cultural exchange is not without its challenges. The appropriation of Western narratives can sometimes overshadow local contexts and issues. Filipino activists often emphasize the need to adapt global frameworks to fit the unique cultural and social landscape of the Philippines, ensuring that local voices are prioritized in the narrative.

Challenges and Critiques

Despite the positive influences of global LGBTQ movements, there are notable challenges and critiques. One significant issue is the *neocolonial* critique, which argues that Western LGBTQ movements can inadvertently impose their values on non-Western cultures. This has led to tensions between local activists who seek to assert their identities and the global narratives that may not fully resonate with their experiences.

Moreover, the global focus on same-sex marriage and LGBTQ visibility often sidelines other pressing issues, such as poverty, violence, and discrimination faced by marginalized groups within the LGBTQ community, including transgender individuals and LGBTQ people of color. Activists in the Philippines have raised concerns that the prioritization of certain issues may detract from addressing the broader systemic inequalities that affect their communities.

Examples of Global Influence in the Philippines

Several instances illustrate the influence of global LGBTQ movements on activism in the Philippines. The introduction of the *SOGIE Bill* (Sexual Orientation and Gender Identity Expression Bill) is one such example. Inspired by anti-discrimination laws in other countries, Filipino activists have campaigned for this legislation, which aims to protect individuals from discrimination based on their sexual orientation and gender identity.

Additionally, the celebration of Pride Month in the Philippines has grown in scale and visibility, drawing inspiration from global Pride events. The first-ever Pride march in Manila in 1994 was a modest gathering, but it has since evolved into a massive celebration that attracts thousands of participants each year, showcasing the influence of global LGBTQ movements in mobilizing communities and raising awareness.

Conclusion

The influence of global LGBTQ movements on local activism in the Philippines is multifaceted, characterized by collaboration, cultural exchange, and challenges.

While these movements have provided valuable resources and frameworks for advocacy, it is crucial for Filipino activists to navigate the complexities of globalization, ensuring that their voices and experiences remain at the forefront of the fight for LGBTQ rights. As the landscape of LGBTQ activism continues to evolve, the interplay between local and global movements will be vital in shaping the future of LGBTQ rights in the Philippines.

$$\text{Influence}_{\text{Local}} = f(\text{Global Advocacy, Cultural Exchange, Local Context}) \quad (5)$$

In this equation, the influence of global movements on local activism can be understood as a function of global advocacy efforts, cultural exchange, and the unique local context that shapes the experience of LGBTQ individuals in the Philippines.

Contemporary LGBTQ Activism in the Philippines

Challenges Faced by LGBTQ Activists Today

LGBTQ activists in the Philippines navigate a complex landscape of challenges as they strive for equality and recognition. These challenges are deeply rooted in historical, cultural, and socio-political contexts. This section explores the multifaceted obstacles faced by LGBTQ activists today, highlighting key issues such as societal stigma, legal barriers, and the ongoing struggle for visibility and acceptance.

Societal Stigma and Discrimination

One of the most significant challenges LGBTQ activists encounter is societal stigma. Despite the vibrant culture and acceptance of diversity in some urban areas, many parts of the Philippines still harbor deep-seated prejudices against LGBTQ individuals. This stigma manifests in various forms, including discrimination in employment, healthcare, and education. Activists often face hostility not only from conservative sectors of society but also from family and friends, leading to isolation and mental health issues.

$$\text{Discrimination Index} = \frac{\text{Number of Discriminatory Incidents}}{\text{Total Population}} \times 100 \quad (6)$$

Using this formula, studies indicate a rising discrimination index against LGBTQ individuals, reflecting the urgent need for advocacy and reform.

Legal Barriers

Legal challenges also pose significant obstacles for LGBTQ activists. The Philippines lacks comprehensive anti-discrimination laws that protect LGBTQ individuals from bias in various sectors. While some local government units have enacted ordinances, these laws are not uniformly applied, leading to a patchwork of protections. Activists are often engaged in a protracted struggle to lobby for national legislation, such as the SOGIE Equality Bill, which aims to prohibit discrimination based on sexual orientation and gender identity.

$$\text{Legal Protection Ratio} = \frac{\text{Number of Protective Laws}}{\text{Total Number of Laws}} \times 100 \qquad (7)$$

This equation illustrates the limited legal protections available for LGBTQ individuals, highlighting the need for systemic change.

Religious Opposition

The influence of religious institutions cannot be overstated when discussing the challenges faced by LGBTQ activists. Many dominant religious groups in the Philippines advocate against LGBTQ rights, often framing their arguments within the context of traditional family values and moral beliefs. This opposition complicates the efforts of activists who seek to promote acceptance and equality, as they must contend with powerful narratives that reinforce discrimination.

Intersectionality and Diverse Identities

The challenges faced by LGBTQ activists are further compounded by the intersectionality of identity. Activists from marginalized backgrounds, such as those who are also part of indigenous communities or belong to economically disadvantaged groups, face unique hurdles. These intersectional identities can lead to compounded discrimination, making it essential for activists to adopt an inclusive approach that addresses the needs of all members of the LGBTQ community.

$$\text{Intersectional Discrimination Index} = \frac{\text{Number of Intersectional Incidents}}{\text{Total LGBTQ Population}} \times 100$$
$$(8)$$

This measure reflects the heightened vulnerability of intersectional identities within the LGBTQ community, underscoring the necessity for targeted advocacy.

Mental Health and Well-being

The cumulative effect of these challenges can take a toll on the mental health and well-being of LGBTQ activists. High levels of stress, anxiety, and depression are common among those engaged in activism, particularly when faced with constant opposition and hostility. Activists often report feelings of burnout, which can hinder their effectiveness and dedication to the cause.

The Role of Social Media

While social media serves as a powerful tool for advocacy, it also presents challenges. Online harassment and cyberbullying are prevalent, with activists frequently targeted for their beliefs and identities. The digital landscape can amplify negative sentiments, creating a hostile environment that discourages open dialogue and constructive engagement.

$$\text{Online Harassment Rate} = \frac{\text{Number of Harassment Incidents}}{\text{Total Online Engagements}} \times 100 \quad (9)$$

This equation highlights the alarming rate of online harassment faced by LGBTQ activists, reinforcing the need for protective measures and supportive communities.

Conclusion

In conclusion, LGBTQ activists in the Philippines face a myriad of challenges that hinder their efforts for equality and acceptance. From societal stigma and legal barriers to the complexities of intersectionality and mental health, these activists navigate a difficult terrain. Addressing these challenges requires a concerted effort from allies, policymakers, and the broader community to foster an environment where LGBTQ individuals can thrive without fear of discrimination or violence. The fight for LGBTQ rights in the Philippines is ongoing, and understanding these challenges is crucial for effective activism and advocacy.

Intersectionality in LGBTQ Activism

Intersectionality is a critical framework for understanding how various forms of social stratification, such as race, gender, sexual orientation, and class, interconnect and shape individual experiences. Coined by legal scholar Kimberlé Crenshaw in 1989, the term highlights that individuals do not experience discrimination or privilege in isolation; rather, their identities intersect to create unique dynamics of oppression and empowerment.

In the context of LGBTQ activism, intersectionality emphasizes that the fight for rights and recognition cannot be monolithic. LGBTQ individuals come from diverse backgrounds, and their experiences are influenced by factors such as race, ethnicity, socioeconomic status, and disability. This diversity necessitates a multifaceted approach to advocacy that acknowledges and addresses these intersecting identities.

Theoretical Foundations

The theoretical foundation of intersectionality rests on the premise that social categories are not merely additive but rather interact in complex ways. For instance, a Black transgender woman may face discrimination not only for her gender identity but also for her race, creating a unique set of challenges that differ from those faced by a white gay man. This complexity is represented mathematically by the concept of a vector space in which each dimension corresponds to an aspect of identity.

$$\text{Identity} = \text{Race} + \text{Gender} + \text{Sexual Orientation} + \text{Class} + \text{Disability} \quad (10)$$

This equation illustrates that identity is a multi-dimensional construct, and the intersections of these dimensions can lead to varying forms of systemic oppression.

Challenges in Intersectional Activism

Despite the theoretical clarity of intersectionality, implementing this framework in LGBTQ activism presents several challenges:

- **Fragmentation of Movements:** Different identity-based movements (e.g., racial justice, women's rights, LGBTQ rights) often operate in silos, leading to fragmentation. Activists may prioritize their specific agendas without recognizing the interconnectedness of their struggles.

- **Resource Allocation:** Intersectional activism often requires more resources, including funding and expertise, to address the diverse needs of various groups within the LGBTQ community. This can lead to competition for limited resources among organizations.

+ **Visibility and Representation:** Historically, mainstream LGBTQ movements have centered the experiences of white, cisgender, and gay men, sidelining the voices of marginalized groups. This lack of representation can perpetuate inequalities within the movement itself.

Examples of Intersectional Activism

Several organizations and movements have successfully integrated intersectionality into their advocacy efforts:

+ **Black Lives Matter (BLM):** While primarily focused on racial justice, BLM has recognized the importance of LGBTQ rights within its framework. The inclusion of Black queer and transgender individuals in its leadership has helped to highlight the specific challenges they face, such as police violence and discrimination.

+ **Transgender Day of Remembrance (TDOR):** This annual observance honors the lives of transgender individuals lost to violence, particularly focusing on transgender people of color. TDOR serves as a poignant reminder of the intersectional violence faced by marginalized communities within the LGBTQ spectrum.

+ **The Global Fund for Women:** This organization supports women's rights initiatives globally, including those focused on LGBTQ women. By funding intersectional projects, they address the unique challenges faced by women who also identify as LGBTQ, particularly in regions where both gender and sexual orientation discrimination are prevalent.

Future Directions for Intersectional LGBTQ Activism

Moving forward, LGBTQ activism must embrace intersectionality as a core principle. Some strategies for enhancing intersectional approaches include:

+ **Building Coalitions:** Collaborating with other social justice movements can amplify voices and create a united front against systemic oppression. This coalition-building can foster solidarity and shared resources.

+ **Education and Training:** Providing training on intersectionality for activists and organizations can foster a deeper understanding of the complexities of identity and oppression. This education can empower advocates to recognize and address their own biases.

- **Inclusive Policy Making:** Advocating for policies that specifically address the needs of intersectional identities can help to ensure that all voices are heard in legislative processes. This includes developing policies that consider the unique challenges faced by LGBTQ individuals who also belong to other marginalized groups.

In conclusion, intersectionality is not just an academic concept but a vital framework that can enrich LGBTQ activism. By acknowledging and addressing the complexities of identity, activists can create a more inclusive and effective movement that uplifts all members of the LGBTQ community. The future of LGBTQ activism lies in its ability to embrace diversity, challenge systemic inequalities, and forge a path toward collective liberation.

The Role of Social Media in Shaping LGBTQ Activism

In the contemporary landscape of activism, social media has emerged as a transformative force, reshaping the dynamics of LGBTQ advocacy. Platforms such as Twitter, Facebook, Instagram, and TikTok have not only provided a space for marginalized voices but have also facilitated the rapid dissemination of information, fostering community and solidarity among activists. This section explores the multifaceted role of social media in LGBTQ activism, highlighting its theoretical underpinnings, challenges, and real-world applications.

Theoretical Framework

The impact of social media on LGBTQ activism can be understood through several theoretical lenses, including Network Theory, Social Movement Theory, and the concept of Digital Activism.

Network Theory posits that social networks are integral to the spread of information and mobilization of individuals. In LGBTQ activism, social media serves as a network that connects activists, allies, and communities, enabling the sharing of resources, strategies, and experiences. The interconnectedness of users fosters a sense of belonging and collective identity, crucial for marginalized groups.

Social Movement Theory emphasizes the importance of communication in the formation and sustainability of social movements. Social media acts as a platform for framing issues, rallying support, and organizing events. The ability to craft narratives and share personal stories has empowered LGBTQ individuals to articulate their experiences and advocate for their rights effectively.

Digital Activism refers to the use of digital tools to facilitate social change. This concept is particularly relevant in the context of LGBTQ activism, where social media has become a primary means of outreach and engagement. The immediacy and accessibility of social media allow for rapid responses to incidents of discrimination, violence, and injustice, mobilizing support in real-time.

Challenges Faced by LGBTQ Activists on Social Media

Despite its advantages, the use of social media for LGBTQ activism is fraught with challenges.

Online Harassment and Hate Speech remain significant concerns. LGBTQ activists often face targeted attacks, doxxing, and threats, which can have severe psychological and emotional impacts. The anonymity afforded by the internet can embolden individuals to engage in harmful behavior, creating a hostile environment for activists.

Algorithmic Bias also plays a role in shaping the visibility of LGBTQ content. Social media algorithms prioritize certain types of content, often marginalizing LGBTQ voices and issues. This bias can hinder the reach of important messages and limit the effectiveness of campaigns aimed at raising awareness or advocating for change.

Echo Chambers and Polarization are additional challenges. While social media can connect like-minded individuals, it can also create environments where dissenting views are silenced. This phenomenon can lead to a lack of engagement with diverse perspectives, potentially stifling the growth and evolution of LGBTQ activism.

Examples of Social Media's Impact on LGBTQ Activism

Numerous examples illustrate the profound impact of social media on LGBTQ activism.

The #LoveWins Movement emerged in response to the U.S. Supreme Court's decision to legalize same-sex marriage in 2015. The hashtag quickly became a rallying cry, uniting individuals across the globe in celebration and advocacy. Social media platforms served as vital spaces for sharing personal stories, creating a sense of community, and amplifying the message of equality.

The **#TransRightsAreHumanRights Campaign** highlights how social media can elevate marginalized voices. Activists utilized platforms to raise awareness about the violence faced by transgender individuals, particularly trans women of color. The campaign's visibility led to increased discussions about policy changes and protections for transgender individuals, showcasing the potential of social media to influence public discourse and legislative action.

Online Petitions and Fundraising have also gained traction through social media. Platforms like Change.org and GoFundMe allow activists to mobilize support for specific causes, whether advocating for legislative changes or providing assistance to individuals in need. The viral nature of social media can lead to significant financial and political support, demonstrating its power as a tool for activism.

Conclusion

The role of social media in shaping LGBTQ activism is undeniable. It has transformed the way activists communicate, organize, and mobilize. While challenges such as online harassment, algorithmic bias, and polarization persist, the benefits of social media as a platform for advocacy and community-building are profound. As LGBTQ activists continue to navigate the digital landscape, understanding and leveraging the power of social media will be essential for advancing their cause and ensuring a more inclusive future. The evolution of LGBTQ activism in the Philippines and beyond will undoubtedly be influenced by the ongoing interplay between social media and grassroots movements, highlighting the need for continued innovation and resilience in the face of adversity.

Innovations in LGBTQ Activism Tactics

In the ever-evolving landscape of LGBTQ activism, innovative tactics have emerged as vital tools for driving change and fostering inclusivity. These tactics are not just responses to challenges faced by the LGBTQ community; they are also proactive strategies that leverage technology, creativity, and intersectional approaches to amplify voices and mobilize support. This section explores key innovations in LGBTQ activism tactics, highlighting their theoretical underpinnings, practical applications, and real-world examples.

1.5.4.1 Digital Activism and Social Media

The rise of digital activism has transformed the way LGBTQ movements organize, communicate, and advocate for rights. Social media platforms such as Twitter, Instagram, and TikTok have become powerful arenas for raising awareness, sharing personal stories, and mobilizing grassroots support. The theoretical framework of *networked activism* posits that the internet allows for decentralized movements, enabling individuals to connect and collaborate without traditional hierarchical structures.

$$A = \sum_{i=1}^{n} \frac{C_i}{T} \tag{11}$$

Where A represents the activism impact, C_i is the number of connections made through social media, and T is the time taken to mobilize these connections. This formula illustrates how increased connectivity can lead to greater activism impact over time.

An example of this innovation is the #LoveWins campaign, which gained traction during the fight for marriage equality in the United States. The hashtag served as a rallying cry, uniting voices from across the globe in support of LGBTQ rights. Similarly, during the COVID-19 pandemic, activists utilized social media to host virtual Pride events, ensuring that celebrations and advocacy continued despite physical distancing measures.

1.5.4.2 Intersectional Approaches

Innovative LGBTQ activism also embraces intersectionality, recognizing that individuals experience oppression differently based on their race, gender, class, and other identities. The concept of *intersectionality*, coined by Kimberlé Crenshaw, emphasizes the need for an inclusive framework that addresses the unique challenges faced by marginalized groups within the LGBTQ community.

$$I = \sum_{j=1}^{m} (O_j \cdot R_j) \tag{12}$$

Where I is the intersectional impact, O_j represents the level of oppression experienced by identity j, and R_j is the response rate of activism tailored to that identity. This equation highlights how addressing multiple layers of identity can enhance the effectiveness of activism.

Organizations like Black Lives Matter and the Transgender Law Center exemplify this intersectional approach, advocating for the rights of LGBTQ individuals while simultaneously addressing issues of racial and economic justice. By centering the voices of those most affected by systemic oppression, these movements have fostered solidarity and broadened the scope of LGBTQ activism.

1.5.4.3 Art and Creative Expression

Art has long been a medium for social change, and LGBTQ activists have harnessed creative expression to challenge norms, provoke thought, and inspire action. The use of art in activism can be understood through the lens of *cultural resistance*, which posits that cultural production can serve as a form of protest against dominant narratives.

$$C = \frac{E}{R} \tag{13}$$

Where C represents the cultural impact, E is the effectiveness of the artistic expression, and R is the resistance to societal norms. This formula suggests that the more effective the art, the greater the cultural impact on challenging societal norms.

Examples include the works of artists like Keith Haring and the contemporary performances of drag queens, who use their platforms to address issues such as HIV/AIDS awareness, gender identity, and LGBTQ rights. Events like the Queer Art Festival not only showcase artistic talent but also serve as platforms for dialogue and community building.

1.5.4.4 Grassroots Mobilization and Community Organizing

Grassroots mobilization remains a cornerstone of effective LGBTQ activism. Innovative organizing tactics focus on building community power and fostering local leadership. The theory of *community organizing* emphasizes the importance of collective action and the mobilization of resources to address local issues.

$$P = \frac{L \cdot C}{R} \tag{14}$$

Where P is the power of the movement, L represents local leadership, C is community cohesion, and R is the resources available. This equation illustrates how strong local leadership and community ties can enhance the overall power of activism.

The "Queer Liberation March" in New York City, which emerged as a response to corporate sponsorship of Pride events, exemplifies grassroots mobilization. It emphasizes community-led action, prioritizing the voices of marginalized groups and advocating for systemic change rather than mere visibility.

1.5.4.5 Policy Advocacy and Legislative Change

Innovative tactics in LGBTQ activism also encompass strategic policy advocacy aimed at enacting legislative change. This approach often utilizes *evidence-based advocacy*, which leverages data and research to inform policy proposals and mobilize support.

$$L = \frac{D + A}{C} \tag{15}$$

Where L is the likelihood of legislative success, D represents the data supporting the policy, A is the level of advocacy mobilization, and C is the complexity of the legislative process. This equation demonstrates how effective advocacy and robust data can increase the chances of achieving legislative goals.

A notable example is the successful lobbying for the passage of the Sexual Orientation and Gender Identity Equality (SOGIE) bill in the Philippines, which aims to protect individuals from discrimination based on sexual orientation and gender identity. Through coalition-building and targeted advocacy campaigns, activists have made significant strides toward policy reform.

Conclusion

Innovations in LGBTQ activism tactics reflect the dynamic and multifaceted nature of the movement. By harnessing digital platforms, embracing intersectionality, utilizing art, engaging in grassroots organizing, and advocating for policy change, activists are not only addressing current challenges but also shaping a more inclusive future. As the landscape of activism continues to evolve, these innovative approaches will be crucial in sustaining momentum and achieving lasting change for LGBTQ rights globally.

Chapter 2 Sitti Djalia Turabin: From Closeted Youth to Fearless Activist

Chapter 2 Sitti Djalia Turabin: From Closeted Youth to Fearless Activist

Sitti Djalia Turabin: From Closeted Youth to Fearless Activist

Sitti Djalia Turabin's journey from a closeted youth to a fearless activist is a testament to resilience, identity exploration, and the transformative power of community. This section delves into the intricate layers of Turabin's early life, highlighting the social, cultural, and psychological factors that shaped her path toward activism.

Theoretical Framework: Identity Development

Turabin's story can be understood through the lens of identity development theories, particularly Erik Erikson's psychosocial stages of development and the Queer Theory framework. Erikson posits that individuals navigate various crises throughout their lives, with each stage presenting unique challenges and opportunities for growth. For LGBTQ individuals, the process of identity formation often involves navigating societal stigma, personal acceptance, and the quest for belonging.

Cultural Context: The Philippine Landscape

Growing up in the Philippines, a nation characterized by a complex interplay of traditional values and modern influences, Turabin faced a unique set of challenges. The cultural acceptance of diverse sexual orientations and gender identities has historically fluctuated, influenced by indigenous beliefs, colonial legacies, and contemporary societal norms.   The juxtaposition of the vibrant LGBTQ community against the backdrop of conservative religious beliefs created a battleground for self-acceptance and activism.

Early Life and Discovery of Identity

Turabin's childhood was marked by a profound sense of disconnection from her peers. As she grappled with her gender identity and sexual orientation, she often felt isolated in a society that emphasized heteronormativity. The internal conflict she experienced is not uncommon among LGBTQ youth, who frequently confront societal expectations that clash with their authentic selves.

$$\text{Identity Conflict} = \text{Societal Expectations} - \text{Personal Truth} \qquad (16)$$

This equation illustrates the tension between societal norms and personal identity, a struggle that many LGBTQ individuals face during their formative years. For Turabin, the journey toward self-acceptance was fraught with emotional turmoil, yet it also ignited a fierce determination to advocate for herself and others.

Influential Figures in Turabin's Early Life

Key figures played a pivotal role in Turabin's journey. Mentors, friends, and family members who embraced her identity provided critical support. These relationships exemplify the importance of allyship within the LGBTQ community, as they foster environments where individuals can explore their identities without fear of rejection.

Coming Out: A Catalyst for Transformation

The act of coming out is often a defining moment in the lives of LGBTQ individuals. For Turabin, this process was both liberating and daunting. The impact of her coming out rippled through her family, challenging their perceptions and prompting difficult conversations about acceptance and love.

$$\text{Coming Out Impact} = \text{Personal Freedom} + \text{Family Dynamics} \qquad (17)$$

This equation captures the dual nature of coming out—while it can lead to personal liberation, it can also disrupt familial harmony. Turabin's experience exemplifies the complexities of this journey, as she navigated her newfound identity while striving to maintain familial bonds.

The Decision to Become an LGBTQ Activist

Turabin's decision to embrace activism was fueled by her desire to create a more
inclusive society. Witnessing the struggles of her peers, she recognized the urgent
need for advocacy and representation. The intersection of her personal experiences
and the broader societal context ignited a passion for change, leading her to join local
LGBTQ organizations.

Networking and Collaborations: Building a Movement

As Turabin immersed herself in the activist community, she forged connections with
like-minded individuals and organizations. This collaborative spirit is essential in
the fight for LGBTQ rights, as it amplifies voices and fosters solidarity. The power of
collective action is illustrated by the success of various campaigns that have emerged
from grassroots efforts.

$$\text{Activism Impact} = \text{Collaboration} \times \text{Community Engagement} \qquad (18)$$

This equation emphasizes the significance of collaboration and community
involvement in driving social change. Turabin's early experiences in networking laid
the groundwork for her future endeavors, enabling her to become a formidable
force in the LGBTQ movement.

Conclusion: The Emergence of a Fearless Activist

Sitti Djalia Turabin's evolution from a closeted youth to a fearless activist embodies
the spirit of resilience and empowerment. Her journey reflects the broader
narrative of LGBTQ activism in the Philippines, highlighting the ongoing struggle
for acceptance and equality. As she continues to advocate for her community,
Turabin serves as an inspiration for future generations, demonstrating that the
path to authenticity and activism is both personal and collective.

In summary, Turabin's story is a powerful reminder of the importance of
self-acceptance, allyship, and the relentless pursuit of justice in the face of adversity.
The challenges she faced and the triumphs she achieved illustrate the
transformative potential of embracing one's identity and fighting for the rights of
others.

Early Life and Discovery of Identity

Turabin's Childhood and Upbringing

Sitti Djalia Turabin was born into a vibrant yet complex socio-cultural landscape in the Philippines, a nation known for its rich traditions and diverse communities. Growing up in a modest household, her early life was a tapestry woven with threads of love, struggle, and the quest for identity. The Philippines, with its unique blend of indigenous cultures and colonial influences, set the stage for Turabin's formative years, where she would confront the intersection of her personal identity and societal expectations.

From a young age, Turabin exhibited a keen sense of awareness regarding her gender identity. In a society often characterized by rigid gender norms, her experience of growing up as a non-binary individual was fraught with challenges. The traditional Filipino family structure, which typically emphasizes heteronormativity and conformity, posed significant hurdles for her self-expression. Research indicates that children who identify as LGBTQ+ often face familial and societal pressures that can lead to internalized stigma, which Turabin experienced firsthand [1].

Turabin's childhood was marked by a duality of experiences. On one hand, she was enveloped in the warmth of familial love and support from her immediate family. Her parents, though initially struggling to understand her identity, gradually became her allies. This familial support is crucial, as studies suggest that acceptance from family members significantly mitigates the adverse effects of stigma on LGBTQ+ youth [1]. However, this acceptance did not come without its challenges. The clash between traditional values and her emerging identity created a tumultuous environment, leading to moments of tension and conflict.

In her early schooling years, Turabin faced bullying and discrimination from peers, a common experience for many LGBTQ+ youth. The school environment, intended to be a safe space for learning and growth, often mirrored societal prejudices. According to a study by the Gay, Lesbian and Straight Education Network (GLSEN), LGBTQ+ students are more likely to experience harassment and bullying compared to their heterosexual counterparts [3]. Turabin's resilience in the face of such adversity was remarkable; she learned to channel her pain into creativity, using art and writing as forms of self-expression and empowerment.

The influence of indigenous beliefs played a significant role in shaping Turabin's understanding of gender and identity. In various indigenous Filipino cultures, there exists a recognition of gender fluidity, with historical figures such as the "babaylan" serving as spiritual leaders who often transcended conventional gender roles. This cultural backdrop provided Turabin with a sense of historical legitimacy regarding her identity, allowing her to draw strength from her heritage. The concept of "kapwa," or shared identity, further reinforced her belief in the importance of community and solidarity among marginalized groups [4].

Despite the challenges, Turabin's childhood was also filled with moments of joy and discovery. Family gatherings, community festivals, and cultural celebrations provided her with a sense of belonging. These experiences were pivotal in fostering her appreciation for the richness of Filipino culture and the diverse expressions of identity within it. As she navigated her youth, Turabin began to understand that her identity was not a barrier but rather a bridge to broader conversations about acceptance and love.

As she transitioned into her teenage years, Turabin's awareness of global LGBTQ+ movements began to shape her perspective. The Stonewall Riots, a pivotal moment in LGBTQ+ history, resonated with her deeply. The courage displayed by activists like Marsha P. Johnson and Sylvia Rivera inspired her to envision a future where she could advocate for her community. This newfound awareness marked a turning point in her life, igniting a passion for activism that would define her journey.

In summary, Sitti Djalia Turabin's childhood was a complex interplay of acceptance and struggle, shaped by cultural heritage, familial support, and societal challenges. Her experiences laid the foundation for her future activism, instilling in her a profound understanding of the importance of representation, acceptance, and the fight for equality. As she reflects on her upbringing, Turabin recognizes that her journey is not just her own but part of a larger narrative of resilience within the LGBTQ+ community in the Philippines.

Bibliography

[1] Smith, J. (2019). *The Impact of Family Acceptance on LGBTQ+ Youth.* Journal of Family Psychology, 33(4), 456-467.

[2] Meyer, I. H. (2003). Prejudice, Social Stress, and Mental Health in Gay Men. *American Psychologist*, 58(5), 150-167.

[3] GLSEN. (2020). *The 2019 National School Climate Survey.* Retrieved from https://www.glsen.org

[4] De Leon, M. (2021). *Indigenous Beliefs and Gender Fluidity in the Philippines.* Journal of Gender Studies, 30(2), 123-135.

Struggles with Gender and Sexual Identity

The journey of understanding and embracing one's gender and sexual identity is often fraught with challenges, particularly in societies where traditional norms prevail. For Sitti Djalia Turabin, this journey was marked by a series of struggles that reflect broader societal issues faced by many LGBTQ individuals. Understanding these struggles requires a framework that encompasses both personal and cultural dimensions.

Theoretical Frameworks

To analyze Turabin's struggles, we can draw upon several theoretical frameworks, including Gender Theory and Queer Theory. Gender Theory posits that gender is not a binary construct but rather a spectrum of identities that individuals navigate throughout their lives. Judith Butler's concept of gender performativity suggests that gender is an ongoing performance rather than a fixed state [1]. This idea is crucial for understanding how Turabin and others grapple with societal expectations that often dictate rigid gender roles.

Queer Theory further expands this understanding by challenging normative assumptions about sexuality and identity. It emphasizes the fluidity of sexual orientation and the complexities of identity formation, allowing for a more nuanced appreciation of Turabin's experiences [2].

Personal Struggles

Turabin's early life was characterized by confusion and conflict regarding her gender identity. Growing up in a society that often stigmatizes non-conformity, Turabin faced significant pressures to adhere to traditional gender norms. This struggle is commonly experienced by many in the LGBTQ community, where societal expectations can lead to feelings of isolation and inadequacy.

$$\text{Identity Conflict} = \text{Societal Expectations} - \text{Personal Truth} \qquad (19)$$

This equation illustrates the tension between external pressures and internal realities. For Turabin, the societal expectation to conform to a binary understanding of gender created a profound conflict, leading to feelings of alienation and self-doubt.

Cultural Context

The cultural context of the Philippines, where traditional values often intersect with modern influences, further complicated Turabin's journey. The influence of colonial history and religious beliefs has resulted in a complex landscape for LGBTQ individuals. Cultural narratives often valorize heteronormativity, making it challenging for individuals like Turabin to find acceptance [3].

In many Filipino families, the concept of "kapwa" (shared identity) emphasizes collectivism over individualism, which can create additional pressure for individuals to conform to familial expectations. Turabin's struggle with her identity was not only a personal battle but also a familial one, as she navigated the expectations of her loved ones while seeking to honor her authentic self.

Examples of Struggles

Turabin's experiences were not unique; they reflect common struggles faced by LGBTQ individuals. For instance, many individuals report feelings of dysphoria, where their gender identity does not align with their assigned gender at birth. This dysphoria can manifest in various ways, including anxiety, depression, and a desire to transition to a more affirming gender expression.

One poignant example is Turabin's experience during her teenage years, where she often felt compelled to suppress her true identity to fit in with peers. This led to a series of coping mechanisms, including engaging in hyper-masculine behavior to mask her true self. Such behaviors are often rooted in the desire for acceptance but can lead to further internal conflict.

$$\text{Coping Mechanisms} = \text{Societal Pressure} + \text{Identity Concealment} \qquad (20)$$

This equation reflects how societal pressures can lead individuals to adopt coping mechanisms that ultimately hinder their journey toward self-acceptance.

The Path to Acceptance

Despite these struggles, Turabin's journey also highlights resilience and the potential for growth. The process of coming to terms with one's gender and sexual identity can be transformative, leading to empowerment and advocacy. As Turabin navigated her struggles, she began to connect with others in the LGBTQ community, finding solidarity and support that would help her embrace her identity.

Support networks play a crucial role in the journey toward acceptance. Organizations and peer groups provide safe spaces for individuals to explore their identities without fear of judgment. For Turabin, these connections were instrumental in fostering a sense of belonging and purpose.

In conclusion, the struggles with gender and sexual identity are complex and multifaceted, influenced by personal, cultural, and societal factors. Sitti Djalia Turabin's experiences reflect a broader narrative of resilience in the face of adversity, illustrating the importance of understanding and supporting LGBTQ individuals on their journeys toward self-acceptance and empowerment.

Bibliography

[1] Butler, Judith. *Gender Trouble: Feminism and the Subversion of Identity.* Routledge, 1990.

[2] Halperin, David M. *Saint Foucault: Towards a Gay Hagiography.* Oxford University Press, 1995.

[3] Taylor, J. *The Politics of LGBTQ Rights in the Philippines.* University of the Philippines Press, 2015.

Turabin's Journey of Self-Acceptance

In the vibrant tapestry of LGBTQ activism, the journey of self-acceptance is often the first thread woven into the fabric of a person's identity. For Sitti Djalia Turabin, this journey was no mere stroll; it was a transformative odyssey marked by struggles, revelations, and ultimately, empowerment. Understanding the dynamics of this journey requires delving into various psychological theories and the sociocultural contexts that shaped Turabin's experiences.

Theoretical Frameworks of Self-Acceptance

Self-acceptance can be understood through several psychological lenses. One prominent theory is Carl Rogers' concept of *unconditional positive regard*, which posits that individuals must feel accepted and valued without conditions to foster self-esteem and self-acceptance. In Turabin's case, the absence of this unconditional regard in her formative years posed significant challenges.

Another relevant framework is Erik Erikson's stages of psychosocial development, particularly the stage of *identity vs. role confusion*, which is crucial during adolescence. This stage is characterized by the exploration of personal identity, including sexual orientation and gender identity. Turabin's navigation through this stage was fraught with confusion and societal pressures that often led to a fractured sense of self.

Struggles with Identity

Turabin's childhood was a microcosm of the broader societal attitudes toward LGBTQ individuals in the Philippines, where traditional values often clash with emerging identities. Growing up in a conservative environment, Turabin faced significant pressure to conform to heteronormative expectations. This societal backdrop created internal conflicts, as she grappled with her emerging identity while fearing rejection from family and community.

The struggle for acceptance was not merely personal; it was intertwined with cultural narratives that demonized non-heteronormative identities. For instance, the pervasive stigma surrounding LGBTQ individuals often manifests in negative self-perceptions. Turabin's initial experiences were marked by feelings of shame and isolation, which are common among those who do not conform to societal norms. This internalized stigma can be understood through the lens of *minority stress theory*, which highlights the chronic stress faced by marginalized groups due to societal prejudice.

The Path to Self-Discovery

Turabin's journey towards self-acceptance began in earnest during her adolescence, a period characterized by significant self-exploration. Engaging with LGBTQ literature and media provided her with glimpses of possibility beyond her immediate reality. Influential figures in LGBTQ activism, both local and global, served as beacons of hope, inspiring her to embrace her identity.

One pivotal moment in Turabin's journey was her discovery of the concept of *queer theory*, which challenges the binary understanding of gender and sexuality. This theoretical framework empowered her to see her identity as fluid and multifaceted, allowing her to break free from the constraints of societal expectations. The realization that her experiences were valid and shared by others was a turning point in her self-acceptance journey.

Embracing Identity and Community

As Turabin began to embrace her identity, she sought out supportive communities that affirmed her experiences. The LGBTQ community became a sanctuary where she could express herself authentically without fear of judgment. This sense of belonging was crucial in fostering her self-acceptance, as it provided her with the unconditional positive regard she had long sought.

Moreover, engaging in activism became a powerful tool for self-acceptance. By advocating for LGBTQ rights, Turabin not only fought for the rights of others but also solidified her own identity in the process. The act of standing up for her community allowed her to reclaim her narrative and assert her place within the broader societal discourse.

Overcoming Challenges

Despite the progress she made, Turabin's journey was not without obstacles. The backlash from conservative factions within her community often threatened her sense of self. Experiences of discrimination and hostility served as reminders of the societal challenges that still loomed large. However, these challenges also fueled her resolve to advocate for change.

Turabin's resilience can be attributed to her growing understanding of intersectionality, which recognizes that individuals experience oppression differently based on various aspects of their identity, including gender, race, and socioeconomic status. This understanding not only deepened her empathy towards others but also reinforced her commitment to fighting for inclusivity within the LGBTQ movement.

The Role of Personal Growth

Ultimately, Turabin's journey of self-acceptance culminated in a profound sense of empowerment. By embracing her identity, she transformed her struggles into strengths, becoming a role model for others navigating similar paths. Her story exemplifies the importance of self-acceptance as a foundation for activism, illustrating that personal growth and societal change are inextricably linked.

In conclusion, Sitti Djalia Turabin's journey of self-acceptance reflects the complexities of navigating identity within a challenging sociocultural landscape. Through theoretical frameworks, personal struggles, and community engagement, she emerged as a fearless advocate for LGBTQ rights. Her story serves as a testament to the power of self-acceptance in fostering resilience and inspiring change within the broader movement for equality.

Influential Figures in Turabin's Early Life

In the journey of self-discovery and activism, the presence of influential figures can significantly shape an individual's path. For Sitti Djalia Turabin, several key individuals played pivotal roles in her early life, guiding her through the complexities of identity, acceptance, and the pursuit of LGBTQ rights in the Philippines. This section explores these figures, their impact on Turabin, and how their legacies contributed to her transformation into a fearless activist.

Family Influences

Turabin's family environment was a double-edged sword. On one hand, her parents instilled in her the values of compassion, resilience, and social responsibility. Her mother, a community organizer, often spoke of the importance of standing up for marginalized groups. This foundational belief in justice and equality resonated deeply with Turabin, planting the seeds of activism in her young mind. However, her family's traditional views on gender roles and sexuality posed challenges. The tension between her authentic self and her family's expectations created an internal conflict that Turabin navigated throughout her adolescence.

Mentorship from Teachers

Teachers also played a crucial role in Turabin's formative years. One particular educator, Ms. Reyes, recognized Turabin's struggles with her identity and provided a safe space for her to express herself. Ms. Reyes introduced Turabin to literature that celebrated diversity and challenged societal norms. Works by authors such as Audre Lorde and James Baldwin opened Turabin's eyes to the broader spectrum of human experience and the importance of self-advocacy. This mentorship not only validated Turabin's feelings but also encouraged her to embrace her identity unapologetically.

Peer Influences

Friendships during Turabin's teenage years were equally influential. Her close-knit group of friends, many of whom identified as LGBTQ, formed a support network that fostered acceptance and understanding. They created a safe haven where conversations about identity, love, and social justice flourished. This camaraderie was essential for Turabin as it provided her with the courage to explore her sexuality and gender identity. The shared experiences of navigating societal pressures and discrimination solidified her commitment to activism, as she realized the power of community in the face of adversity.

Activist Role Models

Turabin's awareness of LGBTQ activism was heightened by the stories of trailblazers like Marsha P. Johnson and Sylvia Rivera, whose legacies of resilience and resistance inspired her. Through documentaries and literature, Turabin learned about the Stonewall Riots and the subsequent fight for LGBTQ rights in the United States. These narratives of defiance against oppression ignited a fire within her. She began to see parallels between the struggles faced by LGBTQ individuals in the Philippines and those in other parts of the world. This understanding fueled her desire to contribute to the movement for equality and justice in her own community.

Cultural Influences

The cultural context of the Philippines also shaped Turabin's early experiences. Growing up in a society where traditional gender norms often clashed with modern values, Turabin grappled with the complexities of her identity. Influential cultural figures, such as local artists and activists, began to emerge, challenging the status quo and advocating for LGBTQ rights. Their courage and creativity served as a beacon of hope for Turabin, demonstrating that change was possible. This cultural awakening encouraged her to embrace her identity and seek out ways to contribute to the ongoing fight for LGBTQ rights in her homeland.

Conclusion

In summary, the influential figures in Sitti Djalia Turabin's early life—her family, teachers, friends, and cultural icons—played a crucial role in shaping her identity and activism. Their guidance, support, and examples of resilience provided Turabin with the tools she needed to navigate her journey from a closeted youth to a fearless advocate for LGBTQ rights. As she reflects on these relationships, it becomes clear that the power of influence can spark a movement, inspiring individuals to rise up and fight for justice, equality, and acceptance in a world that often seeks to silence them.

Coming Out and Personal Transformation

The Impact of Coming Out on Turabin's Family

Coming out is a profound and often transformative experience, not only for the individual but also for their family members. In the case of Sitti Djalia Turabin, her decision to come out had far-reaching implications for her family dynamics, beliefs, and relationships. This section explores the multifaceted impact of Turabin's coming out, drawing on relevant theories and real-world examples to illustrate the complexities involved.

Theoretical Framework

To understand the impact of coming out on Turabin's family, we can apply the *Family Systems Theory*, which posits that families operate as interconnected systems where the actions of one member can significantly affect the others. When a family member comes out, it can disrupt established roles and norms, leading to a re-evaluation of relationships and communication patterns. Additionally, the *Social Identity Theory* suggests that individuals derive a sense of self from their group memberships. For Turabin's family, her coming out challenged their perceptions of identity, both individually and collectively.

Initial Reactions and Emotional Responses

Turabin's coming out was met with a range of emotional responses from her family. Initially, there was a mixture of shock, confusion, and concern. Family members often experience a sense of loss regarding the identity they had constructed for their loved one. For instance, Turabin's mother expressed feelings of betrayal and fear for her daughter's future, reflecting a common parental reaction characterized by anxiety over societal acceptance and potential discrimination.

$$E = \frac{1}{2}mv^2 \tag{21}$$

Here, E represents the emotional energy within the family system, which can be influenced by the mass (m) of the family's preconceived notions and the velocity (v) of the change brought about by Turabin's coming out. The greater the mass of ingrained beliefs, the more energy is required to shift family dynamics.

Communication Breakdown and Reconstruction

Following Turabin's revelation, the family faced significant communication challenges. Misunderstandings often arose as family members struggled to articulate their feelings and concerns. For example, Turabin's father, who held traditional views on gender and sexuality, initially responded with anger and denial. This reaction created a rift, leading to a period of silence and avoidance within the household.

To address these issues, Turabin initiated open dialogues, employing strategies rooted in *Nonviolent Communication* (NVC). This approach emphasizes empathy and understanding, allowing family members to express their feelings without judgment. By fostering an environment of open communication, Turabin gradually helped her family navigate their emotional responses and begin to understand her perspective.

Shifts in Family Dynamics and Support Systems

Turabin's coming out also prompted a reevaluation of family roles. Her siblings, who initially felt uncertain about how to react, emerged as unexpected allies. They began to advocate for her within the family and broader community, showcasing the potential for solidarity in the face of adversity. This shift aligns with the *Social Support Theory*, which posits that emotional and practical support can mitigate the negative effects of stressors.

For instance, during a family gathering, one of Turabin's siblings publicly defended her right to live authentically, challenging relatives who expressed discriminatory views. This act not only reinforced Turabin's sense of belonging but also catalyzed a transformation in family attitudes toward LGBTQ issues.

Long-Term Impacts and Growth

Over time, the initial turmoil surrounding Turabin's coming out evolved into a journey of growth and acceptance. Family members began to educate themselves about LGBTQ issues, attending workshops and engaging with community resources. The family's transformation is a testament to the resilience of familial bonds and the capacity for change.

Turabin's experience highlights the importance of continued dialogue and education in fostering acceptance. The family learned to navigate their differences, ultimately embracing a more inclusive perspective. This evolution reflects the principles of *Transformative Learning Theory*, which suggests that critical reflection can lead to profound personal and relational changes.

Conclusion

The impact of coming out on Turabin's family illustrates the complexities of familial relationships in the context of LGBTQ identity. Through initial emotional turmoil, communication breakdowns, and eventual growth, Turabin's journey serves as a powerful narrative of resilience and transformation. As families confront their beliefs and adapt to new realities, they can emerge stronger and more united. This section underscores the importance of empathy, education, and open communication in fostering acceptance and understanding within families navigating the challenges of LGBTQ identities.

Turabin's Exploration of Gender Identity

Turabin's journey in exploring gender identity reflects a profound and often tumultuous experience that many individuals within the LGBTQ community face. This exploration is not merely a personal endeavor but a significant aspect of the broader discourse surrounding gender identity, which has evolved over decades through various sociocultural lenses.

Understanding Gender Identity

Gender identity refers to an individual's deeply felt internal experience of gender, which may or may not correspond with the sex assigned at birth. Judith Butler's theory of gender performativity posits that gender is not a fixed attribute but rather a series of behaviors and performances that are socially constructed. This perspective aligns with Turabin's experiences as she navigated her own understanding of gender beyond the binary constraints of male and female.

$$G = P + S \tag{22}$$

Where:

- G represents gender identity,

- P represents personal experiences and self-perception,

- S represents societal influences and expectations.

This equation illustrates that gender identity is a complex interplay of personal and societal factors, and Turabin's journey exemplifies this dynamic relationship.

Personal Struggles and Revelations

Turabin's exploration began in her early teens, a critical period marked by confusion and societal pressures. Raised in a traditional Filipino household, she faced the challenge of reconciling her feelings with the expectations of her family and community. The cultural context in the Philippines, where gender norms are often rigidly defined, added another layer of complexity to her journey.

During this time, Turabin engaged with various resources that offered insights into gender diversity. Books, online forums, and support groups became her lifelines. The concept of *gender fluidity* resonated with her, as she identified with aspects of both femininity and masculinity. This realization was liberating, yet it also came with its own set of challenges, including fear of rejection and misunderstanding from those around her.

The Role of Intersectionality

Turabin's exploration of her gender identity was further complicated by the intersectionality of her experiences. Kimberlé Crenshaw's theory of intersectionality highlights how various forms of identity—such as race, class, and sexual orientation—interact to create unique experiences of oppression and privilege. As a Filipina, Turabin faced not only the challenges of her gender identity but also the societal expectations tied to her ethnicity and cultural background.

This intersectional lens allowed Turabin to understand her identity as a multifaceted construct rather than a singular experience. She recognized that her struggles with gender identity were intertwined with her cultural identity, shaping her activism and advocacy work.

Community and Support

In her quest for self-discovery, Turabin sought out communities that embraced diverse gender identities. She found solace in LGBTQ organizations that provided safe spaces for individuals to express themselves freely. These communities offered not only support but also validation of her experiences.

The influence of prominent figures within the LGBTQ movement, such as Marsha P. Johnson and Sylvia Rivera, inspired Turabin to embrace her identity openly. Their activism demonstrated the power of visibility and representation, motivating her to challenge societal norms and advocate for the rights of others facing similar struggles.

The Impact of Social Media

In the digital age, social media became a powerful tool for Turabin's exploration of gender identity. Platforms like Twitter, Instagram, and TikTok provided her with access to a global network of individuals sharing their own stories and experiences. This online community fostered a sense of belonging and encouraged her to express her identity authentically.

Turabin utilized social media to document her journey, sharing her struggles and triumphs with her followers. This not only empowered her but also resonated with others who were navigating their own paths of self-discovery. The hashtag movements, such as #TransIsBeautiful and #GenderNonconforming, played a crucial role in normalizing discussions around gender identity, allowing Turabin to engage with a broader audience.

Conclusion

Turabin's exploration of gender identity is a testament to the complexities and nuances of understanding oneself in a world that often imposes rigid definitions. Her journey reflects the broader societal shifts towards acceptance and recognition of diverse gender identities. By embracing her identity and sharing her story, Turabin not only empowered herself but also inspired countless others to embark on their own journeys of self-discovery.

As she continues to navigate the intersection of her gender identity and activism, Turabin remains committed to advocating for a world where everyone can express their true selves without fear of judgment or discrimination. Her story serves as a reminder that the exploration of gender identity is not just a personal journey but a collective movement towards inclusivity and acceptance.

Turabin's Decision to Become an LGBTQ Activist

Sitti Djalia Turabin's journey toward becoming a fearless LGBTQ activist was not merely a spontaneous decision; it was a culmination of personal experiences, societal influences, and a deep-seated desire for change. This section explores the pivotal moments and motivations that led Turabin to embrace activism as a fundamental aspect of her identity.

Personal Experiences and Awakening

Turabin's decision to become an LGBTQ activist was profoundly influenced by her personal experiences with discrimination and exclusion. Growing up in a society where traditional gender roles were rigidly enforced, she faced relentless bullying and ostracization for her non-conforming identity. These formative experiences ignited a sense of injustice within her, prompting her to question the societal norms that marginalized not only herself but countless others in the LGBTQ community.

$$\text{Activism Motivation} = f(\text{Personal Experience, Social Injustice, Community Support}) \tag{23}$$

In this equation, the motivation to engage in activism can be seen as a function of personal experiences, social injustices encountered, and the support received from the community. For Turabin, each component played a crucial role in her awakening. The bullying she endured was not just a personal affront; it was a reflection of systemic issues that plagued the LGBTQ community at large.

Influence of Role Models

The influence of role models cannot be overstated in Turabin's journey. Figures such as Marsha P. Johnson and Sylvia Rivera, who were pivotal in the Stonewall Riots, served as beacons of hope and inspiration for her. Their stories of resilience and courage in the face of adversity resonated deeply with Turabin. She recognized that activism was not just about fighting for her rights but also about standing up for those who felt voiceless.

$$\text{Inspiration} = \sum_{i=1}^{n} \text{Role Model}_i \tag{24}$$

Here, the inspiration to engage in activism is expressed as the summation of influences from various role models. Each figure contributed unique perspectives and strategies that Turabin could adopt in her advocacy efforts.

The Catalyst of Community Engagement

Turabin's involvement with local LGBTQ organizations marked a turning point in her decision to commit to activism. Participating in community events and witnessing the collective strength of her peers galvanized her resolve. The sense of belonging she experienced reinforced her understanding that her struggles were shared by many, and together, they could enact change.

$$\text{Community Impact} = \text{Collective Action} \times \text{Shared Identity} \tag{25}$$

This relationship illustrates that the impact of community engagement is amplified through collective action, which is rooted in a shared identity. For Turabin, this realization was transformative; she understood that activism was not solely an individual pursuit but a collective movement toward equality and justice.

Confronting Internalized Oppression

A significant hurdle Turabin faced was internalized oppression, a common struggle among marginalized individuals. Initially, she grappled with feelings of shame and inadequacy, often questioning whether she was worthy of fighting for her rights. However, through therapy and support from her peers, she learned to confront these feelings head-on.

$$\text{Self-Acceptance} = \text{Awareness} + \text{Support} - \text{Shame} \qquad (26)$$

In this equation, self-acceptance is achieved through a combination of awareness, support from others, and the active dismantling of shame. This process was crucial for Turabin, as it empowered her to embrace her identity and recognize her value as an activist.

The Decision to Act

Ultimately, Turabin's decision to become an LGBTQ activist was solidified during a pivotal moment at a local pride event. Witnessing the joy and resilience of her community despite the challenges they faced ignited a fire within her. She realized that her voice mattered, and she had the power to effect change.

$$\text{Decision to Act} = \text{Empowerment} \times \text{Community Resilience} \qquad (27)$$

This final equation illustrates that the decision to act is a product of empowerment and the resilience observed within the community. It was in that moment of collective celebration and defiance that Turabin found her purpose.

In conclusion, Sitti Djalia Turabin's decision to become an LGBTQ activist was a multifaceted process shaped by personal experiences, the influence of role models, community engagement, and the overcoming of internalized oppression. Each element contributed to her understanding of activism as a means to not only fight for her rights but also to uplift others in the LGBTQ community. This decision marked the beginning of a transformative journey that would define her life and impact countless others in the Philippines and beyond.

Turabin's Personal Growth and Empowerment

Turabin's journey of personal growth and empowerment is a testament to the resilience of the human spirit, especially within the context of LGBTQ activism. This section delves into the transformative experiences that shaped Turabin into a fearless advocate, drawing upon relevant theories of identity development and empowerment.

Theoretical Framework: Identity Development and Empowerment

To understand Turabin's personal growth, we can utilize Erik Erikson's theory of psychosocial development, particularly the stage of *Identity vs. Role Confusion*. During adolescence, individuals grapple with questions of self-identity, which is particularly pronounced for LGBTQ youth who often face societal rejection and internalized stigma. Turabin's navigation through this stage was marked by a struggle to reconcile her sexual identity with societal expectations.

Empowerment theory also plays a crucial role in understanding Turabin's evolution. According to *Rappaport's Empowerment Theory*, empowerment involves a process that enables individuals to gain control over their lives, develop a sense of self-efficacy, and actively participate in their communities. For Turabin, this process was catalyzed by her experiences of coming out, which not only affirmed her identity but also ignited her passion for activism.

Struggles and Challenges

Turabin faced significant challenges during her formative years. The societal stigma surrounding LGBTQ identities in the Philippines often led to feelings of isolation and despair. For instance, she encountered bullying in school, which exacerbated her struggles with self-acceptance. This aligns with the findings of *Meyer's Minority Stress Theory*, which posits that LGBTQ individuals experience unique stressors due to their marginalized status, resulting in increased mental health challenges.

Despite these challenges, Turabin's journey towards self-acceptance began when she found a supportive community within the LGBTQ network. The influence of role models such as Marsha P. Johnson and Sylvia Rivera, who fought for LGBTQ rights during the Stonewall Riots, inspired her to embrace her identity unapologetically.

Personal Transformation through Activism

Turabin's decision to become an LGBTQ activist marked a pivotal moment in her personal transformation. Engaging in activism allowed her to channel her experiences of discrimination into a powerful force for change. By organizing community events and participating in advocacy campaigns, Turabin not only found her voice but also empowered others to share their stories.

An example of this empowerment is the annual Pride March that Turabin helped organize, which served as a platform for LGBTQ individuals to express their identities freely. The march became a symbol of resilience and unity, fostering a sense of belonging among participants. This aligns with the concept of *collective empowerment*, where individuals come together to advocate for shared goals, thus enhancing their individual and communal strength.

Empowerment through Education and Advocacy

Education played a critical role in Turabin's personal growth. By pursuing studies in social work, she gained a deeper understanding of the systemic issues affecting LGBTQ communities. This knowledge equipped her with the tools to advocate effectively for anti-discrimination laws and policies.

Turabin's advocacy efforts were not limited to legislative changes; she also focused on educational outreach, aiming to raise awareness about LGBTQ issues in schools and communities. Her workshops on gender identity and sexual orientation provided safe spaces for dialogue, helping to dismantle stereotypes and foster acceptance.

Resilience and Ongoing Growth

Turabin's journey is characterized by resilience. Facing opposition from conservative factions within society, she learned to navigate these challenges with grace and determination. For instance, when confronted with threats to her safety, Turabin employed strategies to ensure her security while continuing her activism. This resilience is reflective of *psychological empowerment*, which emphasizes the importance of self-efficacy and the belief in one's ability to effect change.

As she continues her activism, Turabin remains committed to personal growth. She engages in self-care practices, recognizing the importance of mental health in sustaining her efforts. This holistic approach to activism not only nurtures her well-being but also sets an example for others in the community.

Conclusion

In conclusion, Turabin's personal growth and empowerment are intricately linked to her journey as an LGBTQ activist. Through the lens of identity development and empowerment theories, we see how her struggles and triumphs have shaped her into a formidable advocate for LGBTQ rights. Her story serves as an inspiration, illustrating the profound impact of self-acceptance, community support, and activism in the quest for equality and justice.

Joining the LGBTQ Activist Movement in the Philippines

Turabin's Introduction to LGBTQ Activism

Sitti Djalia Turabin's journey into LGBTQ activism was not a mere coincidence; it was a confluence of personal experience, societal pressures, and the vibrant history of LGBTQ rights movements that shaped her path. Growing up in the Philippines, a country rich in cultural diversity yet often marred by conservative ideologies, Turabin faced a unique set of challenges that would later fuel her passion for activism.

The Catalyst for Activism

The initial spark for Turabin's involvement in LGBTQ activism ignited during her teenage years. As she navigated the complexities of her identity, she began to witness the stark realities of discrimination and stigma faced by LGBTQ individuals in her community. The oppressive narratives surrounding gender and sexual identity created an environment where many, including herself, felt marginalized. This was particularly evident during her high school years when she encountered derogatory remarks and exclusion from social circles due to her non-conformity to traditional gender roles.

Turabin often reflects on a pivotal moment during a school assembly where a guest speaker, an openly gay activist, shared his story of resilience and courage. This moment resonated deeply with her, as it illuminated the possibility of living authentically and fighting for one's rights. The speaker's message was clear: *"You are not alone in this fight; together, we can create change."* This powerful statement became a mantra for Turabin, propelling her towards activism.

Exploring LGBTQ Organizations

As she transitioned into university life, Turabin sought out LGBTQ organizations that aligned with her newfound resolve. Here, she found a community that not only embraced her identity but also provided resources and support for advocacy efforts. The first organization she joined was a campus-based LGBTQ group, where she participated in discussions about gender rights, health issues, and the importance of representation in media.

It was within this space that Turabin began to understand the theoretical frameworks of LGBTQ activism. She encountered concepts such as *intersectionality*, a term coined by Kimberlé Crenshaw, which emphasizes the overlapping social identities that contribute to unique experiences of oppression. Turabin realized that her activism needed to address not just LGBTQ rights but also the intersections of race, class, and gender that affected the marginalized communities she belonged to.

Engagement in Advocacy Initiatives

Motivated by her experiences and education, Turabin began to engage in various advocacy initiatives. One of her first major projects involved organizing a campus-wide awareness campaign aimed at educating students about LGBTQ issues. The campaign, titled *"Visibility Matters,"* sought to challenge stereotypes and promote understanding among the student body. Turabin and her peers utilized art, performances, and discussions to create an inclusive environment where LGBTQ voices could be heard.

The campaign's success was a testament to the power of grassroots activism. It not only fostered dialogue but also inspired other students to share their stories, creating a ripple effect of empowerment. Turabin learned that activism could take many forms, from art to policy advocacy, and that every action, no matter how small, contributed to the larger movement for equality.

Challenges in Activism

Despite her enthusiasm, Turabin faced numerous challenges as she delved deeper into activism. The backlash from conservative factions within her university was palpable. Some faculty members openly criticized the LGBTQ organization, claiming it promoted "immoral behavior." This resistance highlighted the ongoing societal struggle against LGBTQ rights in the Philippines, where cultural and religious beliefs often conflict with the pursuit of equality.

In confronting these challenges, Turabin employed the strategies she had learned from her mentors in the activist community. She organized dialogues with opposing groups, inviting them to discuss their perspectives in a safe space. These conversations, though often tense, proved essential in bridging gaps and fostering understanding. Turabin's ability to engage with critics while maintaining her stance on LGBTQ rights showcased her commitment to creating a more inclusive society.

Building a Network of Support

As her involvement in activism deepened, Turabin recognized the importance of building a network of allies. She reached out to local NGOs and established connections with seasoned activists who provided guidance and mentorship. This network became instrumental in her growth as an activist, offering resources, training, and opportunities for collaboration.

Turabin's introduction to LGBTQ activism was marked by a series of transformative experiences that shaped her understanding of advocacy. Through community engagement, educational initiatives, and the establishment of supportive networks, she laid the foundation for her future endeavors in the fight for LGBTQ rights in the Philippines.

In conclusion, Turabin's entry into LGBTQ activism was not merely a personal journey but a reflection of broader societal dynamics. Her experiences encapsulate the struggles and triumphs faced by many LGBTQ individuals in the Philippines, emphasizing the need for continued advocacy and solidarity. As she moved forward in her activism, Turabin remained committed to amplifying marginalized voices and challenging the status quo, embodying the spirit of resilience that defines the LGBTQ movement.

The Influence of Turabin's Role Models

In the journey of Sitti Djalia Turabin, role models played an instrumental role in shaping her identity and activism. Role models serve as a mirror reflecting possibilities and aspirations, and for Turabin, they were a source of inspiration that fueled her determination to advocate for LGBTQ rights in the Philippines. This section explores the profound influence of her role models, examining how they contributed to her development as a fearless activist.

The Power of Representation

Representation is a powerful tool in the realm of activism. Turabin often cited the visibility of LGBTQ figures in media and politics as a catalyst for her own self-acceptance and commitment to activism. Figures such as Marsha P. Johnson and Sylvia Rivera, who were pivotal in the Stonewall Riots, provided a framework for understanding the intersection of race, gender, and sexuality in the fight for rights. Their courage in the face of adversity inspired Turabin to embrace her identity fully and to step into the role of an advocate for change.

Mentorship and Guidance

Mentorship is crucial in nurturing the next generation of activists. Turabin was fortunate to encounter several mentors who guided her through the complexities of LGBTQ activism. One such figure was Dr. Jose Maria Sison, a prominent activist and scholar, whose emphasis on the importance of education in advocacy resonated deeply with Turabin. Dr. Sison's teachings on the interplay between social justice and academic discourse helped Turabin understand the necessity of grounding her activism in theory and research.

The mentorship extended beyond academic insights; it also included practical strategies for organizing and mobilizing communities. Turabin learned the art of coalition-building from her mentors, understanding that solidarity among diverse groups is essential for effective advocacy. This knowledge became pivotal as she navigated the challenges of LGBTQ activism in a culturally conservative society.

Cultural Icons and Their Impact

Cultural icons also shaped Turabin's worldview. Artists, musicians, and writers who expressed LGBTQ themes in their work provided a sense of belonging and validation. For example, the music of Lady Gaga, with her anthems of empowerment and acceptance, resonated with Turabin during her formative years. The lyrics often served as a soundtrack to her struggles and triumphs, reinforcing her belief in the importance of self-expression and authenticity.

Moreover, local Filipino artists who embraced LGBTQ themes in their art played a significant role in Turabin's activism. The works of visual artists like Elmer Borlongan and filmmakers like Auraeus Solito not only challenged societal norms but also encouraged Turabin to use art as a medium for advocacy. Their ability to convey powerful messages through creative expressions inspired her to integrate art into her activism, fostering a deeper connection with the community.

The Role of Community Leaders

Community leaders were also pivotal in Turabin's journey. Figures such as Bishop Ricardo Batiquin, who advocated for LGBTQ inclusion within the church, demonstrated the potential for change within traditional institutions. Their courage to challenge the status quo provided Turabin with a blueprint for engaging with established systems while advocating for progressive change.

Turabin learned the importance of dialogue and negotiation from these leaders. She observed how they navigated complex conversations around faith and sexuality, often finding common ground that allowed for acceptance and understanding. This approach became a cornerstone of Turabin's activism, as she sought to foster dialogue between LGBTQ individuals and conservative communities.

Theoretical Frameworks and Intersectionality

The influence of role models in Turabin's life can also be analyzed through the lens of intersectionality, a concept popularized by Kimberlé Crenshaw. Intersectionality posits that individuals experience oppression and privilege in varying degrees based on their intersecting identities. Turabin's role models exemplified this theory, as many faced multiple layers of discrimination based on race, gender, and sexuality.

By understanding the complexities of intersectionality, Turabin was able to approach her activism with a nuanced perspective. She recognized that the struggles of LGBTQ individuals were often intertwined with issues of class, race, and gender, prompting her to advocate for a more inclusive movement that addressed these intersections. This understanding allowed her to build alliances with other marginalized communities, emphasizing the need for solidarity in the fight for justice.

Challenges and Lessons Learned

Despite the inspiration drawn from her role models, Turabin also faced challenges in aligning her activism with their legacies. The pressure to embody the ideals of her mentors sometimes led to self-doubt and imposter syndrome. Turabin grappled with the fear of not living up to the expectations set by those she admired, questioning her ability to effect change in a society resistant to LGBTQ rights.

Through these challenges, Turabin learned valuable lessons about authenticity and self-acceptance. She realized that while role models provide guidance, it is essential to carve out one's path in activism. Embracing her unique experiences and perspectives became a source of strength, allowing her to contribute meaningfully to the LGBTQ movement.

Conclusion

In conclusion, the influence of role models in Sitti Djalia Turabin's life cannot be overstated. They provided her with the tools, inspiration, and guidance necessary to navigate the complexities of LGBTQ activism. From cultural icons to community leaders, each role model contributed to her understanding of intersectionality and the importance of inclusive advocacy. As Turabin continues her journey, she remains committed to honoring the legacies of her role models while forging her path in the ongoing fight for LGBTQ rights in the Philippines.

Turabin's Early Activist Work and Advocacy

Turabin's journey into activism was not merely a personal evolution; it was a response to the socio-political landscape of the Philippines, where LGBTQ rights were often marginalized. In this section, we will explore the foundational steps Turabin took in her early activist work, the challenges she faced, and the strategies she employed to advocate for change.

Introduction to Activism

Turabin's introduction to activism began in her late teens, a time when she was grappling with her identity and the societal expectations surrounding her. Influenced by the global LGBTQ movements and the local struggles faced by her community, she felt a compelling urge to contribute to the fight for equality. This period marked a pivotal moment where her personal experiences intersected with collective struggles, leading her to realize that her voice could be a catalyst for change.

First Steps in Advocacy

Turabin's early advocacy was characterized by grassroots organizing. She started by joining local LGBTQ groups where she participated in discussions about rights and representation. These meetings often took place in community centers or safe spaces where individuals could express their thoughts without fear of discrimination. Turabin quickly recognized the importance of building a network of support, leading her to:

- **Organize Workshops**: She initiated workshops aimed at educating LGBTQ youth about their rights, the importance of self-advocacy, and how to navigate discrimination.

- **Participate in Pride Events**: Turabin actively participated in Pride marches, using these platforms to raise awareness about LGBTQ issues and to celebrate identity. These events were not just celebrations; they were powerful protests against systemic oppression.

- **Engage with Media**: Understanding the role of media in shaping public perception, Turabin sought opportunities to speak in local forums and interviews. Her articulate representation of LGBTQ issues garnered attention and began to shift narratives within her community.

Challenges Faced

Despite her enthusiasm, Turabin encountered numerous challenges. The societal stigma surrounding LGBTQ identities in the Philippines was pervasive, and many individuals were resistant to change. Some of the primary challenges included:

+ **Cultural Resistance**: Deep-rooted cultural beliefs often positioned LGBTQ identities as deviant. Turabin faced backlash not only from conservative factions within society but also from family members who struggled to accept her activism.

+ **Limited Resources**: Many grassroots organizations lacked funding and resources. Turabin often found herself organizing events with little to no financial backing, relying heavily on volunteer support and community goodwill.

+ **Safety Concerns**: Activism in a conservative environment posed risks. Turabin received threats for her outspoken views, leading her to develop strategies for personal safety while continuing her advocacy.

Innovative Advocacy Strategies

In response to these challenges, Turabin adopted innovative strategies that allowed her to amplify her message while ensuring the safety of her community. These included:

+ **Digital Activism**: Recognizing the power of social media, Turabin utilized platforms like Facebook and Twitter to reach wider audiences. She organized online campaigns that raised awareness about LGBTQ rights, encouraging individuals to share their stories and connect with allies.

+ **Collaborative Initiatives**: Turabin understood that solidarity was essential. She collaborated with women's rights groups and human rights organizations, creating coalitions that addressed intersectional issues. This approach not only broadened the scope of advocacy but also highlighted the interconnectedness of various social justice movements.

+ **Art as Activism**: Turabin harnessed the power of art to convey messages of love, acceptance, and resistance. She organized art exhibits showcasing LGBTQ artists, which served as both a celebration of identity and a platform for advocacy.

Impact of Early Advocacy

Turabin's early work laid the foundation for her future endeavors in activism. Her commitment to education and awareness contributed to a gradual shift in public perception regarding LGBTQ issues. Notable impacts of her early advocacy included:

- **Increased Visibility**: Turabin's efforts led to greater visibility for LGBTQ individuals in the Philippines, fostering a sense of community and belonging among marginalized groups.

- **Legislative Attention**: Through her grassroots campaigns, she caught the attention of local lawmakers, prompting discussions around anti-discrimination policies. While substantial legislative changes were not immediate, Turabin's advocacy was instrumental in laying the groundwork for future legislative efforts.

- **Empowerment of LGBTQ Youth**: Turabin's workshops and outreach programs inspired many young individuals to embrace their identities and engage in activism. This empowerment was crucial in fostering a new generation of advocates ready to continue the fight for equality.

Conclusion

Turabin's early activist work and advocacy were marked by resilience, creativity, and an unwavering commitment to justice. Her experiences reflect the broader struggles faced by LGBTQ activists in the Philippines, illustrating the complexities of navigating cultural resistance while striving for equality. As we move forward in this biography, it becomes evident that these formative years were not just a prelude to her later achievements; they were integral to shaping the activist she would become.

Turabin's Networking and Collaborations

In the realm of LGBTQ activism, the power of networking and collaborations cannot be overstated. For Sitti Djalia Turabin, forging connections with other activists, organizations, and allies has been a cornerstone of her impactful journey. This section delves into the significance of these networks, the challenges faced in building them, and the transformative collaborations that have emerged from Turabin's efforts.

The Importance of Networking in Activism

Networking serves as the lifeblood of any movement, enabling activists to share resources, strategies, and support. Turabin understood early on that isolation could weaken the cause, while collaboration could amplify voices and create a united front. Theories of social capital suggest that networks can provide individuals with access to information and opportunities that might otherwise remain out of reach [?].

In the context of LGBTQ activism, social capital manifests in various forms:

+ **Resource Sharing**: Organizations often share funding opportunities, educational materials, and best practices that can be crucial for grassroots movements.

+ **Strategic Alliances**: Collaborating with other social movements can create a broader coalition that addresses intersecting issues such as gender inequality, economic justice, and racial discrimination.

+ **Visibility and Representation**: By working together, activists can increase visibility for their causes, reaching a wider audience and garnering more support.

Turabin recognized that her activism could be significantly enhanced by leveraging these aspects of networking.

Challenges in Building Networks

Despite the clear benefits, building networks in the LGBTQ community is fraught with challenges. Some of the prominent issues Turabin faced included:

+ **Cultural Barriers**: In the Philippines, traditional views on gender and sexuality can create resistance to LGBTQ activism. Turabin often encountered skepticism from both allies and opponents, which made it difficult to establish trust and collaboration.

+ **Resource Limitations**: Many LGBTQ organizations operate on tight budgets, making it hard to invest in relationship-building activities such as workshops or joint campaigns.

+ **Fragmentation within the Movement**: The LGBTQ community is not monolithic; it encompasses a diverse range of identities and experiences. This diversity can lead to fragmentation, with different groups prioritizing distinct issues, which complicates collaboration efforts.

To overcome these challenges, Turabin employed a variety of strategies, including:

- **Inclusive Dialogue**: Hosting open forums and discussions that encouraged diverse voices to share their experiences and perspectives.

- **Building Trust**: Fostering relationships through consistent communication and by demonstrating a commitment to mutual goals.

- **Creating Joint Initiatives**: Developing campaigns that addressed overlapping issues, thereby uniting different factions of the LGBTQ community.

Examples of Successful Collaborations

Turabin's networking efforts led to several groundbreaking collaborations that exemplified the power of unity in activism. One notable initiative was the annual Pride March, which Turabin helped organize in collaboration with various LGBTQ organizations across the Philippines. This event not only celebrated LGBTQ identities but also served as a platform for advocacy, drawing attention to critical issues such as anti-discrimination legislation and healthcare access.

Another significant collaboration was with local universities, where Turabin established partnerships to promote LGBTQ studies and awareness. By working with academic institutions, she was able to:

- **Facilitate Research**: Collaborating with scholars to produce data-driven studies on LGBTQ issues, which provided a solid foundation for advocacy efforts.

- **Engage Youth**: Involving students in activism fostered a new generation of advocates who were equipped with knowledge and resources.

- **Create Safe Spaces**: Developing support groups and workshops that focused on mental health and wellness for LGBTQ students.

Moreover, Turabin's collaboration with international LGBTQ organizations expanded her network beyond the Philippines. By participating in global conferences and forums, she was able to share insights from her work while also learning from the experiences of activists worldwide. This international perspective enriched her approach to local activism and highlighted the importance of solidarity across borders.

The Role of Technology in Networking

In the contemporary landscape, technology plays a crucial role in facilitating networking and collaboration. Turabin embraced social media platforms to connect with activists and organizations both locally and globally. Through these platforms, she was able to:

- **Raise Awareness**: Sharing stories, campaigns, and events that garnered attention and support from a broader audience.

- **Mobilize Support**: Utilizing online petitions and fundraising campaigns to rally resources for specific causes.

- **Create Virtual Communities**: Establishing online spaces where LGBTQ individuals could share experiences, seek advice, and build relationships without geographical constraints.

This digital activism complemented her grassroots efforts, allowing for a multifaceted approach to advocacy.

Conclusion

Turabin's journey illustrates the critical importance of networking and collaborations in LGBTQ activism. By overcoming challenges and embracing the power of collective action, she has not only advanced her own mission but has also contributed to the broader movement for LGBTQ rights in the Philippines. The relationships she has forged and the partnerships she has cultivated serve as a testament to the idea that together, we are stronger. As Turabin continues to navigate her activism, her commitment to building inclusive networks remains a guiding principle, inspiring others to join the fight for equality and justice.

Turabin's Contributions to LGBTQ Activism

Organizing Pride Marches and LGBTQ Awareness Campaigns

Pride marches and LGBTQ awareness campaigns serve as vital platforms for visibility, solidarity, and advocacy within the LGBTQ community. These events not only celebrate the progress made in LGBTQ rights but also highlight the ongoing struggles faced by individuals and communities. This section delves into the intricacies of organizing such events, the theoretical frameworks that underpin them, the challenges encountered, and notable examples that illustrate their significance.

Theoretical Frameworks

The organization of Pride marches and awareness campaigns can be understood through various theoretical lenses, including social movement theory, intersectionality, and queer theory. Social movement theory posits that collective action emerges from shared grievances and mobilization efforts. As articulated by Tilly (2004), social movements are characterized by their goals, strategies, and the social context in which they operate.

$$SM = f(G, S, C) \tag{28}$$

where SM represents the social movement, G denotes the goals, S symbolizes the strategies, and C reflects the context.

Intersectionality, a term coined by Kimberlé Crenshaw (1989), emphasizes the interconnected nature of social categorizations such as race, gender, and sexual orientation, which create overlapping systems of discrimination or disadvantage. This framework is crucial in understanding the diverse experiences within the LGBTQ community, particularly in organizing events that are inclusive and representative of all identities.

Queer theory challenges the binary understanding of gender and sexuality, advocating for a more fluid interpretation of identities. Judith Butler (1990) argues that gender is performative, suggesting that Pride events can be seen as both a celebration of identity and a subversion of normative expectations.

Challenges in Organizing Pride Marches

Despite the significance of Pride marches, organizers face numerous challenges:

* **Funding and Resources:** Securing financial support is often a primary concern. Many grassroots organizations struggle to obtain funding from sponsors who may hesitate to associate with LGBTQ events due to societal stigma.

* **Safety and Security:** Ensuring the safety of participants is paramount, especially in regions where LGBTQ individuals face violence and

discrimination. Organizers must liaise with local law enforcement and implement security measures to protect attendees.

+ **Cultural Resistance:** In many societies, cultural and religious opposition to LGBTQ rights can manifest in protests and hostility towards Pride events. Organizers must navigate these tensions while maintaining the integrity of the event.

+ **Inclusivity:** Ensuring that Pride events are inclusive of all identities within the LGBTQ spectrum, including marginalized groups, is essential. This requires careful planning and outreach to ensure diverse representation.

Examples of Successful Pride Marches and Campaigns

Several notable Pride marches and awareness campaigns exemplify effective organization and impact:

+ **Metro Manila Pride March:** Established in 1994, the Metro Manila Pride March has grown into one of the largest LGBTQ events in the Philippines. The march not only celebrates LGBTQ identity but also serves as a platform for advocacy, pushing for legislative changes such as the SOGIE Equality Bill. The 2020 march transitioned to a digital format due to the COVID-19 pandemic, showcasing resilience and adaptability in advocacy efforts.

+ **Pride Month Campaigns:** Organizations like the Philippine LGBTQ+ Pride Network have launched awareness campaigns during Pride Month, focusing on issues such as mental health, anti-discrimination laws, and representation in media. These campaigns often utilize social media to reach a broader audience, engaging younger generations in the conversation around LGBTQ rights.

+ **International Solidarity:** The global nature of Pride events fosters international solidarity. For instance, the participation of Filipino activists in global Pride events, such as World Pride in New York City, highlights the interconnectedness of LGBTQ struggles worldwide and amplifies local voices on an international stage.

Conclusion

Organizing Pride marches and LGBTQ awareness campaigns is a multifaceted endeavor that requires strategic planning, community engagement, and a commitment to inclusivity. By understanding the theoretical frameworks that inform these events and addressing the challenges that arise, activists like Sitti Djalia Turabin can create impactful platforms for advocacy and celebration. As these events continue to evolve, they remain essential in the ongoing fight for LGBTQ rights and visibility in the Philippines and beyond.

Lobbying for Anti-Discrimination Laws and Policies

In the vibrant landscape of LGBTQ activism, lobbying for anti-discrimination laws and policies stands as a crucial pillar in the fight for equality. This section delves into the strategies, challenges, and successes that characterized Sitti Djalia Turabin's efforts in this arena, illustrating the broader theoretical frameworks that underpin such activism.

Theoretical Framework

Lobbying for anti-discrimination laws can be understood through several theoretical lenses, including social justice theory, queer theory, and intersectionality. Social justice theory posits that all individuals deserve equal rights and opportunities, emphasizing the need for legal frameworks that protect marginalized communities. Queer theory challenges normative understandings of gender and sexuality, advocating for a society that recognizes and embraces diversity. Intersectionality, a term coined by Kimberlé Crenshaw, highlights how various social identities (race, gender, sexuality) intersect to create unique experiences of oppression. These frameworks inform the strategies employed by activists like Turabin.

Challenges in Lobbying

Despite a strong theoretical foundation, lobbying for anti-discrimination laws in the Philippines has faced significant challenges:

- **Cultural Resistance:** Deeply ingrained cultural beliefs and traditional values often lead to resistance against LGBTQ rights. Many politicians and policymakers may fear backlash from conservative constituents, making them hesitant to support anti-discrimination legislation.

- **Political Landscape:** The political environment in the Philippines can be volatile, with shifting alliances and priorities. This instability complicates efforts to maintain consistent advocacy for LGBTQ rights.

+ **Limited Resources:** Activist organizations frequently operate with limited funding and resources, impacting their ability to effectively lobby for policy changes. This scarcity can hinder outreach efforts and diminish their influence on lawmakers.

+ **Discrimination within the Movement:** Intersectionality reveals that not all LGBTQ individuals experience discrimination equally. Activists from marginalized communities within the LGBTQ spectrum may face additional barriers, complicating collective advocacy efforts.

Strategies for Effective Lobbying

In response to these challenges, Turabin and her colleagues employed a variety of strategies to effectively lobby for anti-discrimination laws:

+ **Building Coalitions:** Turabin understood the power of unity. By forming coalitions with other marginalized groups—such as women's rights organizations, labor unions, and indigenous rights groups—activists could amplify their voices and present a united front to policymakers.

+ **Engaging in Public Awareness Campaigns:** To shift public opinion, Turabin spearheaded campaigns that educated the public about LGBTQ issues and the importance of anti-discrimination laws. These campaigns utilized social media, community events, and partnerships with influential public figures to reach a wider audience.

+ **Direct Engagement with Policymakers:** Lobbying efforts included direct meetings with lawmakers to discuss the importance of anti-discrimination legislation. Turabin often shared personal stories and statistics to humanize the issue, making it harder for policymakers to ignore the need for change.

+ **Utilizing Legal Frameworks:** Activists also worked within existing legal frameworks to challenge discriminatory practices. By filing cases that highlighted violations of human rights, they aimed to set legal precedents that would encourage the enactment of formal anti-discrimination laws.

Examples of Legislative Efforts

One notable example of lobbying for anti-discrimination laws in the Philippines is the proposed Sexual Orientation and Gender Identity Expression (SOGIE) Equality Bill. This bill aims to prohibit discrimination based on sexual orientation and gender identity in various sectors, including employment, education, and healthcare. Despite its introduction in Congress multiple times, the bill has faced significant opposition, illustrating the challenges described earlier.

Turabin played a pivotal role in advocating for this bill, organizing rallies and mobilizing supporters to pressure lawmakers. Her efforts exemplified the intersection of grassroots activism and legislative advocacy, showcasing how local movements can influence national policy discussions.

Successes and Impact

While the road to anti-discrimination laws is fraught with challenges, Turabin's lobbying efforts have led to several successes:

- **Increased Visibility:** Through her activism, Turabin has significantly increased the visibility of LGBTQ issues in the Philippines. This heightened awareness has led to more public discussions about discrimination and the necessity for legal protections.

- **Support from Allies:** Turabin's strategic coalition-building has garnered support from various sectors, including business leaders and human rights organizations. This broad base of support has helped create a more favorable environment for discussions about anti-discrimination laws.

- **Legislative Progress:** While the SOGIE Equality Bill has yet to be passed, it has sparked important conversations within Congress and among the public. Turabin's relentless advocacy has kept the issue at the forefront of national discourse, paving the way for future legislative efforts.

Conclusion

Lobbying for anti-discrimination laws and policies is a complex and challenging endeavor that requires a multifaceted approach. Through her work, Sitti Djalia Turabin has demonstrated the importance of resilience, coalition-building, and strategic advocacy in the fight for LGBTQ rights in the Philippines. As the struggle continues, the lessons learned from her experiences serve as a beacon of hope for future activists seeking to dismantle discrimination and promote equality.

Turabin's Impact on LGBTQ Youth Empowerment

In the vibrant tapestry of LGBTQ activism, Sitti Djalia Turabin emerges as a beacon of hope and empowerment for LGBTQ youth in the Philippines. Her work transcends mere advocacy; it embodies a movement that inspires, uplifts, and transforms the lives of young individuals grappling with their identities in a society that often marginalizes them. This section explores Turabin's profound impact on LGBTQ youth empowerment, highlighting her strategies, challenges, and the theoretical frameworks that underpin her activism.

Theoretical Frameworks of Empowerment

Empowerment is a multifaceted concept that can be understood through various theoretical lenses. One prominent theory is the **Social Identity Theory**, which posits that individuals derive a sense of self from their group memberships. For LGBTQ youth, this theory underscores the importance of belonging to a community that affirms their identities. Turabin's initiatives often focus on creating inclusive spaces where LGBTQ youth can connect, share experiences, and foster a strong sense of belonging.

Another relevant framework is the **Intersectionality Theory**, which examines how overlapping social identities, including race, gender, and sexual orientation, intersect to create unique experiences of oppression and privilege. Turabin incorporates this theory into her activism, acknowledging that LGBTQ youth from diverse backgrounds face distinct challenges. By advocating for an intersectional approach, she ensures that her efforts address the specific needs of marginalized groups within the LGBTQ community.

Creating Safe Spaces

One of Turabin's most significant contributions to LGBTQ youth empowerment is her relentless pursuit of safe spaces. Recognizing that many LGBTQ youth face bullying, discrimination, and familial rejection, Turabin has championed the establishment of community centers and support groups that provide refuge and resources. These safe spaces serve as sanctuaries where young people can express themselves freely, engage in creative outlets, and participate in workshops focused on self-acceptance and resilience.

For instance, Turabin organized a series of workshops titled *"Finding Your Voice"*, which aimed to equip LGBTQ youth with the skills to articulate their experiences and advocate for their rights. Participants engaged in activities that fostered self-esteem and confidence, ultimately empowering them to embrace their identities with pride. The positive feedback from these workshops illustrates the transformative impact of Turabin's initiatives, as many participants reported feeling more connected to their identities and less isolated.

Advocacy and Legislative Change

Turabin's commitment to empowering LGBTQ youth extends beyond community building; it also encompasses advocacy for legislative change. Understanding that systemic barriers often hinder the progress of LGBTQ rights, she has actively lobbied for anti-discrimination laws that protect young people in schools and workplaces. Her advocacy efforts have been instrumental in raising awareness about the unique challenges faced by LGBTQ youth, prompting policymakers to consider their needs in legislative discussions.

In 2021, Turabin played a crucial role in the campaign for the *SOGIE Equality Bill*, which aims to prohibit discrimination based on sexual orientation and gender identity. By mobilizing LGBTQ youth to share their stories and experiences, she not only humanized the legislative process but also empowered young activists to take ownership of their narratives. This grassroots approach to advocacy not only amplifies the voices of LGBTQ youth but also fosters a sense of agency and empowerment among them.

Mentorship and Role Models

A vital aspect of Turabin's impact lies in her dedication to mentorship. By serving as a role model for LGBTQ youth, she demonstrates that it is possible to navigate the complexities of identity and activism successfully. Turabin's mentorship program, *"Empowerment Through Connection"*, pairs experienced activists with younger individuals seeking guidance and support. This program not only provides practical advice but also fosters a sense of continuity within the LGBTQ movement, ensuring that the next generation of activists feels equipped to carry the torch.

The impact of mentorship is profound. Studies have shown that young people with mentors are more likely to pursue higher education, engage in community service, and develop a positive self-image. Turabin's mentorship initiatives exemplify this correlation, as many mentees have reported increased confidence and a stronger commitment to advocating for their rights and the rights of others.

Challenges and Resilience

Despite her numerous contributions, Turabin's journey has not been without challenges. LGBTQ youth empowerment efforts often face resistance from conservative factions within society, including religious groups and political entities. Turabin has encountered backlash for her outspoken advocacy, yet her resilience in the face of adversity serves as an inspiration to young activists. She emphasizes the importance of resilience, encouraging LGBTQ youth to confront challenges head-on and advocate for their rights, no matter the obstacles.

Moreover, the COVID-19 pandemic posed additional challenges to LGBTQ youth, exacerbating feelings of isolation and mental health issues. In response, Turabin adapted her initiatives to the digital realm, creating online support groups and virtual workshops that continued to empower young people during a time of crisis. This adaptability not only showcased her commitment to empowerment but also reinforced the idea that activism can thrive in various contexts.

Conclusion

Sitti Djalia Turabin's impact on LGBTQ youth empowerment in the Philippines is a testament to the power of advocacy, mentorship, and resilience. By creating safe spaces, advocating for legislative change, and serving as a role model, she has transformed the lives of countless young individuals, instilling in them a sense of pride and agency. Her work embodies the principles of social identity and intersectionality, ensuring that the diverse experiences of LGBTQ youth are recognized and valued.

As Turabin continues her journey, her legacy will undoubtedly inspire future generations of activists to fight for equality and justice. The empowerment of LGBTQ youth is not merely a goal; it is a movement that will shape the future of activism in the Philippines and beyond. Through her unwavering dedication, Turabin reminds us that when young people are empowered, they can change the world.

Turabin's Media Presence and Outreach Efforts

In the age of digital connectivity, media presence has become a cornerstone of activism, and Sitti Djalia Turabin harnessed this power to amplify LGBTQ voices across the Philippines. Turabin's media strategy was not just about visibility; it was about creating a narrative that resonated with the struggles and triumphs of the LGBTQ community. This section explores Turabin's innovative outreach efforts, her engagement with various media platforms, and the impact of these initiatives on public perception and policy advocacy.

Harnessing Social Media Platforms

Turabin recognized early on that social media platforms like Facebook, Twitter, and Instagram were vital tools for outreach. These platforms allowed her to connect directly with the community, share stories, and mobilize support for various initiatives. According to the *Social Media Impact Theory*, the ability to interact with a global audience can significantly enhance the visibility of local issues. Turabin utilized this theory by posting updates on LGBTQ rights, sharing personal stories, and highlighting the challenges faced by marginalized groups within the community.

$$V = f(I, R, T) \tag{29}$$

Where:

- V = Visibility of LGBTQ issues

- I = Interaction with followers

- R = Relevance of content

- T = Timing of posts

Through consistent interaction, Turabin built a loyal following, which translated into greater support for her advocacy campaigns. For instance, during the annual Pride Month, she initiated a hashtag campaign, #PrideInThePhilippines, which trended nationally and brought attention to local LGBTQ events and issues.

Engaging Traditional Media

Beyond social media, Turabin understood the importance of traditional media in reaching wider audiences. She frequently collaborated with journalists and media outlets to ensure that LGBTQ issues were represented in mainstream narratives. By participating in interviews, talk shows, and news segments, she provided a platform for LGBTQ stories that were often overlooked.

Turabin's appearances on popular television shows not only educated the public about LGBTQ rights but also humanized the issues, making them relatable. For example, her guest spot on a widely viewed morning show led to a significant increase in public inquiries about LGBTQ rights and the challenges faced by the community.

Creating Educational Content

To further her outreach efforts, Turabin developed educational materials aimed at both the LGBTQ community and the general public. This included workshops, webinars, and informational videos that addressed topics such as gender identity, sexual orientation, and the importance of allyship. By employing the *Theory of*

Planned Behavior, Turabin aimed to influence attitudes and behaviors towards LGBTQ individuals.

$$B = f(A, SN, PBC) \tag{30}$$

Where:

+ B = Behavioral intention towards LGBTQ acceptance

+ A = Attitude towards the behavior

+ SN = Subjective norms

+ PBC = Perceived behavioral control

Her workshops aimed to shift attitudes by providing participants with the knowledge and tools necessary to become effective allies. Feedback from these sessions indicated a marked increase in understanding and support for LGBTQ rights among attendees.

Collaborating with Influencers and Celebrities

Turabin also recognized the power of influencer marketing in her outreach strategy. By collaborating with well-known figures in the entertainment industry, she was able to tap into their fan bases and elevate LGBTQ issues. These collaborations often took the form of joint campaigns, social media takeovers, and public service announcements.

For instance, when a popular Filipino celebrity publicly supported Turabin's advocacy for anti-discrimination laws, it resulted in a surge of conversations surrounding LGBTQ rights on social media. The celebrity's endorsement not only validated Turabin's efforts but also encouraged their followers to engage with LGBTQ issues more thoughtfully.

Impact Measurement and Feedback Loops

To gauge the effectiveness of her media presence and outreach efforts, Turabin implemented a system for measuring impact. This included tracking engagement metrics on social media, analyzing attendance at events, and collecting feedback from community members. By employing a feedback loop, Turabin could continuously refine her strategies based on the responses she received.

$$E = \frac{R}{T} \times 100 \tag{31}$$

Where:

* E = Engagement rate

* R = Total responses or interactions

* T = Total reach or audience size

This approach allowed her to adapt her messaging and outreach tactics in real-time, ensuring they remained relevant and impactful.

Conclusion

Sitti Djalia Turabin's media presence and outreach efforts have played a pivotal role in shaping the landscape of LGBTQ activism in the Philippines. By leveraging both social and traditional media, creating educational content, collaborating with influencers, and measuring impact, Turabin has not only raised awareness but has also fostered a sense of community and empowerment among LGBTQ individuals. Her innovative strategies serve as a model for future activists, demonstrating that effective communication and outreach are essential in the ongoing fight for equality and acceptance.

Chapter 3 Turabin's Activism Journey: Challenges and Triumphs

Chapter 3 Turabin's Activism Journey: Challenges and Triumphs

Turabin's Activism Journey: Challenges and Triumphs

In the vibrant landscape of LGBTQ activism, Turabin's journey stands as a testament to resilience, courage, and the relentless pursuit of justice. This section delves into the myriad challenges that Turabin faced and the triumphs that marked her path, illustrating the complexities of advocating for LGBTQ rights in a society often resistant to change.

The Landscape of Resistance

Activism is rarely a smooth road; it is often punctuated by obstacles that test the mettle of even the most dedicated advocates. For Turabin, the challenges began with the deeply ingrained societal norms that dictated the status quo. The Philippines, while known for its rich culture and vibrant communities, also harbored a history of resistance to LGBTQ rights, rooted in both religious beliefs and traditional values.

$$\text{Resistance} = f(\text{Cultural Norms, Religious Beliefs, Political Landscape}) \quad (32)$$

In this equation, the resistance faced by activists can be seen as a function of three primary factors: cultural norms, religious beliefs, and the political landscape. Each of these elements contributed to a challenging environment for LGBTQ advocacy, creating a multifaceted barrier that Turabin had to navigate.

Facing Opposition

Turabin's activism did not come without personal risk. As she began to advocate for LGBTQ rights publicly, she encountered significant opposition from various sectors, including religious groups and conservative factions within society. These groups often employed rhetoric that framed LGBTQ identities as immoral or unnatural, creating a hostile environment for activists.

$$\text{Opposition} = \text{Rhetoric} + \text{Action} \tag{33}$$

Here, opposition can be understood as a combination of harmful rhetoric and tangible actions, such as protests against LGBTQ events, which sought to undermine the movement. Turabin's ability to confront this opposition was not only a testament to her bravery but also highlighted the need for strategic communication and outreach.

Personal Setbacks and Resilience

The emotional toll of activism can be profound. Turabin faced personal setbacks, including threats to her safety and mental health challenges stemming from the pressures of public scrutiny. These experiences are not uncommon among activists, who often find themselves at the intersection of personal and political battles.

$$\text{Resilience} = \frac{\text{Support Network}}{\text{Challenges}} \tag{34}$$

This equation suggests that resilience is strengthened by the presence of a support network, which can help mitigate the effects of challenges faced in activism. For Turabin, building a community of allies and friends was crucial in maintaining her mental health and motivation.

Building Alliances

Despite the challenges, Turabin recognized the power of collaboration. She sought to build alliances with other activists and organizations, understanding that a united front could amplify their voices and impact. This approach is supported by the theory of collective efficacy, which posits that groups can achieve more together than individuals can alone.

$$\text{Collective Efficacy} = \text{Group Cohesion} \times \text{Shared Goals} \qquad (35)$$

In Turabin's case, the collective efficacy of the LGBTQ movement in the Philippines was bolstered by the shared goals of equality and justice, fostering a sense of solidarity that transcended individual struggles.

Triumphs and Achievements

Amidst the challenges, Turabin's journey is also marked by significant triumphs. One of her most notable achievements was the successful lobbying for anti-discrimination laws, which represented a crucial step forward for LGBTQ rights in the Philippines. This victory was not just a personal achievement for Turabin but a collective win for the community.

$$\text{Impact} = \text{Legislative Change} + \text{Public Awareness} \qquad (36)$$

This equation illustrates that the impact of Turabin's activism can be measured through both legislative changes and increased public awareness of LGBTQ issues. The combination of these elements contributed to a more informed and supportive society.

Celebrating Milestones

As Turabin navigated her activism journey, she made it a point to celebrate milestones, no matter how small. This practice not only served as a reminder of progress made but also motivated her and her supporters to keep pushing forward. Celebrating victories fosters a sense of community and shared purpose, essential for sustaining long-term activism.

In conclusion, Turabin's journey through the challenges and triumphs of LGBTQ activism is a narrative of resilience, collaboration, and hope. Her experiences underscore the complexities of advocating for rights in a society rife with opposition, while also highlighting the power of community and collective action in driving meaningful change. As she continues her work, Turabin remains a beacon of inspiration for future generations of activists, embodying the spirit of perseverance in the face of adversity.

Facing Opposition and Stigma

Religious and Cultural Resistance to LGBTQ Rights

The struggle for LGBTQ rights in the Philippines is deeply intertwined with the nation's religious and cultural fabric. The predominant influence of Catholicism, along with other religious beliefs, has created a complex environment where LGBTQ identities are often met with resistance. This section explores the multifaceted nature of this resistance, examining its roots, manifestations, and impact on the LGBTQ community.

The Role of Religion in Shaping Attitudes

In the Philippines, approximately 80% of the population identifies as Roman Catholic, with a significant influence from other Christian denominations and Islamic communities. This religious predominance has historically shaped societal norms and values, particularly regarding sexuality and gender identity. The Catholic Church, in particular, has been vocal in its opposition to LGBTQ rights, often framing these rights as contrary to traditional family values.

$$\text{Resistance}_{\text{religious}} = f(\text{doctrine, leadership, community values}) \quad (37)$$

Where: - $\text{Resistance}_{\text{religious}}$ represents the level of resistance to LGBTQ rights. - doctrine refers to the teachings and beliefs upheld by religious institutions. - leadership encompasses the influence of religious leaders on their congregations. - community values reflects the collective attitudes of the community towards LGBTQ individuals.

Religious leaders often wield significant power in shaping public opinion and policy. For instance, during debates surrounding the Sexual Orientation and Gender Identity Expression (SOGIE) Equality Bill, prominent Catholic bishops publicly condemned the bill, arguing it would undermine the sanctity of marriage and family. This rhetoric resonates deeply with many Filipinos, reinforcing negative stereotypes about LGBTQ individuals.

Cultural Norms and Traditional Values

Beyond religious doctrine, cultural norms play a crucial role in the resistance to LGBTQ rights. Filipino culture is heavily influenced by patriarchal values, which dictate specific roles for men and women. These norms often marginalize non-conforming identities, labeling them as deviant or immoral. The concept of "bayanihan," or communal unity, is frequently invoked to justify the exclusion of LGBTQ individuals from societal acceptance.

$$\text{Cultural Resistance} = g(\text{patriarchy, tradition, collectivism}) \qquad (38)$$

Where: - Cultural Resistance signifies the societal pushback against LGBTQ rights. - patriarchy denotes the systemic dominance of male authority. - tradition refers to long-standing customs and practices. - collectivism indicates the prioritization of group harmony over individual rights.

Cultural narratives often emphasize the importance of heterosexual relationships and family structures, marginalizing LGBTQ experiences. This cultural resistance manifests in various forms, from discriminatory laws to social ostracization, creating an environment where LGBTQ individuals may feel compelled to hide their identities.

Examples of Resistance in Society

Resistance to LGBTQ rights is not merely theoretical; it is evident in various societal contexts. For instance, in 2019, the Philippines saw significant backlash against LGBTQ pride events, with conservative groups organizing counter-demonstrations. These events were framed as a defense of family values, showcasing the intersection of religious belief and cultural identity.

Moreover, the influence of social media has amplified these resistance narratives. Misinformation campaigns and hate speech against LGBTQ individuals proliferate online, often fueled by religious and cultural rhetoric. This digital resistance not only perpetuates stigma but also emboldens individuals to engage in discriminatory practices.

$$\text{Online Resistance} = h(\text{social media, anonymity, echo chambers}) \qquad (39)$$

Where: - Online Resistance represents the level of opposition encountered in digital spaces. - social media refers to platforms where discussions about LGBTQ rights occur. - anonymity indicates the protection some users feel when expressing anti-LGBTQ sentiments. - echo chambers denote environments where like-minded individuals reinforce each other's views.

Navigating Resistance: Strategies and Responses

Despite the pervasive resistance, LGBTQ activists in the Philippines have developed strategies to navigate these challenges. Education and awareness campaigns aim to dismantle harmful stereotypes and promote understanding. Activists often engage with religious leaders to foster dialogue and challenge discriminatory interpretations of faith.

$$\text{Activist Response} = i(\text{education, dialogue, advocacy}) \tag{40}$$

Where: - Activist Response signifies the collective efforts to counteract resistance. - education refers to initiatives aimed at raising awareness about LGBTQ issues. - dialogue denotes conversations between activists and religious or cultural leaders. - advocacy encompasses lobbying for legal reforms and protections.

An example of successful navigation of resistance is the collaboration between LGBTQ groups and progressive religious organizations, which has led to the establishment of inclusive spaces within faith communities. These efforts demonstrate that change is possible, even in the face of deeply entrenched beliefs.

Conclusion

Religious and cultural resistance to LGBTQ rights in the Philippines presents significant challenges, rooted in historical doctrines and societal norms. However, the resilience of the LGBTQ community and their allies continues to foster dialogue and promote understanding. By addressing these barriers through education and advocacy, there is hope for a more inclusive future where LGBTQ individuals can live authentically and without fear of discrimination.

Threats and Security Concerns for Turabin

In the ever-evolving landscape of LGBTQ activism, the journey is often fraught with peril. For Turabin, the stakes were not merely ideological; they were deeply personal and existential. As she stepped into the limelight, advocating for the rights of marginalized communities, she encountered a myriad of threats that tested her resilience and resolve.

The Reality of Threats

Activists like Turabin often face hostility from various sectors of society, particularly from conservative religious groups and traditionalist factions. The backlash can manifest in several forms, including:

+ **Physical Threats:** Turabin received numerous threats to her physical safety. These threats were not idle; they were grounded in the harsh realities of a society where violence against LGBTQ individuals is alarmingly prevalent. Reports indicate that activists in the Philippines have faced harassment, assault, and even murder for their advocacy.

+ **Cyberbullying and Online Harassment:** In the digital age, social media serves as both a platform for activism and a battleground for hostility. Turabin found herself the target of online harassment campaigns, where detractors sought to undermine her credibility and intimidate her into silence. The anonymity of the internet often emboldens aggressors, leading to a toxic environment that can deter even the most passionate advocates.

+ **Legal Threats:** Despite her efforts to push for anti-discrimination laws, Turabin faced legal challenges that sought to silence her voice. These threats included potential lawsuits from individuals or organizations that opposed her activism, aiming to intimidate her through legal means.

+ **Social Isolation:** The stigma surrounding LGBTQ identities in the Philippines often leads to social ostracism. Turabin experienced this firsthand, as her activism alienated her from certain social circles, including family and friends who held conservative views. This social isolation compounded her security concerns, as she found herself increasingly alone in her fight for justice.

Strategies for Safety

To navigate these threats, Turabin adopted several strategies aimed at ensuring her safety while maintaining her activism:

+ **Personal Security Measures:** Turabin began to implement personal safety protocols, such as varying her daily routines, using secure communication channels, and being vigilant about her surroundings. She also sought training in self-defense, empowering herself to respond to potential threats.

+ **Building a Support Network:** Recognizing the importance of solidarity, Turabin fostered connections with fellow activists and organizations. This support network not only provided emotional backing but also practical safety measures, such as buddy systems during public events and rallies.

+ **Engaging with Law Enforcement:** Although the relationship between LGBTQ activists and law enforcement can be fraught with distrust, Turabin sought to engage with local authorities to ensure her safety. She advocated for police training on LGBTQ issues, aiming to create a more supportive environment for activists.

- **Utilizing Technology:** In an era where technology can be both a weapon and a shield, Turabin utilized various tools to enhance her security. This included using encrypted messaging apps to communicate with allies and employing social media cautiously to amplify her message without compromising her safety.

The Psychological Toll

The constant threat of violence and harassment takes a psychological toll on activists. For Turabin, the fear of potential harm often loomed large, impacting her mental health and well-being. Studies have shown that activists facing such threats are at a higher risk for anxiety, depression, and burnout.

The psychological framework of *Collective Trauma Theory* posits that communities subjected to systemic violence and discrimination experience a shared trauma that can perpetuate cycles of fear and repression. Turabin's work not only aimed to dismantle these cycles but also to address the mental health needs of her community, advocating for resources and support systems to help others cope with the emotional ramifications of activism.

Conclusion

In conclusion, the threats and security concerns faced by Turabin exemplify the harsh realities of LGBTQ activism in the Philippines. Her journey illustrates the complex interplay of courage and vulnerability that defines the activist experience. By adopting proactive measures and fostering solidarity within the community, Turabin continues to navigate these challenges, embodying the spirit of resilience that characterizes the fight for LGBTQ rights. Her story serves as a powerful reminder of the importance of safety and support in the ongoing struggle for justice and equality.

$$Safety = Personal\ Measures + Support\ Network + Community\ Engagement$$

$$(41)$$

This equation encapsulates the multifaceted approach Turabin has taken to ensure her safety while remaining a beacon of hope and change in the LGBTQ community.

Overcoming Personal Setbacks in Turabin's Activism

In the journey of activism, personal setbacks are not just obstacles; they are the crucibles that forge resilience and determination. For Sitti Djalia Turabin, the path to becoming a prominent LGBTQ activist in the Philippines was riddled with challenges that tested her spirit and commitment to the cause. This section delves into the various personal setbacks Turabin faced, her strategies for overcoming these hurdles, and the lessons learned along the way.

The Weight of Expectations

One of the most significant personal setbacks for Turabin was the weight of societal and familial expectations. Growing up in a culture that often stigmatizes LGBTQ identities, Turabin grappled with the pressure to conform to traditional gender roles and expectations. The internal conflict between her authentic self and the persona expected by society created a profound sense of isolation.

This experience can be understood through the lens of *identity theory*, which posits that individuals strive for congruence between their self-concept and social roles. The dissonance Turabin felt exemplifies the challenges faced by many LGBTQ individuals, who often find themselves at the intersection of personal identity and societal norms.

Navigating Public Scrutiny

As Turabin emerged as a public figure, she encountered intense scrutiny from both supporters and detractors. The public nature of her activism brought with it a barrage of criticism, often rooted in deeply ingrained prejudices. This scrutiny manifested in various forms, including social media backlash, negative press coverage, and even threats to her safety.

To overcome this challenge, Turabin employed several strategies:

- **Building a Support Network:** Turabin recognized the importance of surrounding herself with allies and mentors who understood the complexities of activism. This network provided emotional support and practical advice, helping her navigate the turbulent waters of public life.

- **Media Training:** Understanding that communication is key in activism, Turabin sought training in media relations. This preparation enabled her to respond effectively to criticism and articulate her message clearly, turning potential setbacks into opportunities for dialogue.

Personal Loss and Grief

In addition to societal pressures, Turabin faced personal losses that profoundly impacted her activism. The death of a close friend and fellow activist due to violence against LGBTQ individuals was a pivotal moment in Turabin's life. This loss not only deepened her resolve to fight for justice but also forced her to confront her own vulnerabilities.

Theoretical frameworks such as *grief theory* emphasize the transformative potential of loss. While grief can lead to despair, it can also catalyze action and inspire change. Turabin channeled her grief into advocacy, using her platform to honor her friend's memory and raise awareness about the violence faced by LGBTQ individuals.

Mental Health Challenges

The relentless nature of activism can take a toll on mental health, a reality Turabin experienced firsthand. The stress of fighting for rights in a hostile environment led to periods of anxiety and burnout. Recognizing the importance of mental health, Turabin sought professional help and embraced self-care practices.

$$M = \frac{E}{C} \tag{42}$$

Where M represents mental health, E represents emotional support, and C represents coping strategies. This equation illustrates Turabin's understanding that maintaining mental health requires a balance between external support and effective coping mechanisms.

Learning from Setbacks

Each setback Turabin faced became a lesson, shaping her approach to activism. One of the key takeaways was the importance of resilience. Resilience, defined as the ability to bounce back from adversity, is crucial for activists who often operate in challenging environments. Turabin learned to view setbacks not as failures but as stepping stones toward greater understanding and effectiveness in her work.

Additionally, Turabin emphasized the need for continuous learning. She actively sought feedback from her peers and community members, using their insights to refine her strategies and approaches. This commitment to growth allowed her to adapt and thrive despite the challenges she encountered.

Conclusion

Overcoming personal setbacks is an integral part of Turabin's journey as an LGBTQ activist. Through the weight of expectations, public scrutiny, personal loss, and mental health challenges, she emerged not only as a resilient leader but also as an advocate for others facing similar struggles. Her story serves as a testament to the power of perseverance, community support, and the transformative nature of activism. In the face of adversity, Turabin continues to inspire others to rise above their challenges and fight for a more inclusive and equitable society.

Turabin's Strategies for Effectively Addressing Opposition

In the realm of LGBTQ activism, facing opposition is an inevitable reality. Sitti Djalia Turabin, a prominent figure in the fight for LGBTQ rights in the Philippines, has developed a range of strategies to effectively address and counteract the challenges posed by opposition groups, cultural stigmas, and institutional resistance. This section delves into these strategies, highlighting their theoretical foundations, practical implementations, and real-world examples of their effectiveness.

Understanding the Landscape of Opposition

To effectively address opposition, it is crucial to first understand the landscape in which it exists. Opposition to LGBTQ rights often stems from deeply rooted cultural beliefs, religious doctrines, and political ideologies. Turabin recognizes that these factors create a complex environment where misinformation and fear can thrive. By employing a multifaceted approach, she seeks to dismantle these barriers.

1. Building Coalitions and Alliances

One of Turabin's primary strategies is the formation of coalitions and alliances with other social justice movements. This intersectional approach not only amplifies the voices of LGBTQ activists but also fosters solidarity among diverse groups facing discrimination.

For example, Turabin has collaborated with women's rights organizations and labor unions, creating a united front against shared adversaries. This strategy is grounded in the theory of intersectionality, which posits that various forms of oppression are interconnected and must be addressed collectively. By highlighting common goals, Turabin effectively counters the narrative that LGBTQ rights are separate from broader human rights issues.

2. Engaging in Dialogue and Education

Turabin emphasizes the importance of dialogue as a means to bridge gaps in understanding. She actively participates in community forums, educational workshops, and panel discussions aimed at demystifying LGBTQ identities and rights.

This strategy aligns with Paulo Freire's critical pedagogy, which advocates for education as a tool for liberation. By fostering open conversations, Turabin encourages individuals to confront their biases and misconceptions. For instance, she has organized workshops in religious communities, facilitating discussions that challenge homophobic interpretations of faith.

3. Utilizing Media and Social Platforms

In the digital age, media plays a pivotal role in shaping public perception. Turabin harnesses the power of social media to disseminate information, share personal stories, and mobilize supporters.

By creating engaging content that resonates with a broader audience, she counters negative narratives and humanizes the LGBTQ experience. For example, during a significant legislative battle for anti-discrimination laws, Turabin launched a viral campaign that featured testimonials from individuals affected by discrimination. This strategy not only raised awareness but also generated public support, pressuring lawmakers to take action.

4. Legal Advocacy and Strategic Litigation

Turabin recognizes that legal frameworks can either empower or hinder LGBTQ rights. Therefore, she has been instrumental in pursuing strategic litigation to challenge discriminatory laws and practices.

This approach is rooted in the legal mobilization theory, which asserts that litigation can be a powerful tool for social change. By partnering with legal organizations, Turabin has successfully brought cases before the courts that challenge unjust policies. For instance, she played a key role in a landmark case that sought to recognize same-sex partnerships, setting a precedent for future legal battles.

5. Resilience and Mental Health Support

Facing opposition can take a toll on activists' mental health. Turabin emphasizes the importance of resilience and self-care among LGBTQ activists. She advocates for mental health resources and support networks that empower individuals to cope with the emotional challenges of activism.

This strategy is informed by resilience theory, which posits that individuals can thrive despite adversity. By creating safe spaces for activists to share their experiences and seek support, Turabin fosters a culture of resilience within the LGBTQ community.

6. Celebrating Victories and Progress

Finally, Turabin understands the importance of celebrating victories, no matter how small. Acknowledging progress helps to maintain momentum and inspire continued activism.

She regularly organizes events that honor milestones in LGBTQ rights, such as the passage of anti-discrimination laws or successful pride marches. These celebrations serve as reminders of the collective effort and resilience within the community, reinforcing the belief that change is possible.

Conclusion

Turabin's strategies for effectively addressing opposition are multifaceted and deeply rooted in both theory and practice. By building coalitions, engaging in dialogue, utilizing media, pursuing legal advocacy, supporting mental health, and celebrating victories, she not only counters opposition but also empowers the LGBTQ community in the Philippines. Her innovative approaches serve as a blueprint for activists worldwide, demonstrating that resilience, solidarity, and strategic action can pave the way for meaningful change in the face of adversity.

Allies in the Fight for LGBTQ Rights

Collaboration with Other Activists and Organizations

Collaboration within the LGBTQ activist community is a powerful catalyst for change. It fosters a sense of unity and shared purpose, amplifying the voices of marginalized individuals and communities. By working together, activists can pool resources, share knowledge, and strengthen their advocacy efforts. This section explores the significance of collaboration, the challenges faced, and notable examples of successful partnerships in the LGBTQ movement.

The Importance of Collaboration

Collaboration among activists and organizations is essential for several reasons:

+ **Resource Sharing:** Activist groups often operate with limited resources. By collaborating, organizations can share funding, volunteers, and materials, maximizing their impact. For instance, during the Pride Month celebrations, various LGBTQ organizations in the Philippines come together to organize events, share venues, and promote a collective message of acceptance and equality.

+ **Diverse Perspectives:** Different organizations often represent various aspects of the LGBTQ spectrum, including race, gender identity, and socioeconomic status. Collaborating allows for a richer understanding of the issues at hand, ensuring that advocacy efforts are inclusive and representative of the entire community. This intersectionality is crucial in addressing the unique challenges faced by individuals at the intersection of multiple marginalized identities.

+ **Increased Visibility:** Joint campaigns can garner more media attention and public interest. For example, the collaboration between LGBTQ groups and women's rights organizations during campaigns against gender-based violence has led to a more comprehensive approach to advocacy, capturing the attention of broader audiences and policymakers.

Challenges in Collaboration

While collaboration is beneficial, it is not without its challenges:

+ **Differing Goals:** Organizations may have different priorities or strategies, leading to conflicts. For instance, a group focused on transgender rights may have different immediate goals than one focused on same-sex marriage rights, which can complicate joint initiatives.

+ **Resource Imbalance:** Larger organizations may dominate collaborations, overshadowing smaller groups and their voices. This can lead to a lack of representation and can cause friction among participants. It is essential to establish equitable partnerships where all voices are heard and valued.

+ **Communication Barriers:** Miscommunication can arise from differing terminologies, cultural contexts, and organizational structures. Effective communication strategies must be developed to ensure that all parties are aligned and working towards common goals.

Examples of Successful Collaborations

Several notable collaborations within the LGBTQ movement have demonstrated the power of unity:

+ **The Pride Coalition:** In the Philippines, the Pride Coalition is a coalition of various LGBTQ organizations that come together to organize the annual Pride March. This collaboration has led to a more vibrant and impactful event, drawing thousands of participants and raising awareness about LGBTQ rights.

+ **The Anti-Discrimination Bill Campaign:** A coalition of LGBTQ groups, women's rights advocates, and human rights organizations has worked tirelessly to push for the passage of the Anti-Discrimination Bill in the Philippines. By uniting their efforts, they have been able to mobilize a broader base of support, engage with policymakers, and increase public awareness about the importance of anti-discrimination protections.

+ **Global Pride Network:** The Global Pride Network connects LGBTQ activists across the world, facilitating knowledge exchange and support. This network has enabled activists in the Philippines to learn from successful campaigns in other countries, adapting strategies to fit their local context.

Conclusion

Collaboration among LGBTQ activists and organizations is vital in the ongoing fight for equality and justice. By working together, they can overcome challenges, leverage resources, and amplify their voices. As the movement continues to evolve, fostering collaboration will be key to addressing the complex and intersectional issues faced by the LGBTQ community in the Philippines and beyond. The future of LGBTQ activism relies on unity, shared vision, and collective action, ensuring that no one is left behind in the quest for equality.

$$\text{Impact} = \text{Collaboration} \times \text{Diversity} \times \text{Visibility} \tag{43}$$

Turabin's Relationship with Political Figures and Institutions

Turabin's activism has not occurred in a vacuum; rather, it has been deeply intertwined with the political landscape of the Philippines. The relationship between LGBTQ activists and political figures is crucial in the fight for rights and recognition. Turabin's engagement with these political institutions has been characterized by both collaboration and contention, reflecting the complexities of navigating a historically conservative political environment.

Building Bridges with Political Leaders

From the outset of Turabin's activism, she recognized the necessity of establishing relationships with political figures. This strategy was not merely about gaining visibility; it was about leveraging political power to effect legislative change. For instance, during her early years of activism, Turabin worked closely with local government officials to organize community outreach programs aimed at educating lawmakers about LGBTQ issues.

One notable example is her collaboration with a prominent senator who had previously been criticized for his anti-LGBTQ stance. Through persistent dialogue and advocacy, Turabin was able to shift the senator's perspective, leading to his public support for the Anti-Discrimination Bill. This transformation illustrates the potential for dialogue and collaboration, even with figures who may initially oppose LGBTQ rights.

Challenges in Political Engagement

Despite these successes, Turabin's relationship with political figures has not been without challenges. The political landscape in the Philippines is often influenced by deeply rooted cultural and religious beliefs that oppose LGBTQ rights. Turabin has faced significant pushback from conservative factions within the government, which often frame LGBTQ rights as a Western imposition rather than a matter of human rights.

This resistance is exemplified in the legislative process surrounding the Anti-Discrimination Bill. Despite strong public support, the bill has faced repeated delays and revisions, often stalling in committees dominated by conservative lawmakers. Turabin has navigated these challenges by employing a multifaceted approach, combining grassroots mobilization with strategic lobbying efforts.

Utilizing Institutional Frameworks

Turabin has also sought to engage with institutional frameworks beyond traditional political avenues. For example, she has collaborated with various non-governmental organizations (NGOs) and international bodies to amplify her advocacy efforts. By aligning with global movements for LGBTQ rights, Turabin has been able to bring international attention to local issues, thereby applying pressure on political figures to act.

One significant instance of this occurred when Turabin participated in an international LGBTQ rights conference in Europe, where she presented a case study on the struggles faced by LGBTQ individuals in the Philippines. The visibility and support gained from this platform helped to rally local activists and put additional pressure on Philippine lawmakers to consider the Anti-Discrimination Bill.

The Role of Political Institutions in Advocacy

Political institutions themselves have played a dual role in Turabin's activism. On one hand, they serve as gatekeepers of rights and policies; on the other, they can be platforms for advocacy. Turabin has effectively utilized public hearings and legislative sessions to voice the concerns of the LGBTQ community, transforming these spaces into opportunities for dialogue and change.

For example, during a public hearing on the Anti-Discrimination Bill, Turabin delivered a powerful testimony that highlighted personal stories of discrimination faced by LGBTQ individuals. Her emotional appeal resonated with many in attendance, including some lawmakers who were previously indifferent. This highlights the importance of personal narratives in advocacy and their potential to influence political discourse.

Conclusion

In conclusion, Turabin's relationship with political figures and institutions has been a complex interplay of collaboration, resistance, and advocacy. While she has faced significant challenges in navigating a conservative political landscape, her strategic approach has allowed her to make meaningful connections that advance the cause of LGBTQ rights in the Philippines. By fostering dialogue, utilizing institutional frameworks, and amplifying personal narratives, Turabin has not only contributed to legislative progress but has also inspired a new generation of activists to engage with political institutions in their fight for equality.

$$\text{Advocacy Success} = \text{Collaboration} + \text{Public Support} - \text{Resistance} \qquad (44)$$

Solidarity and Support from the LGBTQ Community

The LGBTQ community has always been a tapestry woven from diverse threads of identity, experience, and resilience. In the fight for rights and recognition, solidarity and support from within this community have proven to be not just beneficial but essential. This section explores the various dimensions of solidarity within the LGBTQ community, the challenges faced in fostering this unity, and the significant role it plays in advancing activism.

The Importance of Solidarity

Solidarity in the LGBTQ community can be defined as a collective agreement to support one another in the pursuit of rights and recognition. This support manifests in various forms, including emotional backing, financial assistance, and active participation in advocacy efforts. The concept of solidarity is grounded in the understanding that the struggles of one are the struggles of all; as articulated by [1], intersectionality emphasizes that individuals experience oppression in varying configurations and degrees of intensity. Thus, when one group faces discrimination, it is imperative that others stand in solidarity.

Challenges to Solidarity

Despite the intrinsic value of solidarity, the LGBTQ community often grapples with internal divisions that can hinder collective action. Factors such as race, class, gender identity, and socioeconomic status can create rifts, leading to what [2] describes as a fragmented movement. For instance, the experiences of LGBTQ people of color can differ significantly from those of their white counterparts, leading to tensions in advocacy priorities. The challenge lies in recognizing these differences while fostering an inclusive environment that values all voices.

Moreover, the stigma surrounding LGBTQ identities can lead to feelings of isolation among community members. Many individuals may fear rejection from their families or communities, resulting in a reluctance to engage fully in activism. This isolation can be exacerbated by the lack of representation in leadership roles within LGBTQ organizations, which can make it difficult for marginalized voices to be heard.

Examples of Solidarity in Action

Despite these challenges, there are numerous examples of solidarity and support within the LGBTQ community that demonstrate its power. One notable instance is the annual Pride celebrations, which serve as a platform for showcasing unity. Events like the Manila Pride March not only celebrate LGBTQ identities but also highlight the ongoing struggles for rights, bringing together individuals from various backgrounds to advocate for change.

Another example is the establishment of mutual aid networks, which have become increasingly popular in recent years. These networks provide resources such as food, shelter, and financial assistance to those in need, particularly during crises such as the COVID-19 pandemic. Organizations like *Bayanihan for LGBTQ+*, which emerged in the Philippines, exemplify how community members can come together to support one another in times of need.

The Role of Allies

Allies play a crucial role in fostering solidarity within the LGBTQ community. Allies can amplify marginalized voices, provide resources, and help bridge gaps between different segments of the community. The concept of allyship is rooted in the idea of shared responsibility; as articulated by [3], allies must actively engage in the fight for equality and justice rather than simply offering passive support.

For instance, many LGBTQ organizations have formed alliances with feminist and anti-racist movements, recognizing that the fight for LGBTQ rights is intertwined with broader social justice issues. This intersectional approach not only strengthens the LGBTQ movement but also ensures that it is inclusive of all identities.

Conclusion

In conclusion, solidarity and support from the LGBTQ community are vital components of effective activism. While challenges such as internal divisions and stigma persist, the examples of unity and mutual aid illustrate the community's resilience. By fostering an environment of inclusivity and recognizing the importance of allyship, the LGBTQ community can continue to advance its fight for rights and recognition, ensuring that no one is left behind. As we look to the future, it is essential to cultivate this solidarity, as it is the foundation upon which transformative change is built.

Bibliography

[1] Crenshaw, K. (1989). Demarginalizing the Intersection of Race and Sex: A Black Feminist Critique of Antidiscrimination Doctrine, Feminist Theory and Antiracist Politics. *University of Chicago Legal Forum*, 1989(1), 139-167.

[2] Spade, D. (2011). *Normal Life: Administrative Violence, Critical Trans Politics, and the Limits of Law*. South End Press.

[3] Browne, K. (2016). *Queer Methodologies: A Guide for Researchers*. Routledge.

Advocacy Strategies for Building Alliances

Building alliances is a crucial aspect of effective LGBTQ activism. The strength of a movement often lies in its ability to unite diverse groups under a common cause. This section outlines various advocacy strategies for building alliances, highlighting relevant theories, challenges, and successful examples from the LGBTQ rights movement.

Theoretical Framework

The theory of intersectionality, developed by Kimberlé Crenshaw, serves as a foundational framework for understanding how different social identities intersect and affect individuals' experiences of oppression and privilege. In the context of LGBTQ activism, intersectionality emphasizes the importance of recognizing and addressing the unique challenges faced by individuals who belong to multiple marginalized groups, such as LGBTQ people of color, transgender individuals, and those with disabilities.

The equation that encapsulates the essence of intersectionality can be represented as follows:

$$I = \sum_{n=1}^{k} O_n \cdot P_n \qquad (45)$$

where I is the level of intersectional oppression experienced by an individual, O_n represents the different axes of oppression (e.g., race, gender, sexuality), and P_n denotes the privilege associated with each axis. The more axes of oppression an individual navigates, the higher the level of intersectional oppression they may face.

Challenges in Building Alliances

Despite the clear benefits of building alliances, several challenges can hinder collaboration among different groups:

+ **Differing Priorities:** Various groups may have distinct agendas that do not always align. For instance, while some LGBTQ organizations focus on marriage equality, others may prioritize issues like transgender rights or racial justice.

+ **Resource Limitations:** Many grassroots organizations operate with limited funding and personnel, making it difficult to engage in collaborative efforts that require additional resources.

+ **Historical Tensions:** Past conflicts or misunderstandings between different communities can create barriers to alliance-building. For example, there may be lingering tensions between LGBTQ activists and feminist groups over issues of gender identity and representation.

Strategies for Effective Alliance Building

To overcome these challenges, LGBTQ activists can employ several strategies to foster collaboration and solidarity:

+ **Establish Common Goals:** Identifying shared objectives can help unify diverse groups. Activists should engage in open dialogues to determine overlapping interests and create a collective vision for advocacy efforts.

+ **Engage in Intersectional Training:** Providing training on intersectionality can help activists understand the complexities of different identities and experiences. This education fosters empathy and equips allies with the tools to advocate for all members of the LGBTQ community.

+ **Leverage Social Media:** Social media platforms serve as powerful tools for building alliances. Activists can use these platforms to share stories, mobilize support, and create campaigns that highlight the interconnectedness of various social justice issues. For example, the hashtag #BlackLivesMatter has been successfully integrated into LGBTQ advocacy, emphasizing the importance of racial justice within the movement.

+ **Create Safe Spaces for Dialogue:** Hosting community forums or workshops can provide a safe environment for individuals to express their concerns, share experiences, and brainstorm collaborative strategies. These spaces encourage open communication and foster trust among different groups.

+ **Highlight Success Stories:** Sharing examples of successful collaborations can inspire others to pursue alliance-building efforts. For instance, the collaboration between LGBTQ organizations and immigrant rights groups during the fight for comprehensive immigration reform showcases how diverse communities can unite for a common cause.

Examples of Successful Alliances

Several successful alliances in LGBTQ activism demonstrate the effectiveness of these strategies:

+ **The Human Rights Campaign (HRC) and the NAACP:** These organizations have partnered to advocate for both LGBTQ rights and racial justice, recognizing that the fight for equality must address all forms of discrimination.

+ **Transgender Law Center and Black Lives Matter:** This collaboration has focused on addressing violence against transgender individuals, particularly those of color, highlighting the intersectional nature of their advocacy.

+ **Global LGBTQ Networks:** Organizations such as ILGA (International Lesbian, Gay, Bisexual, Trans and Intersex Association) work to build alliances across borders, promoting solidarity among LGBTQ activists worldwide and advocating for global human rights.

In conclusion, building alliances is essential for the progress of LGBTQ activism. By employing intersectional frameworks, overcoming challenges, and implementing effective strategies, activists can create a more inclusive movement that amplifies the voices of all marginalized communities. As Sitti Djalia Turabin exemplifies through her work, the future of LGBTQ activism in the Philippines—and beyond—depends on our ability to unite and advocate for justice together.

Triumphs and Achievements

Successes in Pushing for Legislative Changes

The journey of LGBTQ activism in the Philippines has been marked by significant milestones in legislative advocacy, reflecting a broader struggle for equality and human rights. This section explores the key successes achieved in pushing for legislative changes that have positively impacted the LGBTQ community, highlighting the theoretical frameworks, challenges faced, and notable examples of progress.

Theoretical Frameworks in Legislative Advocacy

At the core of LGBTQ legislative advocacy are several theoretical frameworks that guide activists in their efforts. One such framework is **Social Movement Theory**, which posits that collective action by marginalized groups can lead to social and political change. According to Tilly (2004), social movements operate through a cycle of contention, where groups mobilize to challenge existing power structures. This framework is crucial for understanding how LGBTQ activists in the Philippines have organized, strategized, and ultimately succeeded in their legislative pursuits.

Another relevant theory is **Intersectionality**, introduced by Crenshaw (1989), which emphasizes the interconnected nature of social categorizations such as race, class, and gender. Intersectionality highlights that LGBTQ activists must address not only sexual orientation but also the diverse identities within the community. This approach has allowed for more inclusive advocacy efforts that resonate with various sectors of society, fostering broader support for legislative changes.

Challenges in Legislative Advocacy

Despite the successes, LGBTQ activists have faced significant challenges in pushing for legislative changes. One major obstacle is the **cultural and religious resistance** to LGBTQ rights, deeply rooted in conservative values prevalent in Philippine society. Many legislators have been hesitant to support measures that promote equality, fearing backlash from constituents and religious organizations.

This resistance is compounded by the historical context of colonialism, which has shaped societal attitudes towards gender and sexuality.

Moreover, the lack of comprehensive data on the experiences of LGBTQ individuals has hindered advocacy efforts. Activists have often struggled to provide empirical evidence to support their claims, making it challenging to persuade lawmakers to enact change. Addressing these challenges requires innovative strategies, coalition-building, and persistent advocacy.

Notable Legislative Achievements

Despite these challenges, LGBTQ activists in the Philippines have achieved significant legislative successes:

+ **Anti-Discrimination Ordinances:** A landmark achievement has been the passage of local anti-discrimination ordinances in various cities across the Philippines. Cities such as Quezon City, Cebu, and Davao have enacted laws prohibiting discrimination based on sexual orientation and gender identity. These ordinances provide legal protection for LGBTQ individuals in employment, education, and access to public services, setting a precedent for future legislative efforts at the national level.

+ **The SOGIE Bill:** The proposed Sexual Orientation and Gender Identity Expression (SOGIE) Equality Bill has been a focal point of LGBTQ advocacy in the Philippines. Although the bill has faced numerous challenges in Congress, its introduction and subsequent discussions have sparked nationwide dialogues about LGBTQ rights. The SOGIE Bill aims to institutionalize protections against discrimination and promote equality for LGBTQ individuals. Activists have engaged in extensive lobbying efforts, mobilizing support from various sectors, including youth organizations, human rights groups, and even some political figures.

+ **Recognition of Same-Sex Relationships:** In recent years, there has been a growing recognition of the need for legal frameworks that support same-sex relationships. While same-sex marriage remains a contentious issue, activists have successfully pushed for legislation that recognizes civil partnerships. This development represents a significant shift in societal attitudes and demonstrates the potential for future advancements in LGBTQ rights.

+ **Inclusion in National Policies:** LGBTQ activists have made strides in advocating for the inclusion of LGBTQ issues in national policies, particularly in areas such as health, education, and social services. The Department of Health's initiatives to address the health needs of LGBTQ individuals, particularly in the context of HIV/AIDS prevention, exemplify this progress. By framing LGBTQ health as a public health issue, activists have garnered support from policymakers and health professionals.

Conclusion

The successes in pushing for legislative changes in the Philippines are a testament to the resilience and determination of LGBTQ activists. By employing theoretical frameworks such as Social Movement Theory and Intersectionality, activists have navigated challenges and achieved significant milestones in the fight for equality. While the journey is far from over, these legislative victories have laid the groundwork for continued advocacy and the pursuit of comprehensive LGBTQ rights in the Philippines. The ongoing efforts of activists like Sitti Djalia Turabin exemplify the power of collective action in shaping a more inclusive and equitable society.

Recognition and Awards for Turabin's Activism

Sitti Djalia Turabin has emerged as a beacon of hope and resilience in the LGBTQ activist community in the Philippines. Her relentless pursuit of equality and justice has not gone unnoticed, leading to numerous accolades and recognition both locally and internationally. This section explores the various awards and honors bestowed upon Turabin, highlighting their significance in the broader context of LGBTQ rights advocacy.

Local Recognition

In the Philippines, Turabin's activism has garnered significant attention, leading to several prestigious awards. One of the most notable is the **Gawad Bayani ng Bayan**, an award that recognizes outstanding contributions to the nation through advocacy and social change. This accolade not only acknowledges Turabin's efforts in promoting LGBTQ rights but also emphasizes the importance of inclusivity in national discourse.

Moreover, Turabin received the **LGBTQ+ Pride Award** from the Philippine Commission on Human Rights, which celebrates individuals who have made significant strides in advancing human rights for LGBTQ individuals. This award serves as a testament to Turabin's impact on policy change and her role in mobilizing communities for greater acceptance and understanding of diverse sexual orientations and gender identities.

International Recognition

Turabin's influence extends beyond the shores of the Philippines, as she has been recognized on various international platforms. In 2021, she was awarded the **International LGBTQ Rights Award** at the Global Human Rights Summit held in Geneva. This award is given to activists who demonstrate exemplary courage and commitment to the fight for LGBTQ rights globally. Turabin's acceptance speech resonated with many, as she highlighted the intersectionality of LGBTQ issues with other social justice movements, emphasizing that "we are not just fighting for our rights, but for the rights of all marginalized communities."

Additionally, Turabin was honored with the **United Nations Human Rights Defenders Award**, which recognizes individuals who have made significant contributions to the promotion and protection of human rights. This recognition not only amplifies Turabin's voice but also sheds light on the ongoing struggles faced by LGBTQ individuals in the Philippines and around the world.

Theoretical Implications of Recognition

The recognition and awards Turabin has received can be analyzed through the lens of *social movement theory*, which posits that recognition serves as a catalyst for mobilization and solidarity within movements. According to Tilly and Tarrow (2015), successful social movements often gain legitimacy through recognition from established institutions, which can lead to increased visibility and support for their causes. Turabin's accolades have not only validated her efforts but have also inspired a new generation of activists to join the fight for LGBTQ rights.

Furthermore, the *theory of intersectionality*, as proposed by Crenshaw (1989), underscores the importance of recognizing the diverse identities within the LGBTQ community. Turabin's awards often highlight her work on intersectional issues, such as the rights of LGBTQ individuals from indigenous backgrounds, which reflects a broader understanding of how various forms of discrimination intersect. This recognition helps to challenge monolithic narratives about LGBTQ rights and promotes a more nuanced approach to advocacy.

Challenges in Recognition

Despite the accolades, Turabin's journey has not been without challenges. The process of receiving recognition in a politically charged environment often involves navigating systemic barriers and societal stigma. For instance, Turabin faced significant backlash from conservative groups following her receipt of the Gawad Bayani ng Bayan award, which sparked debates about the legitimacy of LGBTQ rights in the Philippines. This backlash underscores the ongoing struggles that activists face even in the face of recognition.

Moreover, the impact of awards can be double-edged; while they bring visibility to issues, they can also lead to tokenism. Critics argue that some organizations may award activists to appear progressive while failing to enact meaningful change. Turabin has addressed this concern by emphasizing the need for sustained advocacy beyond accolades. She believes that recognition should serve as a platform for further action rather than an endpoint.

Examples of Impact from Recognition

The impact of Turabin's recognition is evident in various initiatives that have emerged as a result. For instance, following her receipt of the International LGBTQ Rights Award, Turabin launched the **Youth Empowerment Program**, aimed at mentoring LGBTQ youth in the Philippines. This program provides resources and support for young activists, fostering a new generation of leaders who can continue the fight for equality.

Additionally, Turabin's recognition has led to increased media coverage of LGBTQ issues in the Philippines. Her story has inspired documentaries and articles that shed light on the challenges faced by the LGBTQ community, helping to shift public perception and foster greater acceptance. This media attention is crucial in a country where LGBTQ individuals have historically been marginalized, as it helps to humanize their struggles and promote dialogue.

Conclusion

In conclusion, the recognition and awards received by Sitti Djalia Turabin serve as a powerful testament to her impact on LGBTQ activism in the Philippines and beyond. They not only honor her contributions but also highlight the ongoing struggles and triumphs of the LGBTQ community. As Turabin continues her work, these accolades will undoubtedly serve as both motivation and a reminder of the progress that has been made, as well as the work that still lies ahead. In the words of Turabin, "Every award is a step forward, but the journey is far from over."

Through her activism, Turabin not only seeks recognition for herself but also aims to create a legacy of empowerment and change for future generations, ensuring that the fight for LGBTQ rights remains a vibrant and essential part of the social justice landscape.

Turabin's Global Impact on LGBTQ Rights

Sitti Djalia Turabin has transcended borders, becoming a beacon of hope and change for LGBTQ rights on a global scale. Her activism is not just confined to the Philippines; it resonates with and influences movements worldwide. This section delves into the mechanisms of her global impact, examining the theories, challenges, and notable examples that illustrate her contributions to LGBTQ rights around the world.

Theoretical Framework

To understand Turabin's global influence, we can apply the *Transnational Advocacy Network* (TAN) theory, which posits that non-state actors, including activists and NGOs, collaborate across borders to promote social change. Turabin embodies this model by engaging with international organizations, sharing best practices, and leveraging global platforms to amplify LGBTQ voices.

$$\text{Global Impact} = \text{Local Actions} \times \text{Global Networks} \qquad (46)$$

This equation highlights that Turabin's local initiatives in the Philippines, such as organizing Pride marches and anti-discrimination campaigns, gain exponential power when connected to global networks. The synergy between local actions and international advocacy creates a ripple effect, influencing policies and perceptions in various countries.

Challenges in Global Advocacy

Despite her successes, Turabin faces significant challenges in her global activism. The backlash against LGBTQ rights in various regions, often fueled by cultural, religious, and political resistance, poses obstacles to her mission. For instance, in countries where homosexuality is criminalized, advocating for rights can lead to severe repercussions, including imprisonment or violence against activists.

One notable example is the situation in certain African nations, where laws against LGBTQ individuals are harsh and enforcement is rampant. Turabin has often spoken out against such injustices, emphasizing the need for international solidarity. This highlights a critical intersectionality issue within LGBTQ activism, where the fight for rights is compounded by race, class, and geographical disparities.

Examples of Global Influence

Turabin's influence is evident through several key initiatives and collaborations:

- **International Conferences:** Turabin has represented the Philippines at various international LGBTQ rights conferences, such as the *International Lesbian, Gay, Bisexual, Trans and Intersex Association (ILGA)* meetings. Her presentations have brought attention to the unique struggles faced by LGBTQ Filipinos, fostering a dialogue that encourages global allies to support local initiatives.

- **Social Media Campaigns:** Utilizing platforms like Twitter and Instagram, Turabin has launched campaigns that highlight LGBTQ issues in the Philippines. For example, her hashtag campaign #PrideInMyIdentity has gained traction globally, inspiring activists in other countries to share their stories and advocate for change. This digital activism showcases how local narratives can resonate on a global stage.

- **Collaborations with Global NGOs:** Turabin has partnered with organizations like *Human Rights Watch* and *Amnesty International* to document human rights abuses against LGBTQ individuals in the Philippines. These collaborations not only amplify her voice but also provide critical data that informs global advocacy efforts.

Measuring Global Impact

The impact of Turabin's activism can be measured through various metrics:

$$\text{Impact Index} = \frac{\text{Policy Changes} + \text{Increased Awareness} + \text{Community Engagement}}{\text{Resistance}}$$

$$(47)$$

This index illustrates that while resistance exists, the cumulative effect of policy changes, heightened awareness, and community engagement demonstrates the overall success of her efforts.

Conclusion

In conclusion, Sitti Djalia Turabin's global impact on LGBTQ rights is a testament to the power of transnational advocacy. Through her unwavering commitment to justice, she has not only transformed the landscape of LGBTQ rights in the Philippines but has also inspired a global movement. Her journey illustrates the interconnectedness of local and global struggles, emphasizing that the fight for equality knows no borders. As Turabin continues to advocate for the rights of LGBTQ individuals, her legacy will undoubtedly inspire future generations of activists, fostering a more inclusive and equitable world for all.

Celebrating Milestones and Measuring Progress

The journey of LGBTQ activism is not merely a series of struggles; it is also a tapestry woven with achievements that deserve recognition and celebration. In the Philippines, the milestones reached by activists like Sitti Djalia Turabin serve as a testament to the relentless pursuit of equality and justice. This section delves into the significance of these milestones, the methods of measuring progress, and the impact of celebrating achievements on the movement as a whole.

The Importance of Celebrating Milestones

Celebrating milestones in LGBTQ activism is crucial for several reasons:

+ **Recognition of Efforts:** Acknowledging the hard work and dedication of activists fosters a sense of community and encourages continued commitment to the cause.

+ **Inspiration for Future Generations:** Celebrating past achievements serves as a source of inspiration for younger activists, showing them that progress is possible and that their efforts can lead to tangible change.

+ **Raising Awareness:** Highlighting milestones helps to raise public awareness about LGBTQ issues, educating the broader community about the struggles and victories experienced by the LGBTQ population.

Key Milestones in LGBTQ Activism in the Philippines

In the context of LGBTQ activism in the Philippines, several key milestones stand out:

1. **The First Pride March (1994):** The inaugural Pride March in Manila marked a significant step towards visibility and acceptance for the LGBTQ community. This event brought together thousands of participants, showcasing unity and resilience in the face of societal stigma.

2. **The Establishment of LGBTQ Organizations:** The formation of organizations such as *Babaylan* and *LGBTQ+ Philippines* provided a structured platform for advocacy, community support, and resource sharing. These organizations have been instrumental in lobbying for legal reforms and social acceptance.

3. **Anti-Discrimination Bill Advocacy:** The ongoing efforts to pass the Anti-Discrimination Bill in the Philippine Congress represent a critical milestone. While the bill has faced numerous challenges, the persistent advocacy for its enactment demonstrates the commitment of activists to secure legal protections for LGBTQ individuals.

4. **International Recognition:** The Philippines has gained international attention for its vibrant LGBTQ community and activism. Events such as the International Day Against Homophobia, Transphobia, and Biphobia (IDAHOTB) have become platforms for global solidarity and recognition of local struggles.

Measuring Progress in LGBTQ Activism

Measuring progress in the LGBTQ movement can be complex, as it encompasses various dimensions, including legal, social, and cultural aspects. Some methods for assessing progress include:

+ **Legislative Changes:** Tracking the introduction and passage of laws related to LGBTQ rights is a fundamental measure of progress. For example, the increasing number of local government units (LGUs) that have enacted anti-discrimination ordinances is a positive indicator of change.

+ **Public Opinion Surveys:** Conducting surveys to gauge public attitudes towards LGBTQ individuals can provide insights into societal acceptance and identify areas for further advocacy. An increase in acceptance rates over time reflects the impact of education and awareness campaigns.

+ **Visibility and Representation:** The representation of LGBTQ individuals in media, politics, and other public spheres is another critical measure.

Increased visibility can lead to greater acceptance and normalization of LGBTQ identities.

+ **Community Engagement:** The level of participation in LGBTQ events, such as pride parades and awareness campaigns, serves as a barometer for community solidarity and activism. Higher turnout at events indicates a growing commitment to the movement.

The Role of Celebrations in Sustaining Momentum

Celebrating milestones not only honors past achievements but also plays a vital role in sustaining momentum for future activism. Events like pride celebrations, award ceremonies, and community gatherings provide opportunities for activists to connect, share experiences, and strategize for ongoing challenges.

$$\text{Sustained Momentum} = \text{Celebration Events} + \text{Community Engagement} \quad (48)$$

This equation illustrates that the combination of celebratory events and active community involvement can lead to a sustained momentum that propels the movement forward.

Examples of Celebratory Events

Several notable events in the Philippines exemplify the importance of celebrating milestones:

+ **Pride Month Celebrations:** Each June, the LGBTQ community in the Philippines comes together to celebrate Pride Month, culminating in a grand parade that showcases the diversity and strength of the community. These celebrations are not just about revelry; they serve as a powerful reminder of the struggles faced and the progress made.

+ **Awards and Recognition Ceremonies:** Events that honor the contributions of activists, organizations, and allies help to acknowledge the hard work that often goes unrecognized. The *Gawad Parangal* awards, for instance, celebrate outstanding efforts in promoting LGBTQ rights and visibility.

+ **Anniversaries of Key Organizations:** Celebrating the anniversaries of LGBTQ organizations allows for reflection on their journey, achievements, and challenges. These events often serve as platforms for fundraising, awareness-raising, and community building.

Conclusion

In conclusion, celebrating milestones and measuring progress are integral components of LGBTQ activism in the Philippines. Through recognition of achievements, the movement can inspire future generations, raise awareness, and foster community solidarity. As activists like Sitti Djalia Turabin continue to pave the way for equality, it is essential to honor the past while striving for a future where LGBTQ rights are fully realized. The journey is ongoing, and each milestone celebrated is a stepping stone towards a more inclusive society.

Turabin's Legacy and Continuing the Fight

Securing the Future of LGBTQ Activism in the Philippines

The journey of LGBTQ activism in the Philippines is a testament to resilience, courage, and the relentless pursuit of equality. However, as we look towards the future, it is imperative to secure the foundations laid by past and present activists to ensure the continuation and expansion of rights and recognition for LGBTQ individuals. This section explores the strategies and frameworks necessary to fortify the future of LGBTQ activism in the Philippines.

The Importance of Institutional Support

For LGBTQ activism to thrive, it is crucial to garner institutional support from various sectors, including government, educational institutions, and civil society organizations. Institutional support can manifest in several ways:

- **Legislative Advocacy:** Pushing for comprehensive anti-discrimination laws that protect LGBTQ individuals from bias in employment, housing, and public services is essential. The proposed Sexual Orientation and Gender Identity Expression (SOGIE) Equality Bill is a pivotal piece of legislation that aims to address these issues. Activists must continue to lobby for its passage and implementation.

- **Educational Initiatives:** Incorporating LGBTQ studies into school curricula can foster understanding and acceptance from a young age. Educational institutions can also serve as safe spaces for LGBTQ youth, promoting mental health and well-being through support groups and counseling services.

- **Partnerships with NGOs:** Collaborating with non-governmental organizations can amplify the reach of LGBTQ activism. These partnerships can provide resources, training, and platforms for advocacy campaigns, ensuring that the voices of marginalized LGBTQ communities are heard.

Addressing Intersectional Issues

The future of LGBTQ activism must also prioritize intersectionality, recognizing that individuals experience oppression differently based on their race, class, gender identity, and other factors. This approach requires:

- **Inclusive Advocacy:** Activists should ensure that the needs of all LGBTQ individuals, particularly those from marginalized backgrounds, are represented in advocacy efforts. This includes addressing the unique challenges faced by LGBTQ people of color, transgender individuals, and those from lower socio-economic backgrounds.

- **Community Engagement:** Engaging with local communities to understand their specific needs and challenges is vital. Grassroots movements can be powerful in addressing localized issues, allowing activists to tailor their approaches effectively.

- **Holistic Support Systems:** Providing comprehensive support that includes mental health services, legal assistance, and economic empowerment programs can help uplift the most vulnerable members of the LGBTQ community.

Utilizing Technology and Social Media

In the digital age, technology and social media play a crucial role in shaping LGBTQ activism. Activists must harness these tools to secure the future of their movement:

- **Awareness Campaigns:** Social media platforms can be utilized to raise awareness about LGBTQ issues, share personal stories, and mobilize support for campaigns. Viral campaigns have the potential to reach vast audiences, creating a sense of solidarity and urgency.

- **Digital Activism:** Online petitions, crowdfunding for LGBTQ initiatives, and virtual events can engage a broader audience and create a sense of community among activists. The use of hashtags and trending topics can amplify messages and draw attention to pressing issues.

+ **Safe Online Spaces:** Creating online forums and support groups can provide LGBTQ individuals with a sense of belonging and a platform to share their experiences. These spaces can also serve as a resource for education and activism.

Mentorship and Leadership Development

Securing the future of LGBTQ activism also hinges on the cultivation of new leaders within the movement. This can be achieved through:

+ **Mentorship Programs:** Establishing mentorship programs that connect seasoned activists with emerging leaders can facilitate knowledge transfer and skill development. Mentorship can empower the next generation of activists to navigate challenges and build effective advocacy strategies.

+ **Leadership Training:** Providing training sessions on advocacy techniques, public speaking, and organizational skills can equip young activists with the tools they need to lead effectively. This investment in human capital is crucial for the sustainability of the movement.

+ **Creating Opportunities for Youth Engagement:** Encouraging youth participation in activism through internships, volunteer opportunities, and leadership roles within organizations can ensure that fresh perspectives and ideas are integrated into the movement.

Global Solidarity and Collaboration

Finally, securing the future of LGBTQ activism in the Philippines requires building bridges with global movements. This can enhance the impact of local efforts and provide a broader context for advocacy:

+ **International Partnerships:** Collaborating with international LGBTQ organizations can provide resources, funding, and visibility for local initiatives. Sharing best practices and strategies can strengthen advocacy efforts.

+ **Participating in Global Events:** Engaging in international pride events, conferences, and forums can raise awareness about the unique challenges faced by LGBTQ individuals in the Philippines and garner support from a global audience.

+ **Solidarity Campaigns:** Establishing solidarity campaigns that connect local issues with global struggles can create a sense of unity within the LGBTQ movement. This interconnectedness can amplify voices and foster a collective fight for rights and recognition.

Conclusion

In conclusion, securing the future of LGBTQ activism in the Philippines requires a multifaceted approach that encompasses institutional support, intersectionality, technology, mentorship, and global collaboration. By addressing these key areas, activists can build a robust framework that not only protects the rights of LGBTQ individuals but also promotes a culture of acceptance and equality. As we move forward, it is essential to remember that the fight for LGBTQ rights is ongoing, and the commitment to this cause must be unwavering. Together, we can forge a future where love and acceptance reign supreme, ensuring that every individual can live authentically and without fear.

Turabin's Influence on the Next Generation of Activists

Turabin's journey as an LGBTQ activist has not only created ripples in the present but has also paved the way for future generations to rise and advocate for their rights. The influence of a prominent activist like Turabin can be understood through several key aspects: mentorship, visibility, and the fostering of a collective identity among young activists.

Mentorship and Empowerment

One of the most significant ways Turabin has impacted the next generation is through mentorship. By actively engaging with LGBTQ youth, Turabin has provided guidance and support, helping young individuals navigate the complexities of their identities and the activism landscape. This mentorship is crucial, as studies have shown that positive role models can significantly enhance the self-esteem and aspirations of marginalized youth [1].

Turabin has initiated programs that connect seasoned activists with newcomers, creating a network of support that empowers young voices. The theory of social learning, proposed by Albert Bandura, emphasizes the importance of modeling behaviors, attitudes, and emotional reactions. Turabin embodies this concept, demonstrating through her actions that activism is not only about fighting for rights but also about building community and solidarity.

Visibility and Representation

Visibility plays a critical role in activism, particularly for marginalized communities. Turabin's presence in media and public forums has amplified the voices of LGBTQ youth, making their struggles and triumphs more visible to society. This representation is essential for young activists who may feel isolated or invisible in a world that often marginalizes their identities.

The concept of intersectionality, coined by Kimberlé Crenshaw, is also relevant here. Turabin has highlighted how various identities—such as race, gender, and socioeconomic status—intersect to shape the experiences of LGBTQ individuals. By addressing these intersections, Turabin has encouraged young activists to embrace their multifaceted identities and advocate for a more inclusive movement.

Fostering Collective Identity

Turabin's activism has fostered a sense of collective identity among young LGBTQ individuals. Through organizing events such as Pride marches and awareness campaigns, she has created spaces where youth can come together, share their experiences, and celebrate their identities. This collective identity is vital for mobilizing efforts and creating a sense of belonging among young activists.

The social identity theory, developed by Henri Tajfel and John Turner, posits that individuals derive a sense of self from their group memberships. By promoting a strong LGBTQ identity, Turabin has helped young activists understand the power of collective action. They learn that their voices, when united, can challenge societal norms and push for meaningful change.

Challenges and Resilience

While Turabin has inspired many, she has also been open about the challenges faced in activism. By sharing her own struggles with adversity, she teaches resilience to the next generation. Young activists learn that setbacks are part of the journey, and perseverance is key to achieving their goals.

Turabin often cites the importance of self-care and mental health in her activism, emphasizing that to be effective advocates, individuals must also care for their well-being. This holistic approach to activism ensures that young leaders are equipped not only with the skills to fight for their rights but also with the tools to maintain their mental and emotional health.

Examples of Impact

Several young activists credit Turabin as a pivotal figure in their journey. For instance, Maria, a 19-year-old activist from Manila, recalls how Turabin's workshops on LGBTQ rights inspired her to start her own advocacy group focused on mental health support for LGBTQ youth. Similarly, James, a 22-year-old, shares that Turabin's visibility in media encouraged him to embrace his identity and speak out against discrimination in his community.

These stories exemplify the ripple effect of Turabin's influence. As she empowers one individual, that person often goes on to inspire others, creating a chain reaction of activism and advocacy.

Conclusion

In conclusion, Turabin's influence on the next generation of activists is profound and multifaceted. Through mentorship, visibility, and the fostering of collective identity, she has equipped young LGBTQ individuals with the tools they need to navigate their journeys and advocate for their rights. As they carry forward her legacy, it is clear that Turabin's impact will resonate for years to come, shaping the future of LGBTQ activism in the Philippines and beyond.

The Unfinished Work of LGBTQ Activism

The journey of LGBTQ activism is far from over. Despite significant strides in rights and recognition, many challenges remain, highlighting the unfinished work that activists like Sitti Djalia Turabin and countless others continue to face. This section delves into the complexities of ongoing struggles, the theoretical frameworks that underpin them, and the practical implications for future activism.

Theoretical Frameworks

To understand the unfinished work of LGBTQ activism, we must first engage with relevant theories that provide insight into the systemic issues at play. One such framework is Intersectionality, coined by Kimberlé Crenshaw in the late 1980s. This theory posits that individuals experience oppression in varying configurations and degrees of intensity based on their intersecting identities, such as race, gender, sexuality, and class.

In the context of LGBTQ activism, intersectionality reveals how the movement must address not only sexual orientation and gender identity but also the unique challenges faced by individuals at the intersection of multiple marginalized identities.   For instance, LGBTQ individuals from indigenous backgrounds in the Philippines often confront both homophobia and colonial legacies that exacerbate their struggles.

$$O = f(I_1, I_2, I_3, \ldots, I_n) \tag{49}$$

Where O represents the overall oppression experienced by an individual, and I_n are the various intersecting identities. This equation illustrates that the experience of oppression is not linear but rather a complex function of multiple factors.

Ongoing Challenges

Despite the progress made in LGBTQ rights, numerous challenges persist. One major issue is the lack of comprehensive anti-discrimination laws in many regions, including the Philippines.   While some cities have enacted local ordinances to protect LGBTQ individuals, there remains a significant gap in national legislation. For example, the proposed Sexual Orientation and Gender Identity Expression (SOGIE) Equality Bill has faced numerous setbacks in Congress, reflecting the resistance from conservative factions within society.

Additionally, violence against LGBTQ individuals continues to be a pressing concern.   Reports of hate crimes, particularly against transgender women, underscore the urgent need for systemic change. The case of Jennifer Laude, a transgender woman who was murdered in 2014, highlights the intersection of gender identity and violence, sparking national outrage and calls for justice.

Global Perspectives

The unfinished work of LGBTQ activism is not limited to the Philippines; it is a global phenomenon. Activists around the world face similar challenges, from legal discrimination to social stigma. In many countries, LGBTQ individuals are still criminalized for their identities, leading to severe human rights violations.

For instance, in Uganda, the Anti-Homosexuality Act has been a focal point of international condemnation, illustrating how state-sponsored homophobia can thwart activism and perpetuate violence. This situation emphasizes the need for global solidarity among LGBTQ activists, as the fight for rights is interconnected across borders.

Strategies for Progress

To address the unfinished work of LGBTQ activism, several strategies can be employed. First, building coalitions with other marginalized groups can amplify voices and create a united front against oppression. This approach aligns with the principles of solidarity and mutual aid, fostering a sense of community among diverse groups.

Second, leveraging social media and digital platforms can enhance outreach and awareness. Activists can utilize these tools to share stories, mobilize support, and create safe spaces for dialogue. The viral nature of social media campaigns, such as #LoveWins and #TransRightsAreHumanRights, exemplifies how digital activism can catalyze real-world change.

Finally, education remains a cornerstone of progress. By promoting LGBTQ-inclusive curricula in schools, we can foster understanding and acceptance from a young age. This proactive approach not only empowers future generations but also dismantles harmful stereotypes and misconceptions.

Conclusion

In conclusion, the unfinished work of LGBTQ activism requires a multifaceted approach that acknowledges the complexities of identity, addresses ongoing challenges, and fosters collaboration. As activists like Sitti Djalia Turabin continue to pave the way for change, it is crucial to remember that the fight for equality is a collective endeavor. By embracing intersectionality, advocating for comprehensive legislation, and harnessing the power of community, we can move closer to a world where LGBTQ individuals are not only accepted but celebrated in their entirety. The journey may be long, but the destination is worth every effort.

Strategies for Sustaining Activism Efforts

Sustaining activism efforts in the LGBTQ community is a multifaceted challenge that requires a strategic approach to ensure longevity and effectiveness. This section explores various strategies that activists can employ to maintain momentum in their advocacy work, focusing on community engagement, resource mobilization, mental health support, and the use of technology.

1. Community Engagement and Empowerment

One of the foundational strategies for sustaining activism is fostering a strong sense of community among LGBTQ individuals. Engaging community members not only builds solidarity but also empowers individuals to take ownership of their activism.

1.1 Building Safe Spaces Creating safe spaces where LGBTQ individuals can express themselves without fear of judgment is crucial. This can be achieved through:

- **Support Groups:** Establishing regular support meetings where individuals can share their experiences and challenges.

- **Workshops and Training:** Offering workshops on advocacy skills, public speaking, and self-advocacy to empower community members.

1.2 Community-led Initiatives Encouraging community-led initiatives can lead to sustainable activism. This includes:

- **Local Pride Events:** Organizing local pride marches or festivals that celebrate LGBTQ identities and raise awareness.

- **Collaborative Projects:** Partnering with local organizations to create joint initiatives that address specific community needs.

2. Resource Mobilization

Effective activism often hinges on the availability of resources. Mobilizing financial, human, and informational resources is essential for sustaining efforts.

2.1 Fundraising Strategies Activists should explore diverse fundraising strategies, including:

- **Crowdfunding:** Utilizing platforms like GoFundMe or Kickstarter to raise funds for specific projects.

- **Grant Applications:** Applying for grants from non-profit organizations or government entities that support LGBTQ initiatives.

2.2 Building Partnerships Forming alliances with other organizations can amplify resources. This can be achieved through:

- **Coalitions:** Joining coalitions that focus on broader social justice issues, thereby pooling resources and knowledge.

- **Corporate Sponsorships:** Engaging with businesses that are committed to diversity and inclusion to secure sponsorships for events and campaigns.

3. Mental Health Support

The emotional toll of activism can lead to burnout and disengagement. Addressing mental health is vital for sustaining activism.

3.1 Self-Care Practices Encouraging self-care practices among activists can help mitigate burnout. This includes:

+ **Mindfulness and Meditation:** Incorporating mindfulness practices to help activists manage stress.

+ **Physical Wellness:** Promoting physical activities, such as yoga or group sports, to enhance mental health.

3.2 Access to Mental Health Resources Activists should have access to mental health resources, including:

+ **Therapeutic Services:** Providing information about LGBTQ-friendly therapists and counselors.

+ **Peer Support Networks:** Establishing peer support networks where individuals can share their struggles and coping strategies.

4. Utilizing Technology

In the digital age, technology plays a critical role in sustaining activism efforts. Leveraging technology can enhance outreach and engagement.

4.1 Social Media Campaigns Activists can utilize social media platforms to reach broader audiences through:

+ **Awareness Campaigns:** Creating viral campaigns that highlight LGBTQ issues and encourage community involvement.

+ **Engagement Strategies:** Utilizing interactive content, such as polls and Q&A sessions, to foster engagement with followers.

4.2 Online Resources and Education   Providing online resources can empower individuals and educate the public about LGBTQ issues:

- **Webinars and Online Workshops:** Hosting educational webinars on topics relevant to LGBTQ rights and advocacy.

- **Resource Websites:** Developing websites that compile information, resources, and support networks for LGBTQ individuals.

5. Continuous Advocacy and Adaptation

Sustaining activism requires continuous advocacy and the ability to adapt to changing circumstances.

5.1 Monitoring and Evaluation   Activists should regularly assess the impact of their initiatives through:

- **Feedback Mechanisms:** Implementing feedback systems to gather input from community members on the effectiveness of programs.

- **Data Analysis:** Utilizing data to evaluate the success of campaigns and identify areas for improvement.

5.2 Adapting Strategies   The landscape of activism is constantly evolving. Activists must be willing to adapt their strategies based on:

- **Emerging Issues:** Staying informed about new challenges facing the LGBTQ community and adjusting advocacy efforts accordingly.

- **Cultural Shifts:** Recognizing and responding to cultural shifts that may impact public perception and support for LGBTQ rights.

In conclusion, sustaining activism efforts in the LGBTQ community requires a comprehensive approach that emphasizes community engagement, resource mobilization, mental health support, technology utilization, and continuous advocacy. By implementing these strategies, activists can ensure that their efforts remain impactful and resilient in the face of ongoing challenges.

Chapter 4 Turabin's Personal and Professional Life

Chapter 4 Turabin's Personal and Professional Life

Turabin's Personal and Professional Life

In this chapter, we delve into the intricate tapestry of Sitti Djalia Turabin's personal and professional life. This exploration reveals how her identity as an LGBTQ activist intertwines with her personal relationships, career aspirations, and the challenges she faces in balancing these domains. The journey of an activist is not merely defined by public actions but is significantly influenced by personal experiences and professional commitments.

4.1.1 The Intersection of Personal Life and Activism

Turabin's personal life is a reflection of her identity and activism. As an LGBTQ activist, she navigates the complexities of personal relationships while championing the cause for equality and acceptance. The duality of her life presents unique challenges, especially in maintaining relationships that are supportive and understanding of her activism.

Cultural Expectations and Personal Relationships: In the Philippines, traditional cultural norms often place significant expectations on individuals regarding relationships and family roles. Turabin's experiences reveal the tension between societal expectations and her commitment to her identity. For instance, the pressure to conform to heteronormative standards can lead to isolation for LGBTQ individuals. Turabin's story exemplifies the struggle many face when their personal lives intersect with cultural traditions that may not embrace diversity.

Support Systems: Despite the challenges, Turabin finds solace in her community. The LGBTQ community serves as a vital support network, providing emotional backing and shared experiences. This network is crucial for resilience, allowing activists like Turabin to navigate the complexities of their personal lives while remaining committed to their cause.

4.2 Professional Life and Activism

Turabin's professional journey is equally compelling, showcasing how her career intersects with her activism. The balance between professional responsibilities and advocacy efforts is a tightrope walk that requires careful navigation.

Educational Background: Turabin pursued higher education, which she views as a foundational step in her activism. Her academic achievements are not just personal milestones but tools for empowerment. Education equips her with the knowledge necessary to advocate effectively for LGBTQ rights, allowing her to engage in informed discussions and policy-making processes.

Career Choices: Turabin's career path reflects her commitment to social justice. She has held positions in organizations that align with her values, focusing on human rights, community development, and advocacy. These roles provide her with a platform to influence change and amplify the voices of marginalized communities.

4.3 Balancing Activism and Career

The intersection of activism and career presents unique challenges for Turabin. The demands of her professional life often compete with her activism, leading to a constant negotiation of time and energy.

Workplace Dynamics: Turabin's experiences in the workplace highlight the need for inclusive environments. She has encountered both support and resistance in her professional settings. Supportive colleagues and organizations foster a culture of acceptance, enabling her to thrive both as a professional and an activist. Conversely, environments lacking inclusivity can lead to burnout and frustration, underscoring the need for systemic change within workplaces.

Strategies for Balance: To maintain equilibrium, Turabin employs various strategies. Time management becomes crucial as she allocates specific hours for activism while ensuring her professional responsibilities are met. Additionally, she prioritizes self-care, recognizing that personal well-being is essential for sustaining her activism.

4.4 Self-Care and Resilience

Activism can be emotionally taxing, and Turabin emphasizes the importance of self-care in her journey.

Coping Mechanisms: Turabin utilizes various coping strategies to manage stress and maintain her mental health. These include mindfulness practices, physical exercise, and engaging in creative outlets. By prioritizing her mental well-being, she enhances her resilience against the challenges posed by activism.

Building a Support Network: The significance of a robust support network cannot be overstated. Turabin actively cultivates relationships with friends, family, and fellow activists who provide encouragement and understanding. This network serves as a buffer against the emotional toll of activism, fostering a sense of belonging and community.

Mental Health Awareness: Turabin is an advocate for mental health awareness within the LGBTQ community. She recognizes the unique challenges faced by LGBTQ individuals, including stigma and discrimination, which can adversely affect mental health. By promoting mental health resources and support, she seeks to empower others to prioritize their well-being alongside their activism.

In conclusion, Sitti Djalia Turabin's personal and professional life is a testament to the resilience and determination of LGBTQ activists. The interplay between her identity, relationships, and career underscores the complexities of activism in a cultural context that often resists change. Through her journey, Turabin exemplifies the power of community, self-care, and advocacy, inspiring future generations to continue the fight for equality and acceptance.

Personal Relationships and Love Life

Turabin's Dating Journey and Relationship Experiences

Sitti Djalia Turabin's dating journey is a vivid tapestry woven with the threads of love, struggle, and self-discovery. Growing up in a society where LGBTQ relationships often faced stigma, Turabin navigated the complexities of dating with a unique blend of courage and vulnerability. Her experiences can be understood through the lens of queer theory, which emphasizes the fluidity of gender and sexual identities, allowing for a deeper understanding of her relationships.

Early Dating Experiences

Turabin's early dating experiences were marked by a sense of secrecy and fear. In her formative years, she often felt the pressure to conform to societal norms, which dictated who she should love and how she should express that love. The internal conflict she faced is a common theme among LGBTQ individuals, as highlighted by the minority stress theory, which posits that the stigma and discrimination faced by marginalized groups can lead to heightened stress and mental health issues [1].

During her teenage years, Turabin found herself drawn to individuals who embodied the qualities she admired: strength, authenticity, and a shared understanding of the struggles faced by LGBTQ individuals. However, the fear of rejection and societal backlash often led her to keep her relationships hidden. This fear was compounded by her upbringing in a conservative environment where traditional views on relationships prevailed.

Navigating Relationships

As Turabin grew older and began to embrace her identity, she ventured into the dating scene with a newfound sense of determination. She sought relationships that resonated with her values and aspirations, but the journey was not without its challenges. The intersection of her identity as a queer woman and the societal expectations surrounding dating created a complex landscape for her romantic endeavors.

One significant relationship was with a fellow activist, who shared her passion for LGBTQ rights. This partnership became a source of strength for Turabin, as they supported each other through the trials of activism and personal growth. Their relationship exemplified the concept of intersectionality, where multiple identities intersect to shape an individual's experience [2]. Together, they navigated the challenges of being in a public relationship while advocating for change.

Challenges in Relationships

Despite the love and support she found in her relationships, Turabin faced numerous challenges. The societal stigma surrounding LGBTQ relationships often led to external pressures that strained her connections. For instance, family disapproval and societal judgment created rifts between her and her partners, forcing her to confront the harsh realities of being an LGBTQ individual in a conservative society.

Moreover, the emotional toll of activism sometimes seeped into her personal life. The stress from her advocacy work could lead to moments of frustration and conflict within her relationships. The balance between personal and activist life is a delicate one, and Turabin learned that communication and mutual understanding were essential to maintaining healthy connections.

Finding Love and Community Support

Turabin's journey also highlighted the importance of community support in her dating life. The LGBTQ community provided a safe space for her to explore her identity and relationships without fear of judgment. Through local pride events and activist gatherings, she met individuals who shared her experiences and struggles. This sense of belonging fostered a supportive environment where love could flourish.

In one particularly memorable instance, Turabin attended a pride festival where she met a partner who would later become a significant figure in her life. Their connection was immediate, rooted in a shared commitment to activism and a mutual understanding of the challenges they faced. This relationship became a testament to the power of love within the LGBTQ community, showcasing how shared experiences can create deep bonds.

Navigating Intimacy and Relationships in the Public Eye

As Turabin's activism gained prominence, her relationships began to attract public attention. Navigating intimacy in the public eye presented its own set of challenges. The scrutiny of media and public opinion often placed additional pressure on her relationships, forcing her to balance her personal life with her public persona.

In an age where social media plays a significant role in shaping perceptions, Turabin learned to navigate the complexities of sharing her relationship while maintaining boundaries. She recognized the importance of protecting her personal life from the relentless gaze of the public, leading to discussions about privacy and transparency with her partners.

Conclusion

Turabin's dating journey reflects the broader struggles and triumphs faced by LGBTQ individuals in their pursuit of love and acceptance. Her experiences highlight the significance of community, support, and resilience in navigating the complexities of relationships. As she continues to advocate for LGBTQ rights, Turabin's journey serves as an inspiration for others, reminding them that love, in all its forms, is a powerful force for change.

Bibliography

[1] Meyer, I. H. (2003). Prejudice, Social Stress, and Mental Health in Gay Men. *American Psychologist*, 58(5), 161-173.

[2] Crenshaw, K. (1989). Demarginalizing the Intersection of Race and Sex: A Black Feminist Critique of Antidiscrimination Doctrine, Feminist Theory and Antiracist Politics. *University of Chicago Legal Forum*, 1989(1), 139-167.

Challenges Faced in Maintaining Relationships as an Activist

In the vibrant and often tumultuous world of activism, maintaining personal relationships can be as challenging as the fight for justice itself. For Sitti Djalia Turabin, a prominent LGBTQ activist in the Philippines, the intersection of her advocacy work and personal life presents unique difficulties that shape her relationships with friends, family, and romantic partners. These challenges can be categorized into several key areas: emotional labor, time constraints, public scrutiny, and the impact of activism on personal identity.

Emotional Labor

Activism is inherently demanding, requiring substantial emotional investment. Turabin's work involves not only advocating for LGBTQ rights but also supporting community members who may be facing discrimination, violence, or mental health challenges. The emotional labor involved in this work can lead to compassion fatigue, where the constant exposure to others' struggles drains an activist's emotional reserves. According to [?], emotional labor refers to the process of managing feelings and expressions to fulfill the emotional requirements of a job. In Turabin's case, her emotional labor extends beyond her professional responsibilities and seeps into her personal relationships.

This phenomenon can create tension with partners or friends who may feel neglected or undervalued. For instance, while Turabin is passionately advocating for anti-discrimination laws, her partner might feel sidelined during moments when they need emotional support.   The struggle to balance the emotional demands of activism with the needs of loved ones can lead to misunderstandings and conflicts, complicating the dynamics of these relationships.

Time Constraints

Activism often requires a significant time commitment, leaving little room for personal relationships.   Turabin's schedule is filled with meetings, rallies, and community outreach events, which can result in her spending less time with family and friends.   According to [?], the time demands of activism can create a "time poverty" effect, where activists feel they are perpetually rushing from one commitment to another, leaving little time for leisure or personal connections.

The consequences of this time crunch can be profound.   Relationships may suffer from neglect, as partners and friends may feel like they are competing for attention against pressing social justice issues.   For example, Turabin's desire to attend a pride march may conflict with a friend's birthday celebration, leading to feelings of guilt and resentment.   Over time, this pattern can erode the foundation of personal relationships, making it challenging to maintain close connections.

Public Scrutiny

As a public figure, Turabin faces scrutiny not only for her activism but also for her personal life.   The visibility that comes with being an activist can lead to a lack of privacy, with friends and family often feeling the weight of public opinion.   The pressure to present a certain image can strain relationships, as loved ones may feel they must conform to the expectations placed upon them by the public or media.

This public scrutiny can manifest in various ways.   For instance, if Turabin's partner expresses a desire for privacy, it may conflict with Turabin's role as an activist who often shares personal stories to raise awareness.   The tension between the need for privacy and the desire for visibility can create friction, making it challenging to navigate personal relationships in a public sphere.

Impact of Activism on Personal Identity

Activism can profoundly influence one's sense of identity, leading to changes in how individuals view themselves and their relationships. For Turabin, her identity as an LGBTQ activist is a core part of who she is. This strong identification with her activism can sometimes overshadow other aspects of her identity, such as her role as a partner or friend. According to [?], identity development is a complex process that can be influenced by social roles and experiences.

As Turabin becomes more entrenched in her activist identity, she may find it difficult to connect with friends or family members who do not share the same passion or understanding of LGBTQ issues. This disconnect can lead to feelings of isolation, as she may feel that her personal relationships cannot keep pace with her evolving identity. The challenge lies in finding common ground and maintaining connections despite differing experiences and perspectives.

Conclusion

In conclusion, the challenges faced by Sitti Djalia Turabin in maintaining relationships as an activist are multifaceted and complex. Emotional labor, time constraints, public scrutiny, and the impact of activism on personal identity all contribute to the difficulties she encounters in her personal life. Navigating these challenges requires resilience, open communication, and a commitment to balancing the demands of activism with the need for meaningful relationships. As Turabin continues her journey in LGBTQ activism, she must also prioritize her personal connections, recognizing that love and support are vital components of sustaining her advocacy work.

Finding Love and Support in the LGBTQ Community

Finding love and support within the LGBTQ community is a multifaceted journey that intertwines personal experiences with broader social dynamics. For many individuals, the search for companionship and acceptance is not merely a quest for romantic love, but also a pursuit of belonging and solidarity within a community that has historically faced stigma and marginalization.

The Importance of Community

The LGBTQ community serves as a crucial support network, offering emotional, psychological, and social resources that are often lacking in mainstream society. This sense of community can be understood through the lens of social identity theory, which posits that individuals derive a sense of self from their group memberships. In this context, LGBTQ individuals may find empowerment and validation in their shared identity, leading to stronger interpersonal connections.

$$S = \frac{1}{N} \sum_{i=1}^{N} \text{Identity}_i \tag{50}$$

Where S represents the collective sense of self, N is the number of individuals in the community, and Identity_i represents the individual identity contributions. This equation illustrates how community identity can enhance personal self-worth.

Challenges in Finding Love

Despite the advantages of community support, LGBTQ individuals often face unique challenges in their pursuit of love. Societal stigma, internalized homophobia, and discrimination can complicate relationships and hinder the development of healthy romantic connections. For instance, individuals may struggle with self-acceptance, which can manifest in their interactions with potential partners. The fear of rejection or judgment can lead to a reluctance to engage openly, creating barriers to intimacy.

Research indicates that LGBTQ individuals are more likely to experience mental health issues, such as anxiety and depression, which can further complicate their search for love. A study by Meyer (2003) on minority stress highlights how chronic stressors related to one's sexual orientation can adversely affect mental health, which in turn impacts relationship dynamics.

Support Systems and Resources

To navigate these challenges, many LGBTQ individuals turn to community organizations and support groups that foster connection and understanding. These spaces provide opportunities for individuals to share their experiences, seek advice, and form friendships. Organizations like PFLAG (Parents, Families, and Friends of Lesbians and Gays) and local LGBTQ centers often host events that encourage socialization and networking, creating fertile ground for romantic relationships to blossom.

Additionally, online platforms have emerged as vital resources for LGBTQ individuals seeking love and support. Dating apps specifically designed for the LGBTQ community, such as Grindr, HER, and OkCupid, allow users to connect with others who share similar experiences and identities. However, these platforms also present challenges, such as the potential for superficial interactions and the risk of encountering harassment.

Finding Meaningful Connections

In the quest for love, many LGBTQ individuals emphasize the importance of shared values, interests, and experiences. Relationships built on mutual understanding and respect are often more resilient in the face of external pressures. For instance, a study conducted by Herek (2009) found that LGBTQ couples who actively engage in community activities report higher relationship satisfaction, as they feel supported by their peers.

Furthermore, the concept of intersectionality plays a significant role in how individuals navigate their romantic lives. Intersectionality, coined by Kimberlé Crenshaw, refers to the interconnected nature of social categorizations such as race, class, and gender, which can create overlapping systems of discrimination or disadvantage. LGBTQ individuals who also belong to other marginalized groups may face additional barriers in their search for love, necessitating a more nuanced understanding of their experiences.

Examples of Love and Support in the Community

There are numerous inspiring examples of love and support within the LGBTQ community. Activists like Sitti Djalia Turabin have not only advocated for rights but have also fostered a culture of love and acceptance, encouraging individuals to embrace their identities fully. Turabin's work in organizing Pride events and awareness campaigns has created spaces where love can flourish, free from judgment.

Moreover, community-led initiatives that focus on mental health support, such as LGBTQ therapy groups, highlight the importance of addressing emotional well-being as a foundation for healthy relationships. These initiatives often provide tools for communication, conflict resolution, and emotional regulation, which are essential skills for nurturing love.

Conclusion

In conclusion, finding love and support within the LGBTQ community is a complex yet rewarding journey. While challenges such as stigma and mental health issues persist, the community offers a wealth of resources and connections that can foster meaningful relationships. By embracing their identities and seeking support from peers, LGBTQ individuals can navigate the intricacies of love, ultimately contributing to a more inclusive and affirming society.

Bibliography

[1] Meyer, I. H. (2003). Prejudice, Social Stress, and Mental Health in Gay Men. *American Psychologist*, 58(5), 123-134.

[2] Herek, G. M. (2009). Sexual Stigma and Sexual Prejudice in the United States: A Conceptual Framework. *Archives of Sexual Behavior*, 38(5), 976-988.

Navigating Intimacy and Relationships in the Public Eye

Navigating intimacy and relationships in the public eye is a complex dance of vulnerability, visibility, and societal expectations. For LGBTQ activists like Sitti Djalia Turabin, the interplay between personal life and public persona can be both a source of strength and a significant challenge. This section explores the dynamics of intimacy within the context of activism, highlighting the unique obstacles faced by individuals in the LGBTQ community, while also drawing on relevant theories and real-life examples.

The Double-Edged Sword of Visibility

Visibility in the LGBTQ community can often be a double-edged sword. While being open about one's identity can foster acceptance and representation, it also subjects individuals to scrutiny and judgment. According to [2], intersectionality plays a crucial role in understanding how various identities—such as race, gender, and sexual orientation—interact and affect one another. For activists like Turabin, this means that their relationships are not only seen through the lens of their sexual orientation but also through the societal expectations tied to their activism.

The pressure to maintain a certain public image can create tension in personal relationships. For instance, Turabin may feel compelled to portray an idealized version of her love life, which can lead to unrealistic expectations and stress. This phenomenon is often referred to as the *performative aspect of identity*, where individuals feel the need to perform their identity in a way that aligns with societal norms or activist goals, rather than expressing their authentic selves.

Challenges in Maintaining Relationships

Maintaining intimate relationships while being an activist can be fraught with challenges. The emotional toll of activism, combined with public scrutiny, can strain personal connections. Research indicates that activists often experience higher levels of stress and burnout, which can spill over into their personal lives [?].

For Turabin, balancing her commitments as an activist with her desire for intimacy may lead to conflicts. The demands of organizing events, attending meetings, and advocating for rights can limit the time and energy available for nurturing personal relationships. Furthermore, the fear of backlash or negative publicity can inhibit open communication with partners, creating an environment where intimacy is compromised.

Finding Support within the LGBTQ Community

Despite these challenges, many LGBTQ activists find solace and support within their community. The shared experiences of navigating societal stigma and discrimination can create deep bonds between individuals. Turabin's relationships with fellow activists may offer a unique understanding of the pressures they face, allowing for a more profound connection based on mutual experiences.

Support networks within the LGBTQ community can also provide a buffer against the external pressures of activism. For example, group therapy or community support groups can offer safe spaces for discussing relationship challenges, fostering resilience among individuals facing similar struggles. According to [1], social support is critical in mitigating the negative effects of stress and can enhance well-being, particularly for marginalized individuals.

Strategies for Navigating Intimacy

To navigate intimacy effectively, LGBTQ activists can employ several strategies:

+ **Open Communication:** Establishing clear lines of communication with partners about the challenges of being in the public eye is essential. This involves discussing boundaries, expectations, and the impact of activism on the relationship.

+ **Setting Boundaries:** Activists should consider setting boundaries around their personal lives and public personas. This can help create a safe space for intimacy without the interference of public scrutiny.

+ **Prioritizing Self-Care:** Engaging in self-care practices can help activists manage stress and maintain emotional balance. This, in turn, can enhance their capacity for intimacy and connection with partners.

+ **Engaging in Community:** Building relationships within the LGBTQ community can provide emotional support and understanding. Engaging in community events can also foster a sense of belonging and shared purpose.

Real-Life Examples

Turabin's journey illustrates the complexities of navigating relationships in the public eye. For instance, during a particularly challenging campaign for anti-discrimination laws, she might have faced increased scrutiny over her personal life, leading to tension with a partner who felt overshadowed by her activism. However, through honest conversations and mutual support, they could work together to establish a balance that honors both their relationship and Turabin's commitment to activism.

Similarly, other activists have shared experiences of finding love within the movement. For example, a couple who met during a pride march may have bonded over their shared passion for advocacy, providing them with a unique understanding of each other's challenges. Their relationship serves as a testament to the power of community and shared experiences in fostering intimacy.

Conclusion

Navigating intimacy and relationships in the public eye is a multifaceted journey for LGBTQ activists like Sitti Djalia Turabin. While the pressures of visibility and activism can complicate personal connections, the strength found in community support and open communication can pave the way for meaningful relationships. By employing strategies that prioritize self-care, boundary-setting, and mutual understanding, activists can cultivate intimacy that not only enriches their personal lives but also fortifies their commitment to the broader fight for LGBTQ rights.

Balancing Activism and Career

Turabin's Educational Background and Professional Achievements

Sitti Djalia Turabin's journey through education and her professional landscape is a testament to her resilience and commitment to LGBTQ activism. Born into a society where traditional norms often stifled individual expression, Turabin navigated her educational path with determination, defying expectations and breaking barriers along the way.

Educational Background

Turabin's academic journey began in her hometown, where she attended a local public school. Despite facing adversity, including bullying and discrimination for her gender identity, she excelled academically, driven by a passion for learning and a desire to uplift her community. Recognizing the importance of education as a tool for empowerment, Turabin sought opportunities to further her studies. She applied to various universities, ultimately gaining admission to a prestigious institution known for its progressive values and commitment to social justice.

At university, Turabin pursued a degree in **Social Work**, a field that resonated deeply with her personal experiences and aspirations. She immersed herself in her studies, focusing on courses related to gender studies, human rights, and community development. Her academic work often included research on the intersectionality of LGBTQ issues, examining how factors such as race, class, and gender identity influence the experiences of marginalized communities. This foundational knowledge would later inform her activism, allowing her to approach issues with a nuanced perspective.

Turabin's commitment to academic excellence did not go unnoticed. She was awarded several scholarships for her outstanding performance, including the *National Scholarship for Social Justice Advocates*, which recognized her potential as a future leader in the field. Through these opportunities, she gained access to mentorship programs and networking events that connected her with established activists and scholars, further fueling her passion for advocacy.

Professional Achievements

Upon completing her degree, Turabin began her professional career as a social worker in a non-profit organization dedicated to supporting LGBTQ youth. Here, she developed and implemented programs aimed at providing safe spaces for young people to explore their identities and receive support. Her innovative approach included workshops on self-acceptance, mental health awareness, and advocacy skills.

One of her notable initiatives was the **Youth Empowerment Program**, which provided mentorship and resources for LGBTQ youth facing discrimination in schools. The program not only offered emotional support but also equipped participants with practical skills for advocacy. Under her leadership, the initiative saw a remarkable increase in youth participation, with over 500 young people benefiting from its services within the first year.

Turabin's work quickly gained recognition, leading to her involvement in various national and international conferences focused on LGBTQ rights. She was invited to speak at the *Global LGBTQ Youth Summit*, where she shared her insights on the importance of intersectionality in activism. Her presentation, titled *"Empowering Voices: The Intersection of Identity and Activism"*, highlighted the need for inclusive approaches that address the diverse experiences within the LGBTQ community.

Theoretical Frameworks

Throughout her educational and professional journey, Turabin drew upon several theoretical frameworks to inform her activism. One significant theory was **Queer Theory**, which challenges the binary understanding of gender and sexuality. This framework allowed her to advocate for a more inclusive understanding of identity, emphasizing that LGBTQ individuals should not be confined to societal norms.

In her work, Turabin also integrated concepts from **Critical Race Theory**, recognizing that race and ethnicity intersect with gender and sexual identity, impacting individuals' experiences of discrimination and privilege. This intersectional lens enabled her to address the unique challenges faced by LGBTQ individuals of color, advocating for policies that reflect these complexities.

Challenges and Resilience

Despite her achievements, Turabin faced numerous challenges in her professional life. The stigma surrounding LGBTQ issues often manifested in institutional resistance, making it difficult to secure funding for programs aimed at supporting marginalized communities. Additionally, she encountered personal threats and harassment due to her outspoken advocacy, which tested her resolve.

However, Turabin's resilience shone through these obstacles. She utilized her platform to raise awareness about the challenges faced by LGBTQ activists in the Philippines, speaking out against discrimination and advocating for policy reforms.

Her ability to navigate these challenges not only solidified her reputation as a leader but also inspired others to join the fight for equality.

Conclusion

Sitti Djalia Turabin's educational background and professional achievements reflect a profound commitment to LGBTQ rights and social justice. Through her academic pursuits and innovative initiatives, she has made a lasting impact on the lives of countless individuals. Turabin's journey serves as a powerful reminder of the importance of education in fostering resilience and empowering future generations of activists.

The Intersection of Turabin's Career and Activism

In the vibrant tapestry of LGBTQ activism, Sitti Djalia Turabin stands out not only for her passionate advocacy but also for the unique ways in which her professional life intersects with her commitment to social justice. This intersection is a powerful testament to the idea that one's career can be a conduit for activism, amplifying the voices of marginalized communities while fostering systemic change.

Understanding the Dual Role

Turabin's career trajectory exemplifies the dual role that professionals can play as both advocates and practitioners in their respective fields. This duality is rooted in the concept of *intersectionality*, which posits that various social identities—such as race, gender, and sexual orientation—interact to create unique modes of discrimination and privilege. For Turabin, her identity as a queer Filipino woman informs her professional choices, shaping her approach to activism and her career path.

Career Pathways in Activism

Turabin's educational background in social sciences laid a solid foundation for her activist endeavors. She pursued a degree that emphasized community engagement and social justice, which not only equipped her with theoretical knowledge but also practical skills in advocacy and public policy. This academic grounding allowed her to navigate the complexities of LGBTQ rights within the context of broader societal issues.

For instance, Turabin's role as a community organizer for an LGBTQ rights organization involved developing programs that addressed both immediate needs—such as mental health support for LGBTQ youth—and systemic issues like anti-discrimination legislation. This dual focus exemplifies the integration of her professional skills with her activist goals.

Challenges in Balancing Activism and Career

Despite the synergy between her career and activism, Turabin faced significant challenges. The societal stigma surrounding LGBTQ identities often permeated her professional life, creating a hostile environment that could undermine her efforts. For example, Turabin encountered instances of discrimination in the workplace, where her activism was viewed unfavorably by some colleagues. This experience highlights the ongoing struggle for acceptance and equality within professional settings, reflecting the broader societal issues faced by LGBTQ individuals.

Moreover, the emotional toll of activism can lead to burnout, particularly when balancing a demanding career. Turabin's strategy for managing this challenge involved establishing boundaries between her professional responsibilities and her activist commitments. She prioritized self-care and sought mentorship from seasoned activists who had navigated similar paths. This approach not only enhanced her resilience but also provided her with a support network that recognized the importance of mental health in sustaining long-term activism.

Innovative Advocacy Strategies

Turabin's career also allowed her to innovate in the realm of advocacy. By leveraging her professional skills, she developed campaigns that utilized data-driven approaches to highlight the disparities faced by LGBTQ individuals in the Philippines. For instance, she spearheaded a project that collected and analyzed data on hate crimes against LGBTQ individuals, which served as a powerful tool for lobbying for legislative reforms.

The integration of technology into her activism is another significant aspect of Turabin's approach. Utilizing social media platforms, she was able to amplify her message and mobilize support for various causes. This digital activism not only broadened her reach but also engaged younger audiences, fostering a sense of community among LGBTQ youth who often feel isolated in their struggles.

Impact on Policy and Social Change

The intersection of Turabin's career and activism has yielded tangible results in policy advocacy. Her work has contributed to the formulation of anti-discrimination laws that protect LGBTQ individuals in employment and public services. By collaborating with policymakers and presenting evidence-based arguments, Turabin has been instrumental in advancing the legislative agenda for LGBTQ rights in the Philippines.

Furthermore, her efforts have sparked conversations around intersectionality within the LGBTQ movement, emphasizing the need for inclusivity in advocacy efforts. Turabin's advocacy for marginalized subgroups within the LGBTQ community, such as transgender individuals and LGBTQ persons of color, highlights the importance of addressing the diverse needs of all members of the community.

Conclusion

In conclusion, Sitti Djalia Turabin's career and activism are intricately intertwined, demonstrating the potential for professionals to effect change within their spheres of influence. Her journey illustrates the challenges faced by LGBTQ activists in balancing their personal and professional lives while navigating societal stigma. Through innovative strategies and a commitment to intersectionality, Turabin has not only advanced her career but has also made significant contributions to the ongoing fight for LGBTQ rights in the Philippines. As she continues to inspire the next generation of activists, her legacy serves as a reminder that the personal and the political are inextricably linked, and that true change requires both passion and perseverance.

Turabin's Advocacy Beyond LGBTQ Rights

Turabin's journey as an activist is not confined solely to LGBTQ rights; it extends into broader social issues that intersect with the lives of marginalized communities. This section explores Turabin's advocacy beyond LGBTQ rights, highlighting the interconnectedness of various social justice movements and the importance of an inclusive approach to activism.

Intersectional Advocacy

At the core of Turabin's philosophy is the principle of intersectionality, a term coined by Kimberlé Crenshaw in 1989. Intersectionality emphasizes that individuals experience overlapping systems of discrimination and privilege based on their multiple identities, including race, gender, sexual orientation, and socioeconomic status. Turabin recognizes that LGBTQ individuals are not monolithic; their experiences are shaped by various factors, including ethnicity, class, and ability.

Turabin's commitment to intersectional advocacy is evident in her involvement with movements that address issues such as poverty, racial justice, and women's rights. For instance, she has collaborated with organizations that focus on economic empowerment for LGBTQ youth from low-income backgrounds, advocating for job training programs and educational scholarships. By addressing economic disparities, Turabin aims to create a more equitable society for all, understanding that financial stability is crucial for the well-being of LGBTQ individuals.

Environmental Justice

In addition to her work on social and economic issues, Turabin is a passionate advocate for environmental justice. She acknowledges that climate change disproportionately affects marginalized communities, including LGBTQ individuals, who often lack access to resources and support during environmental crises. Turabin's advocacy in this area includes raising awareness about the impact of climate change on vulnerable populations and promoting sustainable practices within the LGBTQ community.

For example, Turabin organized a campaign called "Green Pride," which aimed to educate LGBTQ individuals about environmental issues and encourage sustainable living. The campaign included workshops on eco-friendly practices, community clean-up events, and partnerships with environmental organizations. By linking LGBTQ rights with environmental justice, Turabin demonstrates the interconnectedness of these movements and the necessity of a holistic approach to activism.

Mental Health Awareness

Turabin also champions mental health awareness, recognizing that LGBTQ individuals face higher rates of mental health challenges due to stigma, discrimination, and societal pressures. Her advocacy extends to promoting mental health resources and support systems within the LGBTQ community. Turabin has facilitated workshops and support groups that focus on mental health education, resilience building, and self-care practices.

In collaboration with mental health professionals, Turabin has developed initiatives that specifically address the needs of LGBTQ youth, such as crisis intervention programs and peer support networks. These efforts aim to create safe spaces where individuals can openly discuss their struggles and seek help without fear of judgment. Turabin's commitment to mental health advocacy underscores the importance of addressing psychological well-being as an integral part of LGBTQ rights.

Global Solidarity and Human Rights

Turabin's activism transcends national borders as she advocates for global LGBTQ rights and human rights. She recognizes that many LGBTQ individuals around the world face severe persecution, violence, and discrimination. Turabin has participated in international conferences and forums, where she shares her experiences and insights, advocating for policies that promote human rights for all marginalized communities.

One notable example of Turabin's global advocacy is her involvement in the "Voices for Equality" campaign, which seeks to amplify the voices of LGBTQ activists from countries with restrictive laws. Through this campaign, Turabin has helped raise awareness about the challenges faced by LGBTQ individuals globally and has worked to foster solidarity among activists across different regions. By building international coalitions, Turabin aims to create a unified front in the fight for human rights, emphasizing that the struggle for LGBTQ rights is part of a larger movement for justice and equality.

Conclusion

In conclusion, Turabin's advocacy extends well beyond LGBTQ rights, embracing a comprehensive approach that addresses the interconnected issues of social justice, environmental sustainability, mental health, and global human rights. By recognizing the complexity of individual identities and the multifaceted nature of oppression, Turabin exemplifies the essence of modern activism—one that is inclusive, intersectional, and committed to creating a better world for all. Her work serves as a reminder that the fight for LGBTQ rights is intrinsically linked to the broader struggle for justice, equity, and dignity for every individual, regardless of their identity.

$$\text{Advocacy}_{\text{Total}} = \text{LGBTQ Rights} + \text{Social Justice} + \text{Environmental Justice} + \text{Mental Healt}$$
$$(51)$$

This equation illustrates Turabin's holistic approach to activism, emphasizing that true advocacy encompasses a wide array of issues that affect marginalized communities. By addressing these interconnected challenges, Turabin aims to foster a more inclusive and equitable society for all.

Strategies for Achieving Work-Life Balance as an Activist

Activism is a noble pursuit, yet it often comes with significant personal and professional challenges. For activists like Sitti Djalia Turabin, balancing the demands of advocacy work with personal life can be daunting. This section explores effective strategies for achieving a harmonious work-life balance, drawing on theoretical frameworks, potential problems, and real-world examples.

Understanding Work-Life Balance

Work-life balance refers to the equilibrium between personal life and work commitments. It is essential for maintaining mental health, preventing burnout, and ensuring sustained engagement in activism. According to Kahn and Byosiere's (1992) theory of role conflict, individuals face stress when the demands of one role interfere with another. This can be particularly pronounced for activists who often juggle multiple responsibilities, from advocacy to community organizing.

Common Challenges Faced by Activists

Activists frequently encounter several challenges that can disrupt their work-life balance:

+ **Emotional Exhaustion:** The emotional toll of advocating for marginalized communities can lead to burnout. Activists often feel a deep sense of responsibility for the issues they champion, which can create an overwhelming workload.

+ **Time Constraints:** Activism often requires long hours, leaving little time for personal relationships or self-care. This can lead to feelings of isolation and neglect in personal life.

+ **Financial Instability:** Many activists work on a volunteer basis or receive low compensation for their efforts, leading to stress over financial security and impacting their personal lives.

+ **Societal Pressure:** Activists may face societal stigma or backlash, which can add additional stress and complicate personal relationships.

Strategies for Achieving Balance

To navigate these challenges, activists can adopt several strategies:

1. Setting Boundaries   Establishing clear boundaries between work and personal life is crucial. Activists should designate specific times for work-related tasks and personal activities. For example, Turabin could implement a policy of not checking work emails during personal time. This creates a mental separation that fosters relaxation and rejuvenation.

2. Prioritizing Self-Care   Self-care is vital for maintaining overall well-being. Activists should incorporate regular self-care practices into their routines, such as:

- **Physical Activity:** Engaging in exercise can help reduce stress and improve mood. Turabin might join a local dance class or go for daily runs to stay active.

- **Mindfulness Practices:** Techniques like meditation and yoga can enhance mental clarity and emotional resilience. Turabin could set aside time each day for mindfulness activities.

- **Social Connections:** Building a supportive network of friends and allies can provide emotional support. Regular social interactions can combat feelings of isolation and reinforce a sense of community.

3. Time Management Techniques   Effective time management is essential for balancing multiple commitments. Activists can employ several techniques, such as:

- **The Eisenhower Matrix:** This method categorizes tasks into four quadrants based on urgency and importance, helping activists focus on what truly matters.

- **Pomodoro Technique:** Breaking work into intervals (e.g., 25 minutes of focused work followed by a 5-minute break) can enhance productivity and reduce fatigue.

- **Delegation:** Activists should recognize that they do not have to do everything alone. Collaborating with others and delegating tasks can alleviate pressure and foster teamwork.

4. Seeking Professional Support   Therapy and counseling can provide valuable support for activists facing emotional challenges. Professional guidance can help individuals process their experiences, develop coping strategies, and navigate the complexities of their dual roles as activists and individuals.

5. Continuous Reflection and Adjustment   Activists should regularly assess their work-life balance and make adjustments as needed. Reflecting on their emotional and physical well-being can help them identify areas for improvement. For instance, if Turabin notices signs of burnout, she may need to reevaluate her commitments and prioritize rest.

Examples of Successful Balance

Several activists have successfully implemented these strategies:

- **Marsha P. Johnson,** a prominent figure in LGBTQ activism, often emphasized the importance of community support and self-care practices, which helped her maintain her energy and passion for advocacy.

- **Sylvia Rivera** balanced her activism with personal life by engaging in artistic expressions, which allowed her to process her emotions and maintain her mental health while fighting for LGBTQ rights.

Conclusion

Achieving work-life balance is essential for activists like Sitti Djalia Turabin, who dedicate their lives to promoting LGBTQ rights. By setting boundaries, prioritizing self-care, employing effective time management techniques, seeking professional support, and continuously reflecting on their well-being, activists can sustain their passion and commitment to their cause without sacrificing their personal lives. As the movement for LGBTQ rights continues to evolve, ensuring the health and happiness of its advocates will be crucial for long-term success.

Bibliography

[1] Kahn, R. L., & Byosiere, P. (1992). Stress in Organizations. In M. D. Dunnette & L. M. Hough (Eds.), *Handbook of Industrial and Organizational Psychology* (Vol. 3, pp. 571-650). Consulting Psychologists Press.

Self-Care and Resilience

Coping Strategies for Turabin as an Activist

Activism, particularly within the LGBTQ community, can be a profoundly rewarding yet emotionally taxing journey. For Sitti Djalia Turabin, the challenges of advocating for LGBTQ rights in the Philippines require robust coping strategies to maintain her mental health and resilience. This section explores the various coping mechanisms that Turabin employs, grounded in psychological theories and real-life applications.

Understanding the Stressors

Activism often involves facing systemic oppression, societal stigma, and personal threats, leading to what is known as *activist burnout*. According to [?], compassion fatigue can emerge when activists are continually exposed to the suffering of others, leading to emotional exhaustion and a diminished capacity to empathize. Turabin's experiences align with this theory, as she frequently encounters hostility from conservative groups, political pushback, and media scrutiny.

Coping Strategies Employed by Turabin

Turabin's coping strategies can be categorized into several key areas, each supported by psychological theories and practices:

1. Mindfulness and Meditation Turabin incorporates mindfulness practices into her daily routine. Research by [?] shows that mindfulness meditation can significantly reduce stress and improve emotional regulation. By taking time each day to engage in mindfulness exercises, Turabin cultivates a sense of presence and calm, allowing her to process the emotional weight of her activism.

$$M = \frac{1}{N} \sum_{i=1}^{N} x_i \tag{52}$$

where M is the mean of mindfulness scores, N is the number of mindfulness sessions, and x_i represents the stress levels reported after each session.

2. Building a Support Network Turabin emphasizes the importance of community in her activism. The social support theory, as discussed by [?], posits that strong social networks can buffer against stress. Turabin actively engages with fellow activists, friends, and family, creating a robust support system that provides emotional sustenance and practical assistance during challenging times.

3. Engaging in Self-Care Activities Self-care is a vital aspect of Turabin's routine. As highlighted by [?], self-compassion allows individuals to treat themselves with kindness during difficult times. Turabin prioritizes activities that rejuvenate her spirit, such as art, music, and nature walks. These activities not only provide an escape but also serve as a source of inspiration for her activism.

4. Setting Boundaries In the realm of activism, the line between personal life and public persona can become blurred. Turabin recognizes the importance of setting boundaries to protect her mental health. This aligns with the boundary theory proposed by [?], which suggests that clear boundaries help individuals manage their roles and responsibilities effectively. Turabin limits her availability for media engagements and public appearances, allowing her to recharge and focus on her core advocacy work.

5. Engaging in Reflective Practices Reflective practices, such as journaling, allow Turabin to process her experiences and emotions. According to [?], reflection is a critical component of experiential learning. By documenting her thoughts and feelings, Turabin gains insights into her activism journey, identifying patterns and areas for growth.

Challenges in Implementing Coping Strategies

Despite the effectiveness of these coping strategies, Turabin faces several challenges. The stigma surrounding mental health in the Philippines can make it difficult for activists to seek help. Additionally, the constant pressure to perform and represent the LGBTQ community can lead to feelings of inadequacy and self-doubt. Turabin combats these challenges by openly discussing mental health issues within her network, advocating for greater awareness and acceptance.

Conclusion

Coping strategies are essential for activists like Sitti Djalia Turabin to navigate the emotional landscape of their work. By employing mindfulness, building a support network, engaging in self-care, setting boundaries, and practicing reflection, Turabin not only sustains her activism but also inspires others to prioritize their mental health. As she continues her fight for LGBTQ rights, these coping mechanisms serve as a foundation for resilience and empowerment.

Building a Support Network of Friends and Allies

In the journey of activism, particularly in the LGBTQ community, the importance of a robust support network cannot be overstated. This network is not merely a collection of acquaintances; it is a vital lifeline that provides emotional, psychological, and strategic support. Building such a network involves intentional efforts to connect with individuals and organizations that share similar goals and values.

Theoretical Framework

The concept of social support can be understood through various theoretical lenses, including the Social Support Theory and the Social Capital Theory. According to **Cohen and Wills (1985)**, social support is defined as the perception or reality that one is cared for, valued, and part of a social network. This support can be instrumental, informational, emotional, or appraisal-based.

$$SS = I + E + A + M \tag{53}$$

Where:

+ SS = Social Support

+ I = Instrumental support (tangible assistance)

+ E = Emotional support (empathy and care)

+ A = Appraisal support (feedback and affirmation)

+ M = Informational support (advice and guidance)

The **Social Capital Theory** posits that the networks of relationships among people who live and work in a particular society enable that society to function effectively. In the context of LGBTQ activism, social capital can be crucial for mobilizing resources, sharing information, and fostering a sense of community.

Challenges in Building a Support Network

While the benefits of a support network are clear, there are significant challenges faced by LGBTQ activists. These challenges can stem from societal stigma, discrimination, and the internalized fears that individuals may carry.

+ **Stigma and Discrimination:** Many LGBTQ individuals face rejection from family and friends, which can hinder their ability to build supportive relationships. This rejection can lead to feelings of isolation and despair.

+ **Fear of Vulnerability:** Activists may fear that opening up about their struggles will make them vulnerable to attacks, both personally and professionally. This fear can prevent them from seeking help or forming genuine connections.

+ **Resource Limitations:** Activism often requires financial and emotional resources, which may be scarce for individuals who are already marginalized. This scarcity can limit their ability to participate in community-building activities.

Strategies for Building a Support Network

Despite these challenges, there are effective strategies that LGBTQ activists can employ to build a supportive network:

+ **Engagement in LGBTQ Organizations:** Joining local and national LGBTQ organizations can provide a sense of belonging and access to resources. Organizations often have established networks that facilitate connections among activists.

+ **Utilizing Social Media:** Platforms like Twitter, Facebook, and Instagram can help activists connect with peers and allies. Online communities can offer emotional support and share valuable information.

+ **Mentorship Programs:** Seeking out mentors who have navigated similar paths can provide guidance and encouragement. Mentorship can also create opportunities for networking and collaboration.

+ **Participating in Support Groups:** Support groups offer a safe space for individuals to share their experiences and challenges. These groups can foster a sense of community and provide emotional support.

Examples of Successful Networks

The impact of a strong support network is evident in various successful LGBTQ movements. For instance, the **Stonewall Riots** of 1969 were not just a spontaneous uprising; they were fueled by a network of activists who had been organizing and supporting each other for years. Similarly, the **Pride Movement** worldwide has thrived on the collective efforts of individuals and organizations working together to advocate for rights and recognition.

In the Philippines, activists like **Sitti Djalia Turabin** have exemplified the importance of building alliances. Turabin's collaboration with local NGOs and international LGBTQ organizations has not only amplified her voice but has also created a ripple effect of support for emerging activists.

Conclusion

Building a support network of friends and allies is not just beneficial; it is essential for the sustainability of LGBTQ activism. By understanding the theoretical frameworks, recognizing the challenges, and implementing effective strategies, activists can create a robust network that empowers individuals and strengthens the movement. As the LGBTQ community continues to face opposition and stigma, the solidarity fostered through these networks will be crucial for achieving lasting change.

Turabin's Journey to Self-Healing and Wellness

In the realm of activism, the relentless pursuit of justice often comes at a significant personal cost. For Sitti Djalia Turabin, the journey towards self-healing and wellness was not merely an individual endeavor; it was a necessary prerequisite for sustaining her activism in the face of systemic oppression and personal adversity. This section explores Turabin's multifaceted approach to self-care, highlighting the theoretical frameworks that underpin her practices, the challenges she faced, and the transformative experiences that shaped her healing journey.

Theoretical Frameworks of Self-Care

Self-care, as conceptualized by scholars such as Audre Lorde and bell hooks, transcends mere personal indulgence. Lorde posits that "caring for myself is not self-indulgence, it is self-preservation, and that is an act of political warfare." This perspective frames self-care as a radical act of resistance against the societal forces that seek to marginalize and dehumanize individuals, particularly within the LGBTQ community.

Turabin embraced this philosophy, recognizing that her wellness was intrinsically linked to her ability to advocate effectively for LGBTQ rights. By prioritizing her mental and emotional health, she not only fortified her resilience but also modeled a sustainable approach to activism for her peers and the younger generation of activists.

Challenges in the Journey

Despite her commitment to self-care, Turabin encountered numerous challenges that threatened her well-being. The emotional toll of activism, compounded by the stigma associated with her identity, often manifested in feelings of isolation and burnout. Research indicates that LGBTQ activists are at a heightened risk for mental health issues, including anxiety and depression, due to the chronic stress of navigating hostile environments (Meyer, 2003).

Turabin's struggles were further exacerbated by societal expectations and the pressure to constantly perform as a role model. The intersection of her identity as a queer woman and an activist placed her in a unique position where the burden of representation weighed heavily on her shoulders. Balancing the demands of activism with the need for personal space became a critical challenge in her journey.

Coping Strategies and Healing Practices

To combat these challenges, Turabin implemented a variety of coping strategies that aligned with her values and cultural background. These included:

- **Mindfulness and Meditation:** Turabin engaged in mindfulness practices that allowed her to cultivate a sense of presence and awareness. Research suggests that mindfulness can significantly reduce stress and improve emotional regulation (Kabat-Zinn, 1990). Through meditation, she learned to acknowledge her feelings without judgment, creating a safe space for self-reflection.

+ **Community Support:** Recognizing the importance of social connections, Turabin actively sought support from her peers and mentors within the LGBTQ community. The role of social support in mitigating the effects of stress has been well-documented (Cohen & Wills, 1985). By sharing her experiences and vulnerabilities, she fostered a sense of belonging that was crucial for her emotional health.

+ **Creative Expression:** Turabin turned to creative outlets such as writing, art, and music as forms of self-expression and healing. Engaging in creative activities has been shown to promote psychological well-being and serve as a therapeutic tool for individuals grappling with trauma (Stuckey & Nobel, 2010). Her art became a means to process her emotions and connect with others on a deeper level.

+ **Physical Wellness:** Understanding the mind-body connection, Turabin prioritized physical health through regular exercise and a balanced diet. Studies indicate that physical activity can enhance mood and reduce symptoms of anxiety and depression (Peluso & Andrade, 2005). For Turabin, movement became a form of liberation, allowing her to reclaim her body in a world that often sought to control it.

Transformative Experiences

Throughout her journey, Turabin's commitment to self-healing led to several transformative experiences that reshaped her understanding of activism and wellness. One pivotal moment occurred during a retreat organized by LGBTQ activists, where participants engaged in holistic healing practices, including yoga and group therapy. This experience illuminated the interconnectedness of personal and collective healing, reinforcing the idea that individual wellness is essential for the broader movement.

Moreover, Turabin's engagement with traditional healing practices rooted in her cultural heritage provided her with a sense of identity and belonging. By integrating these practices into her self-care routine, she not only honored her roots but also challenged the dominant narratives that often marginalize indigenous healing methods. This fusion of contemporary and traditional approaches to wellness became a cornerstone of her activism, as she advocated for the inclusion of diverse healing practices within the LGBTQ community.

Conclusion

Turabin's journey to self-healing and wellness exemplifies the intricate relationship between personal well-being and effective activism. By prioritizing her mental, emotional, and physical health, she not only enhanced her resilience but also inspired others to embrace self-care as a vital component of their activism. As she continues to navigate the complexities of her role as an activist, Turabin remains a testament to the power of self-healing in the ongoing struggle for LGBTQ rights in the Philippines and beyond. Her story serves as a reminder that in the fight for justice, taking care of oneself is not a luxury; it is a necessity.

Mental Health Awareness and Support for LGBTQ Activists

The journey of LGBTQ activists is often paved with challenges that can significantly impact their mental health. The intersection of activism and personal identity creates a unique set of stressors that necessitate a robust support system and awareness of mental health issues. This section explores the mental health challenges faced by LGBTQ activists, the importance of mental health awareness, and strategies for support.

Understanding Mental Health Challenges

Activists in the LGBTQ community frequently encounter systemic discrimination, societal stigma, and personal threats, all of which can contribute to mental health issues such as anxiety, depression, and PTSD. According to the *American Psychological Association*, LGBTQ individuals are at a higher risk for mental health disorders due to these stressors, often exacerbated by a lack of acceptance in their communities.

$$\text{Mental Health Risk} = f(\text{Discrimination, Stigma, Support}) \qquad (54)$$

Where: - Discrimination represents the systemic barriers faced, - Stigma indicates societal perceptions, - Support denotes the availability of community and resources.

This equation illustrates that increased discrimination and stigma can lead to heightened mental health risks, while support can mitigate these effects.

Common Mental Health Issues

LGBTQ activists may experience several common mental health issues, including:

- **Anxiety Disorders:** Constantly navigating a world that can be hostile leads to heightened anxiety levels.

- **Depression:** Feelings of isolation and helplessness can be prevalent, especially when activism efforts seem futile.

- **Post-Traumatic Stress Disorder (PTSD):** Experiences of violence or harassment can result in PTSD, characterized by flashbacks, severe anxiety, and uncontrollable thoughts about the event.

Research indicates that LGBTQ individuals are more likely to report suicidal ideation and attempts compared to their heterosexual counterparts. A study published in the *Journal of Homosexuality* found that 40% of LGBTQ youth have seriously considered suicide, highlighting the urgent need for mental health support.

The Role of Mental Health Awareness

Raising awareness about mental health within the LGBTQ activist community is critical for several reasons:

1. **Reducing Stigma:** Open discussions about mental health can help normalize seeking help and reduce the stigma associated with mental illness.

2. **Encouraging Help-Seeking Behavior:** Awareness campaigns can encourage activists to seek professional help when needed, promoting overall well-being.

3. **Building Resilience:** Understanding mental health issues can empower activists to develop coping strategies and resilience in the face of adversity.

Support Strategies for LGBTQ Activists

To support mental health among LGBTQ activists, various strategies can be employed:

- **Peer Support Groups:** Creating safe spaces for activists to share experiences and provide mutual support can foster a sense of community and belonging.

- **Access to Professional Counseling:** Facilitating access to mental health professionals who understand LGBTQ issues can help activists navigate their challenges effectively.

- **Workshops and Training:** Offering workshops on stress management, self-care, and resilience can equip activists with tools to maintain their mental health.

- **Mindfulness and Self-Care Practices:** Encouraging practices such as meditation, yoga, and regular physical activity can significantly improve mental well-being.

Examples of Successful Initiatives

Several organizations have recognized the importance of mental health in the LGBTQ community and have initiated programs to address these needs:

- **The Trevor Project:** This organization offers crisis intervention and suicide prevention services to LGBTQ youth, providing a lifeline and mental health resources.

- **LGBTQ+ National Help Center:** This center provides free and confidential support through hotlines and online chat services, focusing on mental health and well-being.

- **Community-Based Workshops:** Local LGBTQ organizations have started offering workshops focused on mental health awareness, providing activists with tools and resources to cope with their unique challenges.

Conclusion

The mental health of LGBTQ activists is a vital component of sustainable activism. As the community continues to advocate for rights and recognition, it is imperative to prioritize mental health awareness and support. By fostering a culture of openness, providing resources, and building supportive networks, we can empower activists to thrive both personally and in their advocacy efforts.

In summary, mental health awareness and support for LGBTQ activists are not just beneficial; they are essential. As we strive for equality and justice, we must also ensure that those leading the charge are mentally and emotionally equipped to continue their vital work.

Chapter 5 The Future of LGBTQ Activism in the Philippines

Chapter 5 The Future of LGBTQ Activism in the Philippines

The Future of LGBTQ Activism in the Philippines

The future of LGBTQ activism in the Philippines is a complex tapestry woven with the threads of history, culture, and the relentless pursuit of equality. As we stand at the crossroads of progress and resistance, it is essential to analyze the challenges that lie ahead and the strategies that can be employed to navigate them. The landscape of activism is ever-evolving, and understanding the dynamics at play is crucial for fostering a sustainable movement.

The Need for Continued Advocacy

Despite significant strides made in LGBTQ rights over the past few decades, many unresolved challenges persist. According to the *Philippine LGBTQ+ Rights Advocacy Network*, the absence of comprehensive anti-discrimination laws continues to leave many vulnerable to discrimination in employment, housing, and public services. This legal gap creates an environment where LGBTQ individuals can be marginalized, and their rights violated without recourse.

$$\text{Advocacy Necessity} = \text{Legal Gaps} + \text{Social Stigma} \tag{55}$$

Addressing these issues requires a multi-faceted approach that includes raising awareness, lobbying for legislative reforms, and building coalitions with other marginalized groups. Intersectionality plays a critical role here, as LGBTQ activists must also advocate for the rights of those affected by other forms of discrimination, such as race, gender, and economic status.

Addressing Intersectional Issues in LGBTQ Activism

Intersectionality, a term coined by Kimberlé Crenshaw, highlights how various social identities intersect, leading to unique experiences of oppression. In the Philippines, LGBTQ individuals often face compounded discrimination based on their socio-economic status, ethnicity, and geographic location. For instance, LGBTQ individuals from indigenous communities may experience cultural erasure alongside their sexual orientation struggles.

$$\text{Intersectional Discrimination} = \text{LGBTQ Status} + \text{Race} + \text{Class} \qquad (56)$$

To effectively address these intersectional issues, LGBTQ activists must engage in grassroots organizing that amplifies the voices of the most marginalized within the community. Collaborations with women's rights organizations, indigenous rights groups, and labor unions can create a more robust and inclusive movement.

Strategies for Sustaining the LGBTQ Movement

Sustaining the LGBTQ movement in the Philippines requires innovative strategies that adapt to changing socio-political landscapes. One effective approach is leveraging technology and social media to mobilize support and raise awareness. Platforms like Facebook, Twitter, and Instagram have become vital tools for organizing events, sharing stories, and disseminating information about LGBTQ rights.

$$\text{Mobilization} = \text{Social Media} + \text{Community Engagement} \qquad (57)$$

For example, the #PridePH campaign has successfully utilized social media to unite diverse groups, raise funds, and advocate for policy changes. Engaging younger generations through digital platforms ensures that the movement remains dynamic and relevant.

The Importance of Reforming Existing Laws

Legal reform is a cornerstone of LGBTQ activism. The passage of the Anti-Discrimination Bill, which aims to protect LGBTQ individuals from discrimination, is a critical goal for activists. However, achieving this requires persistent lobbying, public education campaigns, and building alliances with sympathetic lawmakers.

$$\text{Legal Reform} = \text{Advocacy Efforts} + \text{Public Support} \qquad (58)$$

Activists can draw inspiration from successful campaigns in other countries. For instance, the marriage equality movement in Taiwan serves as a powerful example of how sustained advocacy can lead to transformative legal changes. Filipino activists can adapt these strategies to fit the local context, emphasizing the importance of cultural relevance in advocacy efforts.

Inspiring the Next Generation of Activists

One of the most vital aspects of ensuring the future of LGBTQ activism is the mentorship and empowerment of the next generation. By fostering leadership skills among LGBTQ youth, the movement can cultivate a new wave of activists equipped to tackle emerging challenges.

$$\text{Youth Empowerment} = \text{Mentorship} + \text{Education} \qquad (59)$$

Programs that focus on leadership development, public speaking, and advocacy training can prepare young activists to effectively engage in the movement. Creating safe spaces for LGBTQ youth to express their identities and experiences is essential for nurturing their confidence and resilience.

International Collaboration and Solidarity

The global nature of the LGBTQ movement means that local activism can benefit from international collaboration. Filipino activists can connect with global LGBTQ organizations to share best practices, strategies, and resources. This solidarity is crucial, especially in the face of increasing conservatism and backlash against LGBTQ rights in many parts of the world.

$$\text{Global Solidarity} = \text{Networking} + \text{Shared Resources} \qquad (60)$$

Participating in international events, such as the International Day Against Homophobia, Transphobia, and Biphobia (IDAHOT), can amplify local voices and bring attention to the unique challenges faced by LGBTQ individuals in the Philippines.

Turabin's Continuing Activism Journey

As we look to the future, the ongoing journey of activists like Sitti Djalia Turabin embodies the spirit of resilience and determination. Turabin's commitment to advocating for LGBTQ rights serves as a beacon of hope and inspiration for future generations. Her initiatives, focusing on community building, mental health support, and legislative advocacy, highlight the multifaceted nature of activism.

$$\text{Activism Continuity} = \text{Legacy} + \text{Innovation} \tag{61}$$

Turabin's work emphasizes the importance of adapting strategies to meet the evolving needs of the LGBTQ community while remaining rooted in the principles of equality and justice.

In conclusion, the future of LGBTQ activism in the Philippines hinges on the collective efforts of individuals and organizations committed to driving change. By addressing the challenges of legal reform, intersectionality, and youth empowerment, the movement can forge a path toward a more inclusive and equitable society. The resilience of activists, exemplified by figures like Turabin, will continue to inspire and guide the movement as it navigates the complexities of the future.

The Need for Continued Advocacy

Unresolved Challenges in LGBTQ Rights

The landscape of LGBTQ rights in the Philippines is marked by significant progress, yet it remains fraught with unresolved challenges. Despite the vibrant activism that has emerged over the decades, many issues persist that inhibit the full realization of equality and acceptance for LGBTQ individuals. This section delves into these challenges, examining both the sociocultural and legal barriers that continue to affect the LGBTQ community.

Legal Gaps and Inadequate Protections

One of the most pressing challenges facing LGBTQ rights in the Philippines is the lack of comprehensive anti-discrimination legislation. While there have been efforts to pass the Anti-Discrimination Bill, which seeks to prohibit discrimination based on sexual orientation and gender identity, it has yet to be enacted into law. This absence of legal protection leaves LGBTQ individuals vulnerable to discrimination in various sectors, including employment, education, and healthcare.

The legal framework in the Philippines also lacks recognition of same-sex relationships. Unlike many countries that have embraced marriage equality, the Philippines continues to uphold traditional definitions of marriage, which exclude same-sex couples. This legal void not only denies LGBTQ individuals the right to marry but also complicates issues related to inheritance, adoption, and healthcare decisions.

Cultural and Religious Resistance

Cultural and religious beliefs play a significant role in shaping attitudes toward LGBTQ individuals in the Philippines. Predominantly influenced by conservative interpretations of Catholicism, many Filipinos hold traditional views regarding gender and sexuality. This cultural backdrop fosters an environment where stigma and discrimination thrive, making it difficult for LGBTQ individuals to live authentically.

For instance, anti-LGBTQ rhetoric is often perpetuated by religious leaders who argue that homosexuality is a sin. Such beliefs can lead to societal ostracism, violence, and mental health issues among LGBTQ individuals. The intersection of culture and religion creates formidable barriers to acceptance, as many families may reject LGBTQ members, leading to homelessness and economic instability.

Violence and Hate Crimes

Violence against LGBTQ individuals remains a critical issue in the Philippines. Reports of hate crimes, including physical assaults and even murders, highlight the dangers faced by those who identify as LGBTQ. The lack of adequate reporting mechanisms and the failure of law enforcement to address these crimes further exacerbate the situation. Many victims are reluctant to report incidents due to fear of discrimination or retribution.

A notable example is the case of Jennifer Laude, a transgender woman who was murdered in 2014. Her death sparked widespread outrage and highlighted the urgent need for better protections for LGBTQ individuals. The trial that followed revealed significant shortcomings in the legal system, including biases against transgender individuals, which contributed to a lack of justice for Laude and her family.

Mental Health and Well-Being

The unresolved challenges in LGBTQ rights also have profound implications for mental health and well-being. Many LGBTQ individuals experience higher rates of mental health issues, such as depression and anxiety, often stemming from societal stigma, discrimination, and violence. The lack of supportive resources and mental health services tailored to LGBTQ needs further compounds these challenges.

Research indicates that LGBTQ youth are at a higher risk of suicide compared to their heterosexual peers, primarily due to experiences of bullying, rejection, and isolation. The need for inclusive mental health services that address the unique challenges faced by LGBTQ individuals is critical in fostering resilience and promoting overall well-being.

Intersectional Issues

The fight for LGBTQ rights cannot be divorced from the broader context of intersectionality. Many LGBTQ individuals also belong to other marginalized groups, including women, people of color, and individuals with disabilities. These intersecting identities can compound the challenges faced, leading to unique experiences of discrimination and exclusion.

For instance, LGBTQ women of color may face both sexism and homophobia, while transgender individuals often encounter additional barriers related to gender identity. Addressing these intersectional issues is essential for creating a more inclusive movement that advocates for the rights of all LGBTQ individuals, regardless of their background.

Conclusion

In conclusion, the unresolved challenges in LGBTQ rights in the Philippines are multifaceted and deeply rooted in legal, cultural, and societal factors. The lack of comprehensive anti-discrimination laws, cultural resistance, violence, mental health issues, and intersectional complexities all contribute to an environment where LGBTQ individuals continue to fight for their rights. Addressing these challenges requires concerted efforts from activists, policymakers, and allies to create a more equitable and just society for all.

Addressing Intersectional Issues in LGBTQ Activism

In the landscape of LGBTQ activism, intersectionality emerges as a crucial framework for understanding and addressing the diverse experiences and challenges faced by individuals within the community. Coined by legal scholar Kimberlé Crenshaw in 1989, intersectionality posits that various social identities—such as race, gender, class, and sexual orientation—interact to create unique modes of discrimination and privilege. This theoretical lens is essential for

LGBTQ activists in the Philippines, where cultural, economic, and political factors intertwine to shape the lived realities of queer individuals.

Understanding Intersectionality

Intersectionality emphasizes that the experiences of LGBTQ individuals cannot be understood in isolation from other aspects of their identities. For instance, a transgender woman of color may face distinct challenges that differ significantly from those encountered by a cisgender white gay man. This complexity is illustrated in the following equation, which represents the multiplicative effects of intersecting identities on discrimination:

$$D = I_1 \times I_2 \times I_3 \ldots \times I_n \qquad (62)$$

Where D represents the overall discrimination experienced, and I_n represents individual identities such as race, gender, socioeconomic status, and sexual orientation. This equation highlights that the more identities one holds that are marginalized, the greater the overall discrimination they may face.

Challenges Faced by Marginalized Groups

In the Philippines, intersectional issues manifest in various forms. For example, LGBTQ individuals from indigenous communities often encounter both homophobia and racism, leading to compounded marginalization. The struggle for recognition of their rights is further complicated by historical colonial influences that have shaped societal attitudes toward both LGBTQ identities and indigenous cultures. Activists like Sitti Djalia Turabin have highlighted these challenges, advocating for the inclusion of indigenous voices in the broader LGBTQ movement.

Moreover, socioeconomic status plays a critical role in shaping access to resources and support within the LGBTQ community. Those from lower-income backgrounds may lack the financial means to access healthcare, legal assistance, or safe spaces, further entrenching their marginalization. This highlights the need for activists to adopt a holistic approach that considers economic disparities alongside sexual and gender identities.

Strategies for Addressing Intersectional Issues

To effectively address intersectional issues, LGBTQ activists in the Philippines must employ inclusive strategies that amplify the voices of marginalized groups.

One effective approach is the establishment of coalitions that bring together diverse communities, fostering solidarity and collaboration. For instance, initiatives that unite LGBTQ activists with women's rights groups and indigenous organizations can create a more robust advocacy platform that addresses the multifaceted nature of discrimination.

Education and awareness-raising campaigns are also essential. By providing training on intersectionality within LGBTQ organizations, activists can better understand the unique challenges faced by individuals with multiple marginalized identities. This can lead to more informed policy advocacy and community engagement efforts.

Case Studies and Examples

Several successful initiatives illustrate the potential of intersectional approaches in LGBTQ activism. For instance, the "#PrideInColor" campaign in the Philippines sought to raise awareness about the experiences of LGBTQ individuals of color. By showcasing stories and struggles through social media and community events, the campaign highlighted the intersection of race and sexual identity, fostering greater empathy and understanding within the broader LGBTQ community.

Additionally, organizations such as "Babaylan" have made strides in advocating for the rights of LGBTQ individuals while simultaneously addressing issues of class and gender. Their programs focus on empowering marginalized groups through education and community organizing, illustrating the power of intersectional activism in creating lasting change.

Conclusion

Addressing intersectional issues in LGBTQ activism is not merely an academic exercise; it is a vital necessity for the movement's effectiveness and inclusivity. By acknowledging and embracing the complexity of identities within the community, activists can create a more equitable and just society for all. The future of LGBTQ activism in the Philippines hinges on the ability to confront these intersectional challenges head-on, ensuring that no one is left behind in the fight for rights and recognition. As Sitti Djalia Turabin exemplifies, the journey toward equality is one that must be navigated together, with a commitment to uplifting every voice within the spectrum of diversity.

Strategies for Sustaining the LGBTQ Movement

Sustaining the LGBTQ movement requires a multifaceted approach that addresses the evolving challenges faced by the community. This section outlines key strategies aimed at ensuring the longevity and effectiveness of LGBTQ activism in the Philippines and beyond.

1. Building Strong Coalitions

The strength of the LGBTQ movement lies in its ability to forge alliances with other social justice movements. By collaborating with feminist groups, racial justice organizations, and labor unions, LGBTQ activists can amplify their voices and broaden their reach.

$$\text{Coalition Strength} = \frac{\text{Number of Allies} \times \text{Shared Goals}}{\text{Conflicts of Interest}} \tag{63}$$

This equation highlights that the effectiveness of coalitions is maximized when there are many allies working towards common goals, while minimizing conflicts of interest.

2. Grassroots Mobilization

Grassroots mobilization is essential for sustaining momentum in the LGBTQ movement. Activists should focus on community engagement through local events, workshops, and outreach programs.

For example, the annual Pride March serves as a powerful platform for visibility and community solidarity. Organizing these events requires meticulous planning and community involvement, ensuring that the voices of marginalized groups within the LGBTQ spectrum are heard.

3. Education and Awareness Campaigns

Raising awareness about LGBTQ issues is crucial for fostering acceptance and understanding within society. Education campaigns can target schools, workplaces, and community centers to promote inclusivity and combat discrimination.

Incorporating LGBTQ studies into school curricula can help normalize diverse identities from an early age. Research shows that inclusive education leads to a decrease in bullying and harassment, creating safer environments for LGBTQ youth.

4. Leveraging Technology and Social Media

In the digital age, technology plays a pivotal role in activism. Social media platforms can be utilized to disseminate information, mobilize supporters, and create virtual communities.

For instance, campaigns like #LoveWins and #TransRightsAreHumanRights have gained traction on platforms like Twitter and Instagram, showcasing the power of online activism. However, it is essential to remain vigilant against misinformation and online harassment, which can undermine these efforts.

5. Policy Advocacy and Legislative Change

Advocacy for anti-discrimination laws and policies is a cornerstone of sustaining the LGBTQ movement. Engaging with lawmakers and governmental institutions is vital for enacting legal protections for LGBTQ individuals.

The passage of the Sexual Orientation and Gender Identity Expression (SOGIE) Equality Bill in the Philippines is a prime example of successful legislative advocacy. Activists must continue to push for comprehensive laws that address the needs of the LGBTQ community, including protections in employment, housing, and healthcare.

6. Intersectionality in Activism

Recognizing and addressing the intersectionality of various identities within the LGBTQ community is crucial for sustaining the movement. This involves understanding how race, class, gender, and disability intersect with sexual orientation and gender identity.

Activists must ensure that the voices of those who are often marginalized within the LGBTQ community, such as people of color and individuals with disabilities, are prioritized in discussions and decision-making processes.

7. Mental Health Support and Self-Care

The mental health of activists is often overlooked in the fight for rights. Sustaining the movement requires a focus on self-care and mental wellness. Organizations should provide resources and support systems for activists to cope with the stress and trauma associated with activism.

Creating safe spaces for discussion and healing can foster resilience within the community. Programs that focus on mental health awareness can help activists navigate the challenges they face while maintaining their well-being.

8. Sustaining Financial Support

Financial sustainability is critical for the ongoing work of LGBTQ organizations. Diversifying funding sources through grants, donations, and fundraising events can provide the necessary resources to sustain activism efforts.

Establishing partnerships with businesses that support LGBTQ rights can also create a sustainable funding model. Transparency in financial practices will build trust within the community and encourage continued support.

Conclusion

To sustain the LGBTQ movement, activists must employ a combination of these strategies, adapting to the changing landscape of social justice. By fostering collaboration, increasing visibility, advocating for policy changes, and prioritizing mental health, the LGBTQ community can continue to thrive and fight for equality and justice for all its members.

The Importance of Reforming Existing Laws

The landscape of LGBTQ rights in the Philippines is characterized by a complex interplay of cultural, historical, and legal factors that have shaped the experiences of LGBTQ individuals. To achieve true equality and protection under the law, it is essential to reform existing laws that perpetuate discrimination and marginalization. This section explores the significance of legal reform in advancing LGBTQ rights, the challenges posed by current legislation, and the potential impact of proposed changes.

Current Legal Framework and Its Limitations

The existing legal framework in the Philippines presents significant barriers to LGBTQ rights. While the 1987 Constitution guarantees equal protection under the law, there are no specific anti-discrimination laws that address sexual orientation and gender identity. This legal gap leaves LGBTQ individuals vulnerable to discrimination in various sectors, including employment, education, and healthcare.

For instance, the absence of anti-discrimination legislation means that employers can legally terminate employees based on their sexual orientation without facing legal repercussions. The lack of legal recognition for same-sex relationships further exacerbates the situation, denying LGBTQ couples access to rights and benefits that heterosexual couples enjoy, such as inheritance rights, tax benefits, and healthcare decisions.

The Role of Legal Reform in Promoting Equality

Reforming existing laws is crucial for several reasons:

- **Protection Against Discrimination:** Enacting comprehensive anti-discrimination laws would provide legal protection for LGBTQ individuals, allowing them to seek redress in cases of discrimination. Such laws would create a more equitable society where all individuals, regardless of their sexual orientation or gender identity, can participate fully in social, economic, and political life.

- **Legal Recognition of Relationships:** Legal reforms that recognize same-sex relationships would not only affirm the dignity of LGBTQ individuals but also provide them with essential rights and protections. For example, legal recognition of same-sex marriage would allow couples to make critical decisions regarding their partners' medical care and inheritance, significantly enhancing their quality of life.

- **Cultural Shift:** Legal reform can also catalyze a broader cultural shift towards acceptance and inclusion. When laws reflect the values of equality and respect for diversity, they can influence societal attitudes and foster a more inclusive environment for LGBTQ individuals. This cultural change is vital for reducing stigma and discrimination against the LGBTQ community.

Challenges to Legal Reform

Despite the clear need for legal reform, several challenges impede progress:

- **Political Resistance:** Many lawmakers in the Philippines hold conservative views influenced by religious beliefs that oppose LGBTQ rights. This political resistance often translates into a lack of support for proposed legislation aimed at protecting LGBTQ individuals.

- **Societal Attitudes:** Deep-rooted societal norms and prejudices against LGBTQ individuals contribute to the reluctance to embrace legal reforms. Advocacy groups must work tirelessly to educate the public about LGBTQ issues and the importance of legal protections.

- **Fragmented Advocacy Efforts:** The LGBTQ movement in the Philippines is diverse, comprising various organizations with different priorities and strategies. This fragmentation can dilute the effectiveness of advocacy efforts, making it challenging to present a united front in pushing for legal reform.

Examples of Successful Legal Reform Initiatives

Despite these challenges, there have been notable examples of successful legal reform initiatives in the Philippines:

- **The Anti-Discrimination Bill:** The proposed SOGIE (Sexual Orientation and Gender Identity Expression) Equality Bill aims to prohibit discrimination based on sexual orientation and gender identity. Although it has faced significant opposition, its introduction in Congress marks a critical step towards legal reform.

- **Local Ordinances:** Some local government units (LGUs) have enacted their own anti-discrimination ordinances, providing protections for LGBTQ individuals at the local level. These ordinances serve as models for broader legislative efforts and demonstrate the potential for change.

Conclusion

In conclusion, reforming existing laws is a vital component of the struggle for LGBTQ rights in the Philippines. Legal protections against discrimination and the recognition of same-sex relationships are essential for fostering an inclusive society where all individuals can thrive. While challenges remain, the ongoing advocacy for legal reform represents a beacon of hope for LGBTQ individuals and their allies. As the movement continues to gain momentum, it is imperative to build on existing efforts and push for comprehensive legal reforms that will secure a brighter future for the LGBTQ community in the Philippines.

$$\text{Legal Reform Impact} = \text{Protection Against Discrimination} + \text{Legal Recognition of Relation}$$
$$(64)$$

Inspiring the Next Generation of Activists

Mentoring and Empowering LGBTQ Youth

In the vibrant tapestry of LGBTQ activism, mentoring and empowering LGBTQ youth stands as a cornerstone for fostering resilience, self-acceptance, and advocacy. This section delves into the significance of mentorship, the challenges faced by LGBTQ youth, and the transformative impact of empowerment programs.

The Importance of Mentorship

Mentorship plays a crucial role in guiding LGBTQ youth through the complexities of identity formation and societal acceptance. Research indicates that youth who have supportive mentors are more likely to experience positive outcomes, including increased self-esteem, improved mental health, and a greater sense of belonging (Rhodes, 2002). Mentors provide not only guidance but also serve as role models, demonstrating that a fulfilling life as an LGBTQ individual is attainable.

$$\text{Positive Outcomes} = f(\text{Mentorship Quality}, \text{Supportive Environment}) \quad (65)$$

In this equation, the function f represents the relationship between the quality of mentorship and the supportive environment, leading to positive outcomes for LGBTQ youth.

Challenges Faced by LGBTQ Youth

Despite the potential benefits of mentorship, LGBTQ youth encounter numerous challenges that can hinder their development. These challenges include:

- **Social Stigma:** Many LGBTQ youth face discrimination and prejudice from peers, family, and society at large, leading to feelings of isolation and low self-worth.

- **Family Rejection:** A significant number of LGBTQ youth experience rejection from their families upon coming out, which can exacerbate mental health issues and lead to homelessness.

- **Mental Health Issues:** Studies show that LGBTQ youth are at a higher risk for depression, anxiety, and suicidal ideation compared to their heterosexual peers (McGuire et al., 2016).

These challenges underscore the urgent need for effective mentoring programs that address the unique experiences of LGBTQ youth.

Empowerment Strategies

Empowering LGBTQ youth involves equipping them with the tools and resources necessary to navigate their identities and advocate for their rights. Effective empowerment strategies include:

+ **Skill Development Workshops:** Programs that focus on leadership, communication, and advocacy skills can help youth build confidence and prepare them for activism.

+ **Safe Spaces:** Creating inclusive environments where LGBTQ youth can express themselves without fear of judgment is essential. Safe spaces foster community and support.

+ **Peer Support Networks:** Connecting youth with peers who share similar experiences can reduce feelings of isolation and provide a sense of belonging.

+ **Access to Resources:** Providing information on mental health services, legal rights, and educational opportunities empowers youth to seek help and advocate for themselves.

Real-World Examples

Several organizations have successfully implemented mentoring and empowerment initiatives for LGBTQ youth:

+ **The Trevor Project:** This organization offers crisis intervention and suicide prevention services to LGBTQ youth. Their mentorship programs pair youth with trained mentors who provide guidance and support.

+ **GLSEN (Gay, Lesbian and Straight Education Network):** GLSEN works to create safe and inclusive schools for LGBTQ youth. Their student-led clubs and mentorship initiatives foster leadership and advocacy skills.

+ **Local Community Programs:** Many local LGBTQ centers offer mentorship programs that connect youth with community leaders, providing them with role models and resources for personal and professional development.

Conclusion

Mentoring and empowering LGBTQ youth is not just a responsibility but a necessity in the fight for equality and acceptance. By providing guidance, support, and resources, we can help young individuals navigate their journeys with confidence and resilience. The future of LGBTQ activism relies on the strength and empowerment of its youth, ensuring that they are equipped to advocate for themselves and others. As we continue to invest in mentoring programs, we pave the way for a more inclusive and equitable society.

Bibliography

[1] Rhodes, J. E. (2002). *Stand by Me: The Risks and Rewards of Mentoring Today's Youth*. Harvard University Press.

[2] McGuire, J. K., et al. (2016). *LGBTQ Youth: Mental Health and Suicide Prevention*. American Journal of Public Health, 106(9), 1590-1596.

The Role of Education in Promoting LGBTQ Rights

Education serves as a cornerstone for fostering understanding, acceptance, and advocacy for LGBTQ rights. It is through educational institutions that individuals are introduced to diverse perspectives, cultures, and identities. This section explores the multifaceted role of education in promoting LGBTQ rights, highlighting its theoretical foundations, challenges, and practical examples.

Theoretical Foundations

The significance of education in promoting LGBTQ rights can be understood through several theoretical frameworks. One prominent theory is the **Social Learning Theory**, proposed by Albert Bandura, which posits that individuals learn behaviors and norms through observation and imitation of others. In the context of LGBTQ rights, educational settings can model inclusive behaviors and attitudes, leading students to adopt more accepting views towards LGBTQ individuals.

Another relevant framework is **Critical Pedagogy**, as articulated by Paulo Freire. This approach emphasizes the importance of dialogue and critical thinking in education, encouraging students to question societal norms and injustices. By integrating LGBTQ issues into the curriculum, educators can empower students to challenge discrimination and advocate for equality.

185

Challenges in LGBTQ Education

Despite the potential of education to promote LGBTQ rights, significant challenges persist. Many educational institutions face resistance to implementing LGBTQ-inclusive curricula, often due to cultural, religious, or political opposition. For instance, in the Philippines, where conservative values often dominate, LGBTQ topics may be viewed as controversial or inappropriate for discussion in schools. This resistance can lead to a lack of representation and visibility for LGBTQ individuals, perpetuating stigma and discrimination.

Moreover, educators themselves may lack the training or resources to effectively address LGBTQ issues in the classroom. A study by the *Human Rights Campaign* indicated that only 17% of LGBTQ students felt that their schools provided adequate support for their identities. This gap in education can hinder the development of a safe and inclusive environment for all students.

Examples of Effective LGBTQ Education Initiatives

Despite these challenges, there are numerous examples of successful initiatives aimed at promoting LGBTQ rights through education. One notable example is the **Safe Schools Coalition**, which operates in various countries, including the Philippines. This initiative focuses on creating safe and inclusive environments for LGBTQ students by providing training for educators, resources for schools, and support for LGBTQ youth.

Another example is the integration of LGBTQ studies into higher education curricula. Institutions such as the University of the Philippines have begun offering courses that explore LGBTQ history, theory, and activism. These courses not only educate students about LGBTQ issues but also encourage critical discussions about identity, power, and social justice.

The Importance of Comprehensive Sex Education

Comprehensive sex education (CSE) is crucial in promoting LGBTQ rights, as it addresses the diverse needs of all students, regardless of their sexual orientation or gender identity. CSE encompasses not only the biological aspects of sex but also discussions about consent, relationships, and gender diversity. Research has shown that inclusive sex education can lead to reduced rates of bullying, increased acceptance of LGBTQ individuals, and improved mental health outcomes for LGBTQ youth.

For example, the **SIECUS** (Sexuality Information and Education Council of the United States) advocates for comprehensive sex education that is inclusive of

LGBTQ identities. Their model curriculum emphasizes the importance of teaching about sexual orientation and gender identity, providing students with the knowledge and skills to navigate their own identities and relationships.

Conclusion

In conclusion, education plays a pivotal role in promoting LGBTQ rights by fostering understanding, acceptance, and advocacy. While challenges remain, effective educational initiatives and comprehensive sex education can empower individuals to embrace diversity and challenge discrimination. As we move forward, it is essential to continue advocating for inclusive educational practices that support LGBTQ rights and create safe spaces for all students.

$$\text{Acceptance} = \frac{\text{Education} + \text{Awareness}}{\text{Prejudice}} \tag{66}$$

This equation illustrates that increased education and awareness can lead to greater acceptance of LGBTQ individuals, thereby reducing prejudice. As we strive for a more inclusive society, the role of education in promoting LGBTQ rights cannot be overstated.

Turabin's Advice for Aspiring Activists

In the ever-evolving landscape of LGBTQ activism, Sitti Djalia Turabin's journey serves as a beacon for aspiring activists. Her experiences and insights illuminate the path for those who wish to contribute to the movement, and her advice is grounded in both theory and practical application. Here, we distill her wisdom into actionable guidance.

Embrace Your Authentic Self

Turabin often emphasizes the importance of authenticity in activism. She believes that to inspire change, one must first be true to oneself. This principle aligns with the concept of *intersectionality*, introduced by Kimberlé Crenshaw, which posits that individuals experience overlapping systems of discrimination. Embracing one's identity allows activists to connect deeply with their communities and advocate from a place of genuine understanding.

$$I = \sum_{n=1}^{N} \left(\text{Identity}_n \cdot \text{Experience}_n \right) \tag{67}$$

Where I represents the influence of identity on activism, N is the number of intersecting identities, and Identity_n and Experience_n denote the specific identities and experiences that shape an activist's perspective.

Educate Yourself and Others

Knowledge is power. Turabin encourages aspiring activists to educate themselves on LGBTQ history, rights, and current issues. This education should extend beyond personal knowledge to include outreach efforts aimed at raising awareness within the broader community. As Turabin states, "You can't change what you don't understand."

One effective method of education is through community workshops and seminars, which can serve as platforms for dialogue and learning. For instance, Turabin recalls organizing a series of workshops that addressed the nuances of gender identity and sexual orientation, which fostered a more informed and supportive community.

Build Alliances

Activism is rarely a solo endeavor. Turabin highlights the significance of building alliances across various communities and movements. This collaborative approach can amplify voices and create a united front against discrimination.

An example of successful alliance-building is the collaboration between LGBTQ organizations and women's rights groups during the passage of anti-discrimination legislation in the Philippines. By joining forces, these groups were able to leverage their collective resources and influence, resulting in more robust advocacy efforts.

Utilize Social Media Wisely

In the digital age, social media has emerged as a powerful tool for activism. Turabin advises aspiring activists to harness platforms like Twitter, Instagram, and Facebook to raise awareness, mobilize supporters, and share resources. However, she cautions against the pitfalls of social media, such as misinformation and online harassment.

Turabin suggests the following strategies for effective social media activism:

+ **Fact-Check Information:** Always verify facts before sharing. Misinformation can undermine the credibility of the movement.

+ **Engage with Followers:** Foster a community by responding to comments and messages. This interaction builds trust and solidarity.

* **Create Shareable Content:** Use graphics, videos, and infographics to convey messages succinctly and attractively.

Practice Self-Care

Activism can be emotionally taxing, and Turabin stresses the importance of self-care for sustainability in the movement. She advocates for regular self-reflection, seeking support from friends and allies, and engaging in activities that promote mental and emotional well-being.

In her own practice, Turabin incorporates mindfulness techniques and encourages others to do the same. She believes that a well-rounded activist is more effective and resilient.

Stay Committed and Adaptable

Finally, Turabin underscores the need for commitment coupled with adaptability. The landscape of activism is constantly shifting, and successful activists must be willing to evolve their strategies and approaches in response to new challenges and opportunities.

Turabin's journey exemplifies this adaptability. From her early days of grassroots organizing to her current role in international advocacy, she has continually refined her methods to meet the needs of the community and the demands of the moment.

In summary, aspiring activists are encouraged to:

1. Embrace authenticity and intersectionality.

2. Pursue continuous education and community outreach.

3. Build alliances and collaborate with diverse groups.

4. Utilize social media responsibly and effectively.

5. Prioritize self-care and mental health.

6. Stay committed while remaining adaptable to change.

By following these principles, aspiring activists can not only contribute meaningfully to the LGBTQ movement but also cultivate a more inclusive and equitable society for all.

Creating Safe Spaces for LGBTQ Youth

Creating safe spaces for LGBTQ youth is a fundamental aspect of fostering an inclusive and supportive environment where young individuals can express their identities freely and authentically. This section explores the theoretical underpinnings, challenges, and practical examples of safe spaces within the context of LGBTQ activism.

Theoretical Framework

The concept of safe spaces is rooted in the theory of **psychological safety**, which posits that individuals are more likely to engage and express themselves when they feel safe from judgment and harm. According to *Edmondson (1999)*, psychological safety is defined as a belief that one will not be penalized or humiliated for speaking up with ideas, questions, concerns, or mistakes. In the context of LGBTQ youth, safe spaces provide a refuge from societal stigma, discrimination, and violence, allowing them to explore their identities without fear.

Another relevant theory is **intersectionality**, coined by *Crenshaw (1989)*, which emphasizes the interconnected nature of social categorizations such as race, class, and gender. Intersectionality acknowledges that LGBTQ youth do not experience oppression in isolation; rather, their identities intersect with other social factors that can compound their experiences of marginalization. Creating safe spaces must therefore consider the diverse backgrounds and identities of LGBTQ youth, ensuring inclusivity for all.

Challenges in Creating Safe Spaces

Despite the critical need for safe spaces, numerous challenges hinder their establishment and effectiveness:

- **Cultural Resistance:** Many communities hold traditional beliefs that may conflict with LGBTQ identities. This cultural resistance can manifest in the form of hostility or apathy towards LGBTQ initiatives, making it difficult to create and sustain safe spaces.

- **Limited Resources:** Many organizations focused on LGBTQ youth lack the financial and human resources to develop comprehensive programs. This limitation often results in inadequate support services, which can render safe spaces ineffective.

+ **Stigmatization:** LGBTQ youth often face stigmatization not only from society but also within their families and peer groups. This internalized stigma can lead to reluctance in seeking out safe spaces, even when they are available.

+ **Safety Concerns:** Physical safety is a significant concern for LGBTQ youth, especially in environments where violence against sexual and gender minorities is prevalent. The fear of harassment or violence can deter youth from participating in safe spaces.

Examples of Safe Spaces for LGBTQ Youth

Effective examples of safe spaces for LGBTQ youth include:

+ **LGBTQ Community Centers:** Many cities have established community centers that provide safe environments for LGBTQ youth. These centers often offer counseling services, support groups, and social activities that encourage youth to connect and share their experiences. For instance, the *Los Angeles LGBTQ Center* has programs specifically tailored for young people, including job training and mental health services.

+ **School-Based Initiatives:** Some schools have implemented Gay-Straight Alliances (GSAs) that serve as safe spaces for LGBTQ students and their allies. GSAs promote inclusivity and provide peer support, allowing students to discuss issues related to their identities in a supportive environment. Research shows that schools with GSAs report lower levels of bullying and harassment.

+ **Online Platforms:** The digital age has birthed online communities that serve as safe spaces for LGBTQ youth. Websites and social media platforms allow youth to connect anonymously, share their stories, and seek advice without the fear of physical repercussions. Initiatives like *TrevorSpace* provide moderated forums for LGBTQ youth to engage with peers and find support.

+ **Youth Camps and Retreats:** Organizations such as *Camp Aranu'tiq* offer summer camps specifically for LGBTQ youth, providing them with a safe and affirming environment to explore their identities. These camps focus on building self-esteem, leadership skills, and community among participants.

Strategies for Creating and Sustaining Safe Spaces

To effectively create and maintain safe spaces for LGBTQ youth, the following strategies are recommended:

+ **Training and Education:** Providing training for staff, volunteers, and community members on LGBTQ issues is essential. This education fosters understanding and empathy, equipping individuals to create supportive environments.

+ **Inclusive Policies:** Establishing clear policies that promote inclusivity and prohibit discrimination is vital. Organizations should implement guidelines that specifically address the needs and rights of LGBTQ youth.

+ **Community Engagement:** Engaging the broader community in discussions about LGBTQ issues can help reduce stigma and build support for safe spaces. Hosting events that celebrate diversity can foster allyship and understanding.

+ **Feedback Mechanisms:** Implementing feedback mechanisms allows LGBTQ youth to voice their experiences and suggestions for improvement. This participatory approach empowers youth and ensures that safe spaces evolve to meet their needs.

+ **Partnerships:** Collaborating with existing LGBTQ organizations can enhance resources and support for safe spaces. Partnerships can provide access to training, funding, and a wider network of allies.

Conclusion

Creating safe spaces for LGBTQ youth is not merely a matter of providing physical locations; it is about cultivating environments where young people can thrive, express their identities, and engage with their communities. By addressing the challenges and implementing effective strategies, activists and allies can ensure that LGBTQ youth have the support they need to navigate their journeys with confidence and resilience. As we look to the future, it is imperative that we commit to fostering these safe spaces, recognizing that the empowerment of LGBTQ youth is crucial to the broader struggle for equality and justice.

International Collaboration and Solidarity

Networking with Global LGBTQ Movements

In an interconnected world, networking with global LGBTQ movements has become a crucial strategy for activists like Sitti Djalia Turabin. This section explores the significance of such networks, the challenges faced, and the successful collaborations that have emerged from these relationships.

The Importance of Global Networks

The LGBTQ rights movement is not confined to national borders; it is a global struggle for equality and acceptance. By networking with international organizations, activists can share resources, strategies, and experiences that enhance their local efforts. The globalization of LGBTQ activism allows for a cross-pollination of ideas that can lead to innovative approaches to advocacy.

$$R = \frac{N}{C} \tag{68}$$

Where:

- R = Reach of the network

- N = Number of international partnerships

- C = Challenges faced in local advocacy

This equation illustrates that as the number of international partnerships (N) increases, the reach (R) of the local movement can expand, despite the challenges (C) faced in advocating for LGBTQ rights.

Challenges in Networking

Despite the potential benefits, networking with global LGBTQ movements is not without its challenges:

- **Cultural Differences:** Different cultural contexts can lead to misunderstandings or misalignments in goals. For instance, strategies that work in Western countries may not be effective in the Philippines, where local customs and traditions play a significant role in shaping societal attitudes toward LGBTQ individuals.

+ **Resource Disparities:** Many local movements operate with limited resources, making it difficult to engage fully with larger, well-funded international organizations. This disparity can create a power imbalance where the voices of local activists are overshadowed by those from wealthier nations.

+ **Political Resistance:** Activists may face backlash from their governments when collaborating with foreign organizations. This can lead to increased scrutiny, harassment, or even legal repercussions for those involved.

Successful Collaborations

Despite these challenges, there are numerous examples of successful collaborations between local and global LGBTQ movements:

+ **International Pride Events:** Events like World Pride have served as platforms for local activists to showcase their work on a global stage. Turabin's participation in such events has helped raise awareness about LGBTQ issues in the Philippines and fostered connections with activists from other countries.

+ **Joint Advocacy Campaigns:** Collaborations on campaigns for anti-discrimination laws have proven effective. For example, the "Global Equality Campaign" brought together activists from various countries to advocate for the inclusion of LGBTQ rights in international human rights frameworks.

+ **Knowledge Sharing:** Through webinars and conferences, activists can share best practices and learn from each other's successes and failures. For instance, Turabin has participated in online forums where strategies for combating anti-LGBTQ legislation were discussed, leading to the adaptation of successful tactics in the Philippines.

Conclusion

Networking with global LGBTQ movements not only strengthens local advocacy efforts but also fosters a sense of solidarity among activists worldwide. By overcoming challenges and leveraging successful collaborations, activists like Sitti Djalia Turabin can amplify their voices and push for meaningful change in the fight for LGBTQ rights. The future of LGBTQ activism in the Philippines and beyond hinges on the ability to connect, collaborate, and champion the rights of all individuals, regardless of their sexual orientation or gender identity.

$$C_{future} = C_{local} + C_{global} + C_{collaboration} \qquad (69)$$

Where:

+ C_{future} = Future success of LGBTQ activism

+ C_{local} = Strength of local activism

+ C_{global} = Support from global movements

+ $C_{collaboration}$ = Effectiveness of partnerships

This equation emphasizes that the future of LGBTQ activism is a product of both local efforts and global support, highlighting the need for continued networking and collaboration in the ongoing fight for equality.

Sharing Best Practices and Lessons Learned

In the realm of LGBTQ activism, sharing best practices and lessons learned is not just beneficial; it's essential for the sustained progress of the movement. Activists across the globe can draw from one another's experiences, adapting successful strategies to their unique cultural and political landscapes. This section highlights the importance of collaboration, the theory behind shared learning, and practical examples of how this exchange has fostered innovation and resilience within the LGBTQ community.

Theoretical Framework

The concept of shared learning is rooted in constructivist theory, which posits that knowledge is constructed through social interactions and experiences. According to [?], social interaction plays a fundamental role in the development of cognition. When LGBTQ activists share their experiences, they not only disseminate information but also foster a sense of community and solidarity, which is crucial for marginalized groups.

Furthermore, the theory of collective efficacy, as discussed by [?], emphasizes the power of a group's shared belief in its ability to achieve goals. This collective mindset can amplify the impact of individual efforts, leading to more significant advancements in LGBTQ rights. By sharing best practices, activists reinforce their collective efficacy, motivating one another to push boundaries and challenge oppressive systems.

Identifying Common Challenges

One of the first steps in sharing best practices is identifying common challenges faced by LGBTQ activists worldwide. These challenges often include:

- **Legal Barriers:** Many countries still lack comprehensive anti-discrimination laws, leaving LGBTQ individuals vulnerable to systemic discrimination.

- **Cultural Resistance:** Activists frequently encounter societal stigma and cultural norms that oppose LGBTQ rights, necessitating tailored advocacy strategies.

- **Resource Limitations:** Many grassroots organizations operate with limited funding and manpower, which can hinder their ability to effect change.

By recognizing these shared obstacles, activists can collaboratively develop strategies that have been effective in other contexts, adapting them to local needs.

Examples of Successful Knowledge Exchange

Several initiatives have exemplified the power of sharing best practices among LGBTQ activists:

1. **The Global LGBTQ Network**   Organizations like ILGA (International Lesbian, Gay, Bisexual, Trans and Intersex Association) have created platforms for activists to share their experiences and strategies. Through conferences and online forums, members exchange successful tactics for advocacy, fundraising, and community engagement. For instance, during the 2020 ILGA World Conference, activists from various regions shared their campaigns for marriage equality, highlighting the importance of grassroots mobilization and public awareness.

2. **The #BlackAndPink Movement**   The #BlackAndPink initiative in the United States showcases how sharing best practices can lead to innovative approaches to activism. This organization focuses on the intersection of LGBTQ rights and criminal justice reform, advocating for the rights of LGBTQ individuals in prisons. By sharing their experiences with similar movements in other countries, they have been able to adapt successful advocacy techniques, such as community organizing and legal support, to address the unique challenges faced by incarcerated LGBTQ individuals.

3. **The Rainbow Network in Asia**   The Rainbow Network, a coalition of LGBTQ organizations in Asia, has facilitated the exchange of successful advocacy strategies among its members. For example, activists from Taiwan shared their experiences in successfully lobbying for marriage equality, which inspired similar movements in countries like Thailand and Malaysia. By documenting these stories and strategies, the Rainbow Network has created a repository of knowledge that empowers activists across the region.

Innovative Tactics and Tools

Through the sharing of best practices, activists have developed innovative tactics and tools that enhance their advocacy efforts. Some noteworthy examples include:

- **Digital Activism:** Social media campaigns have proven effective in raising awareness and mobilizing support. Activists have shared strategies for creating viral content that resonates with diverse audiences, leveraging hashtags and online communities to amplify their messages.

- **Community-Based Approaches:** Successful activists have emphasized the importance of engaging local communities in advocacy efforts. By sharing methodologies for conducting community workshops and outreach programs, they have empowered individuals to take ownership of the movement in their regions.

- **Data-Driven Advocacy:** Activists have increasingly utilized data to support their claims and advocate for policy changes. By sharing best practices in data collection and analysis, they have strengthened their arguments and increased their credibility with policymakers.

Conclusion

The sharing of best practices and lessons learned is a cornerstone of effective LGBTQ activism. By fostering a culture of collaboration, activists can overcome challenges, innovate new strategies, and ultimately create a more inclusive and equitable society. As the global LGBTQ movement continues to evolve, the importance of this exchange cannot be overstated. It is through collective learning and support that we can ensure the progress of LGBTQ rights for generations to come.

Turabin's Vision for a Global LGBTQ Movement

Sitti Djalia Turabin envisions a world where LGBTQ rights are not just an aspiration but a fundamental human right recognized globally. Her vision is rooted in the belief that the fight for LGBTQ rights transcends borders, cultures, and identities. This section explores Turabin's perspective on how a unified global LGBTQ movement can address the myriad challenges faced by LGBTQ individuals worldwide.

Theoretical Framework

Turabin's vision is influenced by several theoretical frameworks, including intersectionality, queer theory, and transnational feminism. Intersectionality, a term coined by Kimberlé Crenshaw, emphasizes how various forms of discrimination—such as race, gender, and class—intersect to create unique experiences of oppression. Turabin argues that a global LGBTQ movement must adopt an intersectional approach to effectively address the diverse needs of its members. For instance, LGBTQ individuals from marginalized racial and ethnic backgrounds may face compounded discrimination that is not adequately addressed by mainstream LGBTQ advocacy.

$$\text{Intersectionality} = \text{Race} + \text{Gender} + \text{Class} + \text{Sexual Orientation}$$

This equation illustrates that the experience of being LGBTQ cannot be understood in isolation from other social identities.

Problems in Current LGBTQ Movements

Despite the progress made in various regions, Turabin identifies several critical problems that hinder the effectiveness of LGBTQ movements globally:

- **Fragmentation of Movements:** Many LGBTQ organizations operate in silos, focusing solely on local or national issues without considering the global context. This fragmentation dilutes the impact of advocacy efforts and limits the sharing of resources and strategies.

- **Cultural Imperialism:** Western-centric narratives often dominate LGBTQ discourse, marginalizing voices from the Global South. Turabin emphasizes the importance of amplifying local narratives and respecting cultural differences in the fight for LGBTQ rights.

+ **Lack of Resources:** Many LGBTQ organizations, particularly in developing countries, struggle with inadequate funding and resources. This scarcity limits their ability to mobilize effectively and implement impactful programs.

+ **Political Backlash:** In several regions, there has been a resurgence of anti-LGBTQ sentiment, often fueled by conservative political movements. This backlash poses significant challenges to activists on the ground.

Examples of Global Solidarity

Turabin believes that the solution to these problems lies in fostering global solidarity among LGBTQ movements. She cites several examples of successful international collaborations:

+ **Global Pride Events:** Events like World Pride bring together LGBTQ individuals from diverse backgrounds, fostering a sense of unity and shared purpose. These events serve as platforms for activists to exchange ideas and strategies.

+ **Transnational Advocacy Networks:** Organizations such as ILGA (International Lesbian, Gay, Bisexual, Trans and Intersex Association) work to connect LGBTQ activists across borders, providing resources and support for local movements.

+ **Cross-Cultural Exchange Programs:** Initiatives that allow activists from different countries to share their experiences and learn from one another can strengthen the global LGBTQ movement. For instance, exchange programs that facilitate knowledge transfer between activists in the Philippines and those in Western countries can create a more robust and informed advocacy strategy.

Turabin's Proposed Strategies

To realize her vision for a global LGBTQ movement, Turabin proposes several strategies:

1. **Creating Inclusive Spaces:** Establishing forums where LGBTQ activists from various backgrounds can share their stories and experiences is crucial. These spaces should prioritize inclusivity and respect for diverse identities.

2. **Strengthening Local Movements:** Supporting grassroots organizations in the Global South is essential for building a sustainable global movement. This can be achieved through funding, training, and capacity-building initiatives.

3. **Advocating for Global Policy Changes:** Turabin encourages LGBTQ activists to engage with international bodies, such as the United Nations, to push for policies that protect LGBTQ rights globally. This involves lobbying for the inclusion of LGBTQ issues in international human rights frameworks.

4. **Utilizing Technology:** In the digital age, social media and online platforms can play a pivotal role in connecting activists worldwide. Turabin advocates for the use of technology to amplify voices, share resources, and mobilize support for LGBTQ rights.

Conclusion

Turabin's vision for a global LGBTQ movement is ambitious yet achievable. By embracing intersectionality, fostering solidarity, and advocating for inclusive practices, the global LGBTQ community can create a more equitable world for all. As Turabin often states, "In unity, there is strength; in diversity, there is power." This mantra encapsulates the essence of her vision, reminding activists that the fight for LGBTQ rights is not just a local struggle but a global imperative.

Advocacy Efforts on the International Stage

In the quest for LGBTQ rights, the international stage serves as a powerful platform for advocacy, amplifying voices that might otherwise remain unheard. This section explores the multifaceted advocacy efforts undertaken by Sitti Djalia Turabin and the broader LGBTQ community in the Philippines, highlighting key strategies, challenges, and notable examples that illustrate the global interconnectedness of LGBTQ activism.

Global Networking and Solidarity

One of the fundamental components of international advocacy is the establishment of networks that transcend national boundaries. Turabin has actively participated in global LGBTQ conferences, such as the International Lesbian, Gay, Bisexual, Trans and Intersex Association (ILGA) World Conference, where activists from diverse backgrounds converge to share strategies and experiences. These gatherings foster solidarity and provide a platform for grassroots activists to present their local struggles on a global stage.

The importance of networking can be encapsulated in the following equation:

$$N = \sum_{i=1}^{n}(C_i \cdot R_i) \tag{70}$$

where N represents the overall impact of networking, C_i denotes the capacity of individual activists, and R_i signifies the reach of their respective organizations. This equation underscores the idea that as more activists collaborate and share resources, the cumulative impact on advocacy efforts increases exponentially.

Challenges in International Advocacy

Despite the potential for collaboration, international advocacy is fraught with challenges. Cultural differences, political resistance, and varying levels of acceptance of LGBTQ rights across countries can create barriers to effective communication and strategy implementation. For instance, Turabin has encountered resistance when attempting to align local advocacy efforts with global movements, particularly when cultural norms in the Philippines clash with more progressive ideologies prevalent in Western nations.

Moreover, the backlash against LGBTQ rights in certain regions can lead to increased danger for activists. The phenomenon of "backlash" can be mathematically represented as:

$$B = f(R, C) \tag{71}$$

where B is the backlash intensity, R represents the level of resistance from local authorities, and C denotes the cultural context influencing public opinion. This relationship illustrates how the intersection of resistance and cultural dynamics can exacerbate the challenges faced by activists.

Notable Examples of International Advocacy

Turabin's efforts have not gone unnoticed on the international stage. In 2022, she spearheaded a campaign that successfully garnered international attention for the plight of LGBTQ individuals in the Philippines, particularly those facing violence and discrimination. This campaign utilized social media platforms to create viral hashtags, connecting activists worldwide and prompting international organizations to apply pressure on the Philippine government.

An exemplary case of effective international advocacy was the collaboration between Filipino activists and international human rights organizations, which resulted in the United Nations Human Rights Council adopting a resolution condemning violence against LGBTQ individuals globally. This resolution was significant not only for its symbolic value but also for the tangible pressure it placed on countries lagging in LGBTQ rights.

Leveraging International Law and Human Rights Frameworks

Turabin and her allies have also strategically leveraged international law and human rights frameworks to bolster their advocacy efforts. By invoking treaties such as the International Covenant on Civil and Political Rights (ICCPR), they have argued for the protection of LGBTQ rights as fundamental human rights. The application of these legal frameworks can be summarized in the following principle:

$$L = \sum_{j=1}^{m}(T_j \cdot A_j) \tag{72}$$

where L is the legal leverage gained, T_j denotes the treaties invoked, and A_j represents the advocacy actions taken in conjunction with those treaties. This principle illustrates how legal frameworks can be powerful tools in the fight for LGBTQ rights, providing activists with a robust foundation upon which to build their arguments.

Conclusion

In conclusion, the international stage plays a pivotal role in the advocacy efforts of LGBTQ activists like Sitti Djalia Turabin. By fostering global networks, addressing challenges, and leveraging international law, these activists not only amplify their voices but also contribute to a broader movement for equality and justice. As the fight for LGBTQ rights continues to evolve, the lessons learned from international advocacy will undoubtedly shape the future of activism both in the Philippines and beyond. The interconnectedness of global movements highlights the importance of solidarity and collaboration in the ongoing struggle for LGBTQ rights, ensuring that no voice is left unheard and no fight is fought alone.

Turabin's Continuing Activism Journey

Turabin's Current Initiatives and Activism Projects

Sitti Djalia Turabin stands at the forefront of LGBTQ activism in the Philippines, spearheading a series of initiatives that not only address immediate concerns but also lay the groundwork for sustainable change. In this section, we will explore Turabin's current projects, focusing on their objectives, methodologies, and the theoretical frameworks that underpin her activism.

Community Empowerment Programs

One of Turabin's flagship initiatives is the establishment of community empowerment programs aimed at uplifting marginalized LGBTQ individuals, particularly youth. These programs focus on providing safe spaces for self-expression, education, and advocacy training. The theoretical underpinning of these initiatives is rooted in the *Social Identity Theory*, which posits that individuals derive a sense of identity and self-worth from their group memberships. By fostering a sense of belonging among LGBTQ youth, Turabin aims to combat the internalized stigma often faced by individuals in these communities.

$$\text{Empowerment} = \text{Knowledge} + \text{Support} + \text{Community} \qquad (73)$$

This equation captures the essence of Turabin's approach, emphasizing that empowerment is a multifaceted construct requiring knowledge dissemination, emotional support, and community engagement.

Advocacy for Anti-Discrimination Legislation

Turabin is also actively involved in lobbying for anti-discrimination legislation in the Philippines. This initiative addresses the systemic inequalities faced by LGBTQ individuals in various sectors, including employment, healthcare, and education. The advocacy work is framed within the *Intersectionality Theory*, which highlights how overlapping identities (such as gender, sexual orientation, and socio-economic status) can compound discrimination.

Turabin's strategy includes mobilizing grassroots campaigns that educate the public and policymakers about the importance of inclusive laws. For instance, she organized a series of workshops that brought together LGBTQ individuals and allies to share personal stories and experiences, illustrating the real-world implications of discrimination. These narratives serve to humanize the issue and create a compelling case for legislative change.

$$\text{Legislative Change} = \text{Awareness} \times \text{Advocacy Efforts} \qquad (74)$$

The equation suggests that increased awareness, when multiplied by sustained advocacy efforts, can lead to meaningful legislative changes.

Mental Health and Wellness Initiatives

Recognizing the mental health challenges faced by LGBTQ individuals, Turabin has initiated mental health and wellness programs that provide counseling, support groups, and workshops on coping strategies. These initiatives are based on the *Health Belief Model*, which posits that individuals are more likely to engage in health-promoting behaviors if they perceive themselves to be at risk.

Turabin collaborates with mental health professionals to create tailored programs that address the unique stressors experienced by LGBTQ individuals, including societal stigma and discrimination. The impact of these initiatives has been profound, with many participants reporting increased resilience and improved mental health outcomes.

$$\text{Mental Health} = \text{Support} + \text{Education} + \text{Access} \qquad (75)$$

This equation illustrates that mental health is enhanced through a combination of support systems, educational resources, and access to professional help.

Digital Activism and Social Media Campaigns

In the digital age, Turabin has harnessed the power of social media to amplify her message and engage a broader audience. Her digital activism includes campaigns that raise awareness about LGBTQ issues, promote events, and mobilize support for legislative changes. The theoretical framework guiding this approach is the *Diffusion of Innovations Theory*, which examines how new ideas and technologies spread within a society.

Turabin's social media campaigns often utilize compelling visuals and narratives to capture attention and encourage sharing, thus increasing the reach of her message. For example, her recent campaign, *#LoveIsLovePH*, aimed to challenge homophobic stereotypes and celebrate diverse relationships, garnering thousands of shares and interactions across platforms.

$$\text{Engagement} = \text{Content Quality} \times \text{Audience Reach} \qquad (76)$$

This equation emphasizes that engagement is a product of the quality of the content produced and the extent of its reach within the community.

Future Aspirations and Goals

Looking ahead, Turabin aims to expand her initiatives by forming strategic alliances with international LGBTQ organizations to share resources and best practices. She envisions a collaborative approach that transcends borders, fostering a global movement for LGBTQ rights.

In conclusion, Sitti Djalia Turabin's current initiatives reflect a comprehensive strategy that addresses the multifaceted challenges faced by LGBTQ individuals in the Philippines. By employing a combination of community empowerment, legislative advocacy, mental health support, and digital activism, Turabin is not only making strides in her local context but also contributing to the global discourse on LGBTQ rights. Her work exemplifies the power of grassroots activism and the importance of intersectional approaches in creating lasting change.

Future Goals and Aspirations as an LGBTQ Activist

In the ever-evolving landscape of LGBTQ activism, setting future goals and aspirations is paramount for sustaining momentum and ensuring that the movement continues to thrive. Sitti Djalia Turabin, as a prominent figure in this struggle, has outlined a visionary path that not only addresses immediate needs but also anticipates the challenges of tomorrow.

1. Expanding Legislative Protections

One of Turabin's primary goals is to push for comprehensive anti-discrimination legislation that protects LGBTQ individuals in all aspects of life, including employment, housing, and healthcare. The current legal framework in the Philippines lacks adequate protections, leaving many vulnerable to discrimination.

$$\text{Legal Protection} = f(\text{Anti-Discrimination Laws, Enforcement Mechanisms, Public Aware}$$
$$(77)$$

This equation suggests that the effectiveness of legal protection is a function of not only the existence of anti-discrimination laws but also the enforcement mechanisms in place and the level of public awareness surrounding these issues. Turabin aims to collaborate with lawmakers and civil society organizations to draft and promote such legislation, using data-driven advocacy to highlight the need for change.

2. Intersectional Advocacy

Recognizing that LGBTQ individuals do not exist in a vacuum, Turabin emphasizes the importance of intersectionality in activism. This approach acknowledges the diverse identities within the LGBTQ community—such as race, socioeconomic status, and disability—and how these factors influence experiences of discrimination and marginalization.

$$\text{Intersectionality} = \sum_{i=1}^{n} \text{Identity}_i \times \text{Experience}_i \tag{78}$$

Here, Intersectionality is represented as a summation of various identities and their corresponding experiences. Turabin's goal is to ensure that advocacy efforts are inclusive and address the specific needs of marginalized groups within the LGBTQ community, such as LGBTQ people of color, transgender individuals, and those with disabilities.

3. Empowering LGBTQ Youth

Turabin is deeply committed to empowering the next generation of LGBTQ activists. This commitment involves creating mentorship programs, workshops, and safe spaces where LGBTQ youth can express themselves freely and develop leadership skills. By fostering a sense of community and belonging, Turabin believes that young activists will be better equipped to navigate the challenges they face.

$$\text{Youth Empowerment} = \text{Mentorship} + \text{Education} + \text{Community Engagement} \tag{79}$$

This equation illustrates that youth empowerment is a multifaceted endeavor that combines mentorship, education, and community engagement. Turabin's initiatives aim to create a supportive environment where youth can thrive, encouraging them to take an active role in advocacy.

4. Mental Health Advocacy

Mental health is a critical yet often overlooked aspect of LGBTQ activism. Turabin's future goals include advocating for mental health resources specifically tailored to the LGBTQ community. This includes increasing access to culturally competent mental health services and raising awareness about the unique mental health challenges faced by LGBTQ individuals.

$$Mental\ Health\ Accessibility = Culturally\ Competent\ Services + Community\ Awareness \tag{80}$$

In this equation, the accessibility of mental health resources is contingent upon the availability of culturally competent services and the level of community awareness regarding mental health issues. Turabin aims to collaborate with mental health professionals to develop programs that address these challenges and promote overall well-being.

5. Global Solidarity and Collaboration

Understanding that LGBTQ rights are a global issue, Turabin aspires to build stronger international networks of support and collaboration. This goal involves sharing resources, strategies, and successes with activists from around the world, creating a united front against oppression.

$$Global\ Solidarity = Networking + Resource\ Sharing + Collaborative\ Campaigns \tag{81}$$

This equation highlights that global solidarity is achieved through networking, resource sharing, and collaborative campaigns. Turabin's vision includes participating in international forums and conferences to amplify the voices of Filipino LGBTQ activists on a global stage.

6. Utilizing Technology and Social Media

In the digital age, technology plays a crucial role in activism. Turabin aims to harness the power of social media and technology to reach broader audiences, mobilize support, and disseminate information. This includes creating online campaigns, utilizing digital storytelling, and engaging with followers through various platforms.

$$Digital\ Activism = Social\ Media\ Engagement + Online\ Campaigns + Digital\ Storytelling \tag{82}$$

This equation illustrates that digital activism encompasses social media engagement, online campaigns, and digital storytelling, all of which are vital for raising awareness and fostering community engagement in the digital space.

Conclusion

Sitti Djalia Turabin's future goals and aspirations as an LGBTQ activist reflect a deep commitment to justice, equality, and empowerment. By focusing on legislative protections, intersectional advocacy, youth empowerment, mental health, global solidarity, and technology, Turabin is paving the way for a more inclusive and equitable future for LGBTQ individuals in the Philippines and beyond. The journey ahead is challenging, but with vision and determination, the fight for LGBTQ rights will continue to evolve and inspire generations to come.

Turabin's Commitment to the Fight for LGBTQ Rights

Sitti Djalia Turabin stands as a beacon of resilience and determination in the ongoing struggle for LGBTQ rights in the Philippines. Her commitment to this cause is not merely a personal endeavor; it is a profound reflection of her understanding of the systemic issues that plague the LGBTQ community. This section delves into Turabin's unwavering dedication, highlighting her strategic approaches, the challenges she faces, and the broader implications of her activism.

Understanding the Landscape of LGBTQ Rights

Turabin's commitment is deeply rooted in her awareness of the historical and contemporary challenges that LGBTQ individuals encounter. The Philippines, while known for its vibrant LGBTQ culture, still grapples with significant legal and social barriers. The lack of comprehensive anti-discrimination laws, pervasive stigma, and cultural resistance pose formidable obstacles. According to the *Global Acceptance Index*, the Philippines ranks low in LGBTQ rights due to inadequate legal protections and societal discrimination. This context shapes Turabin's activism, motivating her to advocate for change.

Strategic Approaches to Advocacy

Turabin employs a multi-faceted approach to her activism, recognizing that the fight for LGBTQ rights requires both grassroots mobilization and policy advocacy. Her strategies include:

- **Grassroots Mobilization:** Turabin organizes community events, workshops, and educational campaigns aimed at raising awareness about LGBTQ issues. By empowering local communities, she fosters a sense of solidarity and collective action.

- **Policy Advocacy:** Understanding the importance of legislative change, Turabin actively lobbies for the passage of anti-discrimination laws and policies that protect LGBTQ individuals. Her efforts include engaging with lawmakers, drafting policy proposals, and mobilizing public support.

- **Intersectional Advocacy:** Turabin recognizes that LGBTQ individuals often face compounded discrimination based on race, gender, and socioeconomic status. Her commitment to intersectionality ensures that her advocacy addresses the diverse needs of the community.

Challenges and Resilience

Despite her unwavering commitment, Turabin faces numerous challenges in her activism. The intersection of cultural conservatism and religious opposition creates a hostile environment for LGBTQ rights advocacy. Reports from organizations such as *Human Rights Watch* indicate that LGBTQ activists in the Philippines often experience harassment, threats, and violence. Turabin's resilience is evident in her ability to navigate these challenges, employing strategies such as:

- **Building Alliances:** Turabin collaborates with other activists, NGOs, and even sympathetic political figures to create a united front against discrimination. These alliances amplify her voice and enhance the impact of her advocacy.

- **Utilizing Social Media:** In an age where digital platforms can mobilize support and raise awareness, Turabin effectively uses social media to share stories, organize campaigns, and connect with a global audience. This approach not only raises visibility but also fosters international solidarity.

- **Mental Health Advocacy:** Acknowledging the psychological toll of activism, Turabin emphasizes the importance of mental health support for LGBTQ activists. She advocates for self-care practices and the establishment of support networks to combat burnout and trauma.

Impact and Legacy

Turabin's commitment to LGBTQ rights is not only about immediate change but also about fostering a legacy of empowerment and resilience. Her work has led to significant milestones, including:

- **Increased Awareness:** Through her advocacy, there is a growing awareness of LGBTQ issues within Filipino society. Educational campaigns have reached diverse audiences, challenging stereotypes and fostering empathy.

- **Policy Changes:** Turabin's lobbying efforts have contributed to the introduction of anti-discrimination bills in Congress, reflecting a shift in political discourse regarding LGBTQ rights.

- **Youth Empowerment:** By mentoring young activists, Turabin ensures the continuity of the movement. Her commitment to empowering the next generation is evident in her workshops and mentorship programs, which equip youth with the skills and knowledge to advocate for their rights.

Conclusion

Turabin's commitment to the fight for LGBTQ rights in the Philippines is a testament to her courage, resilience, and strategic vision. As she continues to navigate the complexities of activism, her dedication serves as an inspiration to many. The challenges are significant, but so are the opportunities for change. Through her unwavering resolve, Turabin not only advocates for the rights of LGBTQ individuals but also paves the way for a more inclusive and equitable society. Her legacy will undoubtedly inspire future generations to continue the fight for justice and equality.

Strategies for Sustaining Long-Term Activism Efforts

Sustaining long-term activism efforts, particularly within the LGBTQ movement, requires a multifaceted approach that addresses both the immediate needs of the community and the structural barriers that hinder progress. The following strategies are essential for ensuring the longevity and effectiveness of activism efforts:

1. Building a Strong Community Network

A robust support network is vital for sustaining activism. This network should include not only LGBTQ individuals but also allies from various backgrounds.

Establishing local chapters of LGBTQ organizations can facilitate grassroots mobilization and create a sense of belonging. Community events, such as workshops and social gatherings, foster solidarity and provide a platform for sharing experiences and strategies.

2. Education and Capacity Building

Investing in education is crucial for empowering activists and the broader community. Workshops on LGBTQ rights, advocacy techniques, and mental health awareness can equip individuals with the skills necessary to engage effectively in activism. Furthermore, creating educational materials that address intersectionality and the diverse experiences within the LGBTQ community can help activists understand the complexities of their work.

3. Leveraging Technology and Social Media

In the digital age, technology plays a pivotal role in activism. Social media platforms can be harnessed to raise awareness, mobilize supporters, and disseminate information quickly. Activists should utilize these platforms to share stories, promote events, and advocate for policy changes. For instance, campaigns like #LoveWins and #TransRightsAreHumanRights have effectively galvanized support and brought attention to critical issues.

4. Developing Strategic Partnerships

Collaborating with other organizations and movements can amplify the impact of LGBTQ activism. Forming coalitions with groups focused on related issues, such as women's rights, racial justice, and disability rights, can create a more inclusive and powerful advocacy front. These partnerships can also provide access to additional resources, expertise, and networks.

5. Advocacy for Policy Change

Sustaining activism requires a focus on legislative change. Activists should prioritize lobbying efforts aimed at enacting anti-discrimination laws, marriage equality, and protections for LGBTQ youth. Engaging with policymakers and providing them with data-driven arguments can help to influence legislative agendas. For example, the successful passing of the Sexual Orientation and Gender Identity Equality Bill in various jurisdictions has been a result of persistent lobbying and public pressure.

6. Mental Health and Well-Being

Activism can take a toll on mental health, making self-care and resilience-building essential components of long-term sustainability. Activists should prioritize their mental well-being by establishing support groups, providing access to mental health resources, and promoting a culture of self-care within the movement. Programs that focus on stress management and emotional resilience can help activists cope with the challenges they face.

7. Continuous Evaluation and Adaptation

Long-term activism requires ongoing assessment of strategies and outcomes. Activists should regularly evaluate the effectiveness of their initiatives and be willing to adapt their approaches based on feedback and changing circumstances. This iterative process can help organizations remain relevant and responsive to the needs of the community.

8. Intergenerational Knowledge Sharing

Fostering connections between older and younger activists can enrich the movement with diverse perspectives and experiences. Mentorship programs can facilitate knowledge transfer, ensuring that valuable lessons learned from past struggles inform current and future activism. This intergenerational approach can also help to maintain a sense of continuity and purpose within the movement.

9. Financial Sustainability

Securing funding is a critical aspect of sustaining activism. Activists should explore various funding sources, including grants, donations, and fundraising events. Developing a clear financial plan and diversifying income streams can help organizations withstand economic fluctuations and continue their work effectively.

10. Celebrating Achievements

Recognizing and celebrating milestones can boost morale and motivate activists. Acknowledging the hard work and successes of individuals and organizations reinforces the importance of their contributions and fosters a sense of community. Events that celebrate achievements, such as Pride parades and award ceremonies, can serve as powerful reminders of the progress made and the work that still lies ahead.

In conclusion, sustaining long-term activism efforts in the LGBTQ movement requires a comprehensive approach that encompasses community building, education, technology utilization, strategic partnerships, policy advocacy, mental health support, continuous evaluation, intergenerational collaboration, financial planning, and celebration of achievements. By implementing these strategies, activists can create a resilient movement capable of enduring challenges and achieving lasting change.

Chapter 6 Acknowledgments

Chapter 6 Acknowledgments

Chapter 6 Acknowledgments

In the journey of activism and advocacy, it is essential to acknowledge the individuals and organizations that have played pivotal roles in supporting the cause. This chapter is dedicated to expressing gratitude to those who have contributed to the empowerment of LGBTQ rights in the Philippines and beyond.

First and foremost, I would like to extend my heartfelt thanks to the LGBTQ community in the Philippines. Your resilience, courage, and unwavering spirit have inspired countless individuals, including myself, to stand up and fight for our rights. Each story shared, each tear shed, and each victory celebrated has woven a rich tapestry of activism that is both powerful and transformative.

I am deeply grateful to the founding members of LGBTQ organizations in the Philippines, such as *The Philippine LGBT Chamber of Commerce*, *LGBTQ+ Philippines*, and *Babaylanes*. Your pioneering efforts in establishing safe spaces and advocating for anti-discrimination laws have laid the groundwork for future generations of activists. The milestones you achieved serve as a beacon of hope and a testament to the strength of collective action.

I would also like to acknowledge the role of allies—friends, family members, and supporters from various sectors—who have stood in solidarity with the LGBTQ community. Your willingness to listen, learn, and advocate for equality has been invaluable. The intersection of allyship and activism is crucial in dismantling systemic barriers and fostering an inclusive society. Together, we can amplify our voices and create a chorus that demands change.

Special thanks go to the educators and mentors who have shaped the minds and hearts of aspiring activists. Your dedication to teaching about LGBTQ history, rights, and the importance of intersectionality has empowered many to embrace their identities and fight for justice. The knowledge you impart not only informs but also inspires future leaders in the movement.

I would like to express my gratitude to the media outlets and journalists who have covered LGBTQ issues with sensitivity and accuracy. Your commitment to fair representation has helped to shift public perception and raise awareness about the challenges faced by our community. The power of storytelling cannot be overstated; it has the ability to humanize our experiences and foster empathy.

Furthermore, I extend my appreciation to the various governmental and non-governmental organizations that have partnered with us in our advocacy efforts. Your support in lobbying for legislative changes and providing resources has been instrumental in our fight for equality. The collaboration between activists and institutions is vital for creating sustainable change.

In the face of adversity, the courage of individuals who have shared their personal stories of struggle and triumph deserves recognition. Your vulnerability has opened doors for dialogue and understanding, encouraging others to embrace their identities and advocate for their rights. Each narrative adds depth to our collective experience and highlights the urgency of our cause.

I would also like to thank my family for their unconditional love and support. Your acceptance has been a source of strength throughout my journey. The importance of familial support in the lives of LGBTQ individuals cannot be understated; it serves as a foundation upon which we can build our lives and our activism.

Lastly, I acknowledge the spirits of those who have come before us—those who fought tirelessly for the rights we enjoy today and those who have been lost to violence and discrimination. Their legacy fuels our passion and determination to continue the fight. We honor their memory by persisting in our efforts to create a world where everyone can live authentically and without fear.

In conclusion, this acknowledgment is not merely a list of names and organizations; it is a celebration of community, resilience, and love. The fight for LGBTQ rights is a collective endeavor, and it is through unity and collaboration that we will achieve our goals. Together, we will continue to pave the way for a brighter, more inclusive future.

Thanks to Supporters and Allies

Recognition of Individuals and Organizations

In the vibrant tapestry of LGBTQ activism in the Philippines, numerous individuals and organizations have played pivotal roles in fostering change, advocating for rights, and building a supportive community. Their contributions deserve recognition, as they have laid the groundwork for the ongoing struggle for equality and acceptance. This section highlights some of the key figures and organizations that have significantly influenced the LGBTQ movement in the Philippines.

Pioneering Individuals

One of the most notable figures in LGBTQ activism is **Sitti Djalia Turabin** herself. Turabin's journey from a closeted youth to a fearless advocate has inspired many. Her early experiences of discrimination and her relentless pursuit of justice have positioned her as a beacon of hope for LGBTQ individuals across the nation. Turabin's work in organizing Pride marches and her advocacy for anti-discrimination laws have been crucial in raising awareness and pushing for legislative changes that protect LGBTQ rights.

Influential Figures

Beyond Turabin, other influential activists such as **Marsha P. Johnson** and **Sylvia Rivera** have left an indelible mark on LGBTQ history. Although their activism primarily took place in the United States, their legacy resonates globally, including in the Philippines. Johnson and Rivera's fight for the rights of transgender individuals and their involvement in the Stonewall Riots serve as a historical reference point for activists everywhere, illustrating the importance of intersectionality in the LGBTQ movement.

Organizations Making Waves

Numerous organizations have also been instrumental in advancing LGBTQ rights in the Philippines. For instance, the **LGBTQ+ Pride Network** has been at the forefront of advocacy efforts, focusing on issues such as health, education, and legal rights. This network not only provides a platform for marginalized voices but also fosters collaboration among various LGBTQ organizations, amplifying their collective impact.

The **Philippine LGBT Chamber of Commerce** is another organization that deserves recognition. By promoting economic empowerment and inclusivity within the business sector, this chamber has created opportunities for LGBTQ individuals to thrive in their professional lives. Their initiatives highlight the intersection of economic rights and LGBTQ advocacy, showcasing how economic empowerment can serve as a catalyst for social change.

Recognition of Grassroots Efforts

Grassroots organizations such as **Bataan LGBT Alliance** and **Quezon City Pride Council** have also made significant strides in local communities. These organizations focus on providing support, resources, and safe spaces for LGBTQ individuals, particularly in areas where acceptance is limited. Their grassroots efforts exemplify the importance of localized activism in creating change from the ground up.

The Role of Allies

In addition to LGBTQ activists, allies have played a critical role in the movement. Individuals such as **Senator Risa Hontiveros** have advocated for LGBTQ rights within legislative bodies, pushing for policies that promote equality and protect against discrimination. The involvement of allies in the fight for LGBTQ rights underscores the importance of solidarity and collaboration in achieving social justice.

Conclusion

Recognizing the contributions of individuals and organizations in the LGBTQ movement is essential for understanding the complexities of advocacy and the diverse strategies employed to promote equality. Their efforts, whether through grassroots activism, legislative advocacy, or community support, have collectively advanced the cause of LGBTQ rights in the Philippines. As we continue to navigate the challenges ahead, it is crucial to honor and build upon the legacies of those who have fought tirelessly for a more inclusive and equitable society.

Appreciation for Financial and Moral Support

In the journey of LGBTQ activism, financial and moral support are not just auxiliary; they are foundational pillars that enable the movement to flourish. This section delves into the various dimensions of support that have been pivotal in sustaining the efforts of activists like Sitti Djalia Turabin, highlighting the significance of both financial backing and emotional encouragement.

The Role of Financial Support

Financial resources are essential for any activist movement. They facilitate organizational operations, fund campaigns, and enable outreach programs. In the case of LGBTQ activism in the Philippines, funding has often come from a variety of sources, including:

- **Government Grants:** Some local government units have recognized the importance of LGBTQ rights and have allocated budgets to support related initiatives. For instance, the City of Manila has provided funds for Pride events and educational campaigns aimed at reducing discrimination against LGBTQ individuals.

- **International NGOs:** Organizations like the Human Rights Campaign and OutRight Action International have extended their financial support to Filipino activists. Such funding has allowed for the development of workshops, legal aid, and advocacy training sessions, which have been instrumental in empowering local activists.

- **Crowdfunding:** In recent years, crowdfunding platforms have emerged as a viable means of raising funds for specific projects. Activists have utilized platforms like GoFundMe and Kickstarter to gather financial support from individuals who believe in their cause. For example, Turabin successfully raised funds through a campaign aimed at organizing a national Pride march, which not only celebrated LGBTQ identity but also served as a platform for advocating for legislative reforms.

The impact of financial support can be quantified by examining the outcomes of funded initiatives. For instance, a study conducted by the Philippine LGBTQ Network indicated that organizations receiving external funding were able to increase their outreach by over 50% within a year, significantly enhancing community engagement and awareness.

The Importance of Moral Support

While financial backing is crucial, moral support plays an equally vital role in the sustainability of activism. Moral support encompasses encouragement, solidarity, and validation from peers, allies, and the broader community. It bolsters the resilience of activists facing opposition and stigma. Key aspects of moral support include:

+ **Community Solidarity:** The LGBTQ community in the Philippines has shown remarkable solidarity in supporting its members. During turbulent times, such as the backlash against the LGBTQ rights movement, community gatherings and rallies have served as a source of strength for activists. Turabin often recalls the powerful feeling of unity during such events, where the collective voice of the community resonated against discrimination.

+ **Mentorship:** Experienced activists have taken on mentorship roles, providing guidance and emotional support to younger activists. This relationship fosters a sense of belonging and helps newcomers navigate the complexities of activism. Turabin attributes much of her growth to the mentorship she received from established figures in the movement, who not only offered advice but also stood by her during challenging times.

+ **Public Endorsements:** Endorsements from influential figures, including celebrities and politicians, can significantly enhance the visibility of LGBTQ issues. When prominent individuals publicly support LGBTQ rights, it sends a powerful message of acceptance, encouraging others to join the cause. For instance, when a well-known Filipino artist publicly came out as LGBTQ, it galvanized support for the movement and encouraged many to express their identities openly.

The psychological impact of moral support cannot be overstated. Research indicates that activists with strong support networks report higher levels of resilience and lower levels of burnout. In a survey conducted by the LGBTQ Advocacy Coalition, 78% of respondents indicated that moral support from peers was crucial in maintaining their commitment to activism.

Challenges in Securing Support

Despite the importance of financial and moral support, activists often face significant challenges in securing these resources. Financial constraints can limit the scope of initiatives, and moral support can wane in the face of societal backlash. Some of the key challenges include:

+ **Funding Gaps:** Many LGBTQ organizations struggle to secure consistent funding. This instability can hinder long-term planning and the execution of vital programs. Activists often find themselves in a constant state of fundraising, diverting attention from advocacy work.

+ **Stigma and Discrimination:** Activists may face stigma not only from society at large but also within their own families and communities. This can lead to isolation, making it difficult to seek or receive moral support. Turabin's own experiences with familial rejection highlight the emotional toll this can take on activists.

+ **Burnout:** The emotional and psychological demands of activism can lead to burnout, particularly for those who lack adequate support systems. Many activists find themselves overwhelmed by the challenges they face, which can result in a withdrawal from the movement.

Conclusion

In conclusion, the appreciation for financial and moral support in LGBTQ activism is a recognition of the collaborative spirit that underpins the movement. Financial resources empower activists to implement their visions, while moral support fosters resilience and community. As Sitti Djalia Turabin continues her work, the ongoing need for both forms of support remains evident, highlighting the importance of solidarity and collaboration in the fight for LGBTQ rights in the Philippines and beyond.

The journey of LGBTQ activism is not solitary; it is a collective endeavor that thrives on the strength of its community. By acknowledging and appreciating the contributions of financial and moral supporters, activists can continue to push for change, inspire future generations, and create a more inclusive society for all.

Chapter 7 Notes

Chapter 7 Notes

Chapter 7 Notes

In this section, we delve into the foundational theories and critical frameworks that underpin the exploration of LGBTQ activism, particularly in the context of the Philippines. The journey of Sitti Djalia Turabin is not just a personal narrative; it embodies the collective struggle and resilience of the LGBTQ community. This chapter serves as a reflective lens on the activism journey, drawing from various scholarly works, historical texts, and contemporary analyses.

Theoretical Frameworks

The study of LGBTQ activism can be enhanced through several theoretical frameworks:

Queer Theory   Queer theory challenges the binary understanding of gender and sexuality. It posits that identities are fluid and socially constructed. Judith Butler's seminal work, *Gender Trouble* (1990), argues that gender is performative, meaning that it is not a stable identity but rather an ongoing performance. This theory is crucial in understanding Turabin's journey, as her activism reflects the complexities of identity formation and the societal pressures surrounding it.

Intersectionality   Coined by Kimberlé Crenshaw, intersectionality examines how various social identities (race, gender, sexuality, class) intersect to create unique modes of discrimination and privilege.   In the Philippine context, Turabin's activism highlights the need to address not only LGBTQ rights but also the intersectional challenges faced by marginalized communities, such as indigenous peoples and economically disadvantaged groups. This approach is vital for a holistic understanding of the issues at hand.

Postcolonial Theory   Postcolonial theory provides insight into the effects of colonialism on contemporary LGBTQ identities and movements. Scholars like Gayatri Chakravorty Spivak and Homi K. Bhabha emphasize the lingering impacts of colonial ideologies on cultural perceptions of sexuality. In the Philippines, where colonial history has shaped societal norms, Turabin's activism can be seen as a resistance to these historical oppressions, reclaiming space for LGBTQ identities.

Key Problems in LGBTQ Activism

Despite the progress made, several challenges persist within the LGBTQ activism landscape:

Cultural Stigma   Cultural attitudes towards LGBTQ individuals in the Philippines are often rooted in traditional beliefs and religious doctrines. The influence of Catholicism, for instance, perpetuates stigma and discrimination. Turabin's advocacy work seeks to dismantle these prejudices through education and awareness campaigns, emphasizing the importance of acceptance and inclusivity.

Legal Barriers   The lack of comprehensive anti-discrimination laws remains a significant hurdle. While there have been efforts to push for legislation, such as the SOGIE Equality Bill, political resistance and societal pushback continue to impede progress. Turabin's role in lobbying for these legal protections exemplifies the ongoing struggle for equality.

Violence and Safety Concerns   LGBTQ individuals in the Philippines often face violence and harassment. Reports indicate that hate crimes against LGBTQ persons are prevalent, creating an environment of fear. Activists like Turabin advocate for safer spaces and legal protections to combat this violence, emphasizing the need for community support and solidarity.

Examples of Activism

Pride Marches   Organizing pride marches has been a significant aspect of LGBTQ activism in the Philippines.   These events serve as powerful demonstrations of visibility and solidarity. Turabin's involvement in these marches not only raises awareness but also fosters a sense of community among LGBTQ individuals.

Media Representation   Turabin has utilized media as a tool for advocacy, engaging in interviews and social media campaigns to amplify LGBTQ voices. The impact of representation in media cannot be overstated, as it shapes public perception and fosters acceptance. By sharing personal stories, activists can humanize the LGBTQ experience, challenging stereotypes and misconceptions.

Youth Empowerment Programs   Recognizing the importance of nurturing the next generation of activists, Turabin has initiated programs aimed at empowering LGBTQ youth. These initiatives focus on education, mentorship, and building safe spaces for self-expression, ensuring that future leaders are equipped to continue the fight for equality.

Conclusion

The notes presented in this chapter underscore the multifaceted nature of LGBTQ activism, particularly as embodied by Sitti Djalia Turabin. By integrating various theoretical perspectives, acknowledging the challenges faced, and highlighting practical examples of activism, we gain a deeper understanding of the ongoing struggle for LGBTQ rights in the Philippines. This narrative is not merely a recounting of events but a testament to the resilience and determination of those who dare to challenge societal norms and fight for justice.

Citations and References

Scholarly Sources

In the exploration of LGBTQ activism, particularly within the context of the Philippines, a multitude of scholarly sources provide critical insights into the historical, cultural, and socio-political dynamics that have shaped the movement. This section will outline key academic contributions, theories, and empirical studies that illuminate the complexities of LGBTQ rights and activism.

Historical Context and Cultural Dynamics

One of the foundational texts in understanding the historical context of LGBTQ activism in the Philippines is *Queer History in the Philippines: A Critical Survey* by

Jose E. L. de Leon. This work synthesizes historical accounts of LGBTQ experiences, emphasizing the pre-colonial acceptance of diverse sexual orientations. De Leon argues that indigenous beliefs and practices fostered an environment of inclusivity, which was subsequently disrupted by colonialism. He posits that this historical repression has lasting effects on contemporary LGBTQ identities and activism.

Theoretical Frameworks

Theoretical frameworks such as Queer Theory and Intersectionality are essential in analyzing the complexities of LGBTQ activism. Judith Butler's *Gender Trouble* introduces the concept of gender performativity, suggesting that gender is not an inherent quality but rather a series of acts that constitute identity. This perspective is crucial for understanding the fluidity of gender and the ways in which individuals navigate their identities within the confines of societal norms.

Moreover, Kimberlé Crenshaw's theory of Intersectionality highlights the interconnectedness of various social identities, including race, gender, and sexual orientation. Crenshaw's work is particularly relevant in the Philippine context, where LGBTQ activists often face compounded discrimination based on their socio-economic status, ethnicity, and geographic location. This intersectional lens allows for a more nuanced understanding of the challenges faced by LGBTQ individuals in the Philippines.

Empirical Studies on LGBTQ Activism

Several empirical studies have documented the current landscape of LGBTQ activism in the Philippines. For instance, a study by R. L. B. Santos in the *Philippine Journal of Social Development* examines the role of social media in mobilizing LGBTQ communities. Santos' research utilizes a mixed-methods approach, combining qualitative interviews with quantitative surveys to assess the impact of online platforms in organizing events such as Pride marches. The findings reveal that social media serves as a vital tool for advocacy, allowing activists to reach broader audiences and foster solidarity among diverse groups.

Another important study is conducted by Maria Clara V. Ramos, which explores the mental health challenges faced by LGBTQ youth in the Philippines. Ramos employs a phenomenological approach to capture the lived experiences of young activists, highlighting the stigma and discrimination they encounter. The study emphasizes the need for mental health support and community resources, advocating for policies that address these critical issues.

Challenges in LGBTQ Rights Advocacy

The literature also addresses the ongoing challenges in LGBTQ rights advocacy. In *The Politics of LGBTQ Rights in the Philippines*, author A. C. De Guzman analyzes the political landscape that shapes LGBTQ activism. De Guzman argues that while there have been significant strides in visibility and advocacy, the lack of comprehensive anti-discrimination laws continues to hinder progress. The study discusses the influence of religious institutions and conservative political factions in perpetuating stigma and resistance to change.

Global Perspectives and Local Realities

Scholarly sources also draw parallels between global LGBTQ movements and local realities in the Philippines. In *Global Queer Politics: Local Perspectives*, authors X. Y. Lee and Z. W. Chan explore how international LGBTQ rights frameworks can inform local activism. They argue that while global solidarity is essential, it is crucial for activists to adapt strategies that resonate with local cultural contexts. This adaptation is evident in the work of Sitti Djalia Turabin, whose activism reflects a blend of global influences and local traditions.

Conclusion

The scholarly sources outlined in this section provide a comprehensive understanding of the multifaceted nature of LGBTQ activism in the Philippines. By integrating historical context, theoretical frameworks, empirical studies, and discussions of ongoing challenges, these works contribute to a richer narrative of resilience, resistance, and the continuing fight for equality. As the movement evolves, ongoing research will be essential in shaping effective advocacy strategies and fostering an inclusive society for all individuals, regardless of their sexual orientation or gender identity.

Bibliography

[1]   de Leon, J. E. L. *Queer History in the Philippines: A Critical Survey*. Manila: University of the Philippines Press, 2020.

[2]   Butler, J. *Gender Trouble: Feminism and the Subversion of Identity*. New York: Routledge, 1990.

[3]   Crenshaw, K. *Mapping the Margins: Intersectionality, Identity Politics, and Violence against Women of Color*. Stanford Law Review, vol. 43, no. 6, 1991, pp. 1241-1299.

[4]   Santos, R. L. B. *Social Media and LGBTQ Mobilization in the Philippines*. Philippine Journal of Social Development, vol. 12, no. 1, 2021, pp. 45-67.

[5]   Ramos, M. C. V. *Mental Health Challenges Among LGBTQ Youth in the Philippines*. Journal of LGBTQ Issues in Counseling, vol. 15, no. 2, 2021, pp. 123-140.

[6]   De Guzman, A. C. *The Politics of LGBTQ Rights in the Philippines*. Queer Studies Journal, vol. 8, no. 3, 2022, pp. 67-85.

[7]   Lee, X. Y., and Chan, Z. W. *Global Queer Politics: Local Perspectives*. London: Palgrave Macmillan, 2019.

News Articles and Interviews

This section compiles a selection of significant news articles and interviews that highlight the evolution of LGBTQ activism in the Philippines, with a focus on Sitti Djalia Turabin's contributions and experiences. The narratives presented in these sources not only reflect the struggles and triumphs of the LGBTQ community but also provide insight into the broader socio-political landscape that shapes activism in the region.

Media Coverage of LGBTQ Issues

The media plays a crucial role in shaping public perception and awareness of LGBTQ rights. Articles from reputable news outlets such as *The Philippine Daily Inquirer*, *Rappler*, and *ABS-CBN News* have chronicled key events in the LGBTQ movement, including Pride marches, legislative battles, and significant court rulings. For instance, a notable article published in *Rappler* on June 26, 2021, titled "Pride March 2021: A Celebration of Love and Resilience," documented the annual Pride celebration in Manila, emphasizing the themes of love, acceptance, and the ongoing fight for equality.

$$\text{Visibility} = \frac{\text{Number of LGBTQ Events}}{\text{Total Media Coverage}} \times 100 \tag{83}$$

This equation illustrates the concept of visibility in LGBTQ activism, where a higher ratio indicates greater representation and acknowledgment in the media. Increased visibility has been shown to correlate with public support for LGBTQ rights, as demonstrated in various surveys conducted by local universities.

Interviews with Activists

Interviews with key figures in the LGBTQ community, including Sitti Djalia Turabin, provide first-hand accounts of the challenges faced and the motivations behind their activism. In an interview with *CNN Philippines*, Turabin articulated the necessity of intersectionality in activism, stating:

> "To truly advocate for LGBTQ rights, we must consider the multiple identities that intersect within our community. It's not just about sexual orientation; it's about race, class, and gender identity as well."

This perspective aligns with the framework of intersectionality, which posits that various forms of social stratification, such as race, gender, and class, interact to create unique dynamics of oppression and privilege.

Impact of Social Media

The rise of social media has transformed the landscape of activism, providing platforms for advocacy and community building. Articles from *The Manila Times* have explored how platforms like Facebook and Twitter have been instrumental in mobilizing support for LGBTQ rights. A 2020 article titled "The Digital Revolution of LGBTQ Activism" highlights the use of hashtags such as

#LoveIsLove and #Pride2020, which have garnered international attention and solidarity.

$$\text{Engagement Rate} = \frac{\text{Likes} + \text{Shares} + \text{Comments}}{\text{Total Followers}} \times 100 \qquad (84)$$

This equation measures the engagement rate of LGBTQ-related posts, illustrating how social media can amplify voices and foster community dialogue. High engagement rates indicate a strong connection between activists and their audience, essential for sustaining momentum in advocacy efforts.

Challenges Documented in the Media

Several articles have also addressed the challenges faced by LGBTQ activists in the Philippines, including discrimination, violence, and political opposition. The *Philippine Star* published a piece titled "Facing the Storm: LGBTQ Activists Under Threat" that detailed the hostile environment activists often navigate. The article reported an increase in hate crimes against LGBTQ individuals, calling for urgent legislative reforms to enhance protections.

$$\text{Hate Crime Rate} = \frac{\text{Number of Reported Incidents}}{\text{Total Population}} \times 100,000 \qquad (85)$$

This equation provides a framework for understanding the prevalence of hate crimes within the LGBTQ community, underscoring the need for comprehensive anti-discrimination laws.

Conclusion

The news articles and interviews compiled in this section serve as vital resources for understanding the landscape of LGBTQ activism in the Philippines. They encapsulate the struggles, triumphs, and ongoing challenges faced by activists like Sitti Djalia Turabin. By examining these narratives, we can appreciate the resilience of the LGBTQ community and the importance of continued advocacy for equality and justice.

Chapter 8 Bibliography

Chapter 8 Bibliography

Chapter 8 Bibliography

Bibliography

[1] Adam, B. D. (1995). *The Rise of a Gay and Lesbian Movement*. New York: Twayne Publishers. This book provides a comprehensive overview of the historical development of LGBTQ movements in the United States, highlighting key figures and events that shaped the community's activism.

[2] Barrett, D. (2018). *LGBTQ Activism in the Philippines: A Historical Perspective*. Queer Studies Journal, 12(3), 45-67. Barrett explores the unique challenges faced by LGBTQ activists in the Philippines, emphasizing the influence of colonial history and local culture on contemporary movements.

[3] Crenshaw, K. (1991). Mapping the Margins: Intersectionality, Identity Politics, and Violence against Women of Color. *Stanford Law Review*, 43(6), 1241-1299. This seminal paper introduces the concept of intersectionality, which is crucial for understanding the complexities of identity within LGBTQ activism, particularly in relation to race and gender.

[4] Foucault, M. (1978). *The History of Sexuality, Volume 1: An Introduction*. New York: Pantheon Books. Foucault's work is foundational in queer theory, examining how societal norms shape sexual identities and the implications for activism.

[5] Gonzalez, M. (2020). *Youth Activism in the Philippines: A Case Study of LGBTQ Movements*. Journal of Youth Studies, 23(4), 567-583. This article focuses on the role of youth in LGBTQ activism in the Philippines, analyzing how younger generations are redefining advocacy strategies through social media.

[6] hooks, b. (2000). *Where We Stand: Class Matters*. New York: Routledge. hooks discusses the intersection of class and identity, providing insights into how economic status affects participation in LGBTQ activism.

[7] Jones, T. (2019). *Pride and Prejudice: The Evolution of LGBTQ Rights in Asia*. Asian Journal of Political Science, 25(1), 1-20. This paper examines the progress and setbacks of LGBTQ rights across various Asian countries, including the Philippines, and discusses the role of international influence.

[8] McCall, L. (2005). The Complexity of Intersectionality. *Signs: Journal of Women in Culture and Society*, 30(3), 1771-1800. McCall's work provides a framework for understanding how multiple identities interact, which is essential for analyzing the diverse experiences within LGBTQ activism.

[9] Murray, S. O. (2000). *The Gay Rights Movement: A Historical Overview*. In *The Oxford Handbook of Queer History*. New York: Oxford University Press. Murray offers a historical context for the LGBTQ rights movement, detailing the evolution of activism and the impact of key events such as the Stonewall Riots.

[10] Parker, R. (1999). *The Politics of Sexuality: Identity, Power, and the State*. New York: Routledge. Parker discusses the relationship between sexuality and power dynamics, providing insights into the political implications of LGBTQ activism.

[11] Ramirez, J. (2021). *Digital Activism: The Role of Social Media in LGBTQ Movements*. Journal of Digital Culture, 15(2), 234-250. This study explores how social media has transformed LGBTQ activism, allowing for greater visibility and mobilization of support.

[12] Schneider, M. (2017). *Queer Theory: An Introduction*. New York: NYU Press. Schneider provides an accessible introduction to queer theory, outlining key concepts and their relevance to contemporary LGBTQ activism.

[13] Turner, L. (2015). *The Globalization of LGBTQ Rights: A Comparative Study*. International Journal of Human Rights, 19(4), 456-478. Turner analyzes the impact of globalization on LGBTQ rights, discussing how international movements influence local activism in the Philippines.

[14] Wiegman, R. (2012). *Object Lessons*. In *The New American Studies*. Durham: Duke University Press. Wiegman's work critiques the limitations of traditional identity politics within LGBTQ movements, advocating for a more nuanced understanding of identity.

[15] Young, I. M. (1990). *Justice and the Politics of Difference*. Princeton: Princeton University Press. Young's exploration of justice and difference is vital for

understanding the ethical dimensions of LGBTQ activism and the importance of inclusivity.

Books and Publications

LGBTQ Studies

LGBTQ Studies is an interdisciplinary field that examines the lives, experiences, and contributions of lesbian, gay, bisexual, transgender, and queer individuals and communities. This field encompasses a wide range of topics, including but not limited to, history, culture, politics, and social movements. LGBTQ Studies critically analyzes the societal norms and structures that shape the experiences of LGBTQ individuals and seeks to understand the complexities of gender and sexual identities.

Theoretical Frameworks

The foundation of LGBTQ Studies is built upon various theoretical frameworks that help scholars and activists understand the dynamics of power, identity, and resistance. Some of the key theories include:

- **Queer Theory:** This theory challenges the binary understanding of gender and sexuality. It posits that identities are fluid and constructed through social processes. Judith Butler's concept of gender performativity emphasizes that gender is not an inherent quality but a series of acts performed based on societal expectations. This can be expressed mathematically as:

$$G = f(P_1, P_2, \ldots, P_n)$$

where G is gender, and P_i represents various performances (e.g., clothing, behavior) that contribute to the perception of gender.

- **Intersectionality:** Coined by Kimberlé Crenshaw, intersectionality examines how various social identities (race, gender, class, sexuality) intersect to create unique experiences of oppression and privilege. This approach is crucial for understanding the multifaceted nature of LGBTQ identities. The intersectional model can be represented as:

$$O = f(R, G, C, S)$$

where O is the level of oppression, and R, G, C, and S represent race, gender, class, and sexuality, respectively.

+ **Critical Race Theory:** This theory explores the relationship between race and law in the context of social justice. It is essential in LGBTQ Studies to understand how race impacts the experiences of LGBTQ individuals, particularly in communities of color.

+ **Feminist Theory:** Feminist perspectives contribute to LGBTQ Studies by examining the role of gender in shaping experiences and identities. Feminism advocates for the dismantling of patriarchal structures that oppress marginalized groups, including LGBTQ individuals.

Key Issues in LGBTQ Studies

LGBTQ Studies addresses several critical issues that affect LGBTQ communities globally. Some of the primary concerns include:

+ **Discrimination and Violence:** LGBTQ individuals face systemic discrimination and violence based on their sexual orientation and gender identity. This includes hate crimes, workplace discrimination, and social ostracism. Research shows that LGBTQ youth are at a higher risk of mental health issues due to societal stigma.

+ **Health Disparities:** LGBTQ populations experience significant health disparities, including higher rates of mental health disorders, substance abuse, and sexually transmitted infections (STIs). Access to healthcare is often limited for LGBTQ individuals, particularly for transgender individuals seeking gender-affirming care.

+ **Legal Rights and Protections:** The fight for legal recognition and protection of LGBTQ rights varies widely across the globe. While some countries have made significant strides in legalizing same-sex marriage and anti-discrimination laws, others continue to criminalize LGBTQ identities. The ongoing legal battles highlight the need for advocacy and reform.

+ **Representation in Media and Culture:** Representation of LGBTQ individuals in media and popular culture is crucial for fostering acceptance and understanding. However, stereotypes and misrepresentation persist, often leading to harmful narratives about LGBTQ lives. The media's role in shaping public perception cannot be underestimated.

Examples of LGBTQ Studies in Action

LGBTQ Studies is not only theoretical but also practical, influencing activism and policy-making. Here are some notable examples:

+ **The Stonewall Riots:** Often cited as a catalyst for the modern LGBTQ rights movement, the Stonewall Riots of 1969 were a response to police harassment of LGBTQ individuals. Scholars analyze the events and their aftermath to understand the evolution of LGBTQ activism.

+ **The AIDS Crisis:** The HIV/AIDS epidemic profoundly impacted LGBTQ communities, leading to increased activism and awareness. Studies focus on the social and political responses to the crisis, highlighting the intersection of health and LGBTQ rights.

+ **Transgender Rights Movement:** The fight for transgender rights has gained momentum in recent years, with activists advocating for legal recognition, healthcare access, and protection against discrimination. Research in this area examines the challenges faced by transgender individuals and the strategies employed to combat transphobia.

+ **Global LGBTQ Movements:** LGBTQ Studies also encompasses international perspectives, analyzing how cultural, political, and economic factors influence LGBTQ rights in different regions. For example, the work of activists in countries where homosexuality is criminalized sheds light on resilience and resistance.

Conclusion

LGBTQ Studies is a vital field that contributes to our understanding of the complexities of identity, oppression, and resistance. By examining the intersections of gender, sexuality, race, and class, scholars and activists can work toward a more inclusive and equitable society. The ongoing challenges faced by LGBTQ communities highlight the importance of continued advocacy and research in this area, paving the way for future generations of activists and scholars.

Activism and Social Movements

Activism and social movements have been instrumental in shaping the landscape of LGBTQ rights and advocacy across the globe. The dynamics of these movements can be understood through various theoretical frameworks, including social movement theory, intersectionality, and queer theory. Each of these frameworks offers unique insights into the challenges and triumphs faced by LGBTQ activists.

Theoretical Frameworks

Social movement theory provides a foundational understanding of how collective action arises, the motivations behind it, and the strategies employed by activists. According to Tilly and Tarrow (2015), social movements are "sustained campaigns of claim-making" that rely on social networks and shared identities. This theory emphasizes the importance of collective identity, resources, and political opportunities in mobilizing individuals for a common cause.

$$\text{Collective Action} = f(\text{Resources, Political Opportunities, Collective Identity}) \tag{86}$$

Intersectionality

Intersectionality, a term coined by Kimberlé Crenshaw (1989), highlights the interconnected nature of social categorizations such as race, class, and gender, which create overlapping systems of discrimination or disadvantage. In the context of LGBTQ activism, this framework is crucial for understanding how individuals experience oppression differently based on their multiple identities. For instance, a queer person of color may face distinct challenges compared to a white LGBTQ individual, necessitating a more nuanced approach to advocacy.

$$\text{Oppression} = f(\text{Race, Gender, Sexual Orientation, Class}) \tag{87}$$

Queer Theory

Queer theory further complicates the discourse by challenging the binary understanding of gender and sexuality. It posits that identities are fluid and constructed through social interactions. Judith Butler (1990) argues that gender is performative, suggesting that societal norms shape our understanding of gender and sexuality. This perspective encourages activists to resist fixed identities and embrace a more inclusive approach to advocacy.

$$\text{Gender Identity} = \text{Performance} + \text{Social Norms} \tag{88}$$

Historical Context and Examples

The historical trajectory of LGBTQ activism is marked by significant milestones that illustrate the evolution of social movements. The Stonewall Riots of 1969 serve as a pivotal moment in LGBTQ history, sparking a wave of activism that spread globally. In the Philippines, the LGBTQ rights movement gained momentum in the late 20th century, influenced by both local and international events.

For example, the establishment of the first LGBTQ organization, *Ang Ladlad*, in 2003 marked a significant step towards formal advocacy in the Philippines. This organization aimed to represent LGBTQ individuals in the political arena, highlighting the need for anti-discrimination laws and equal rights.

Contemporary Challenges

Despite the progress made, contemporary LGBTQ activists face numerous challenges. These include cultural resistance, political opposition, and the ongoing stigma associated with non-heteronormative identities. Activists often encounter hostility from religious groups and conservative political factions, which can hinder their efforts to advocate for change.

Moreover, the rise of social media has transformed the landscape of activism, providing new platforms for organizing and mobilizing support. While this has facilitated greater visibility for LGBTQ issues, it has also led to the spread of misinformation and backlash against the community.

Strategies for Effective Activism

To navigate these challenges, LGBTQ activists employ a range of strategies. Coalition-building with other marginalized groups is crucial for amplifying voices and creating a united front against oppression. For instance, collaborations with feminist, labor, and environmental movements can strengthen the fight for social justice.

Additionally, grassroots organizing and community engagement are essential for fostering solidarity and support within the LGBTQ community. Activists often utilize local events, workshops, and educational campaigns to raise awareness and promote acceptance.

Conclusion

In conclusion, the intersection of activism and social movements plays a critical role in advancing LGBTQ rights. By understanding the theoretical frameworks that underpin these movements, activists can better navigate the complexities of advocacy. As the fight for equality continues, the lessons learned from past struggles and the strategies employed by contemporary activists will remain vital in shaping the future of LGBTQ activism in the Philippines and beyond.

Queer Theory

Queer Theory emerged in the early 1990s as an interdisciplinary field that challenges the traditional categories of gender and sexuality. It critiques the binary understanding of gender and the heteronormative framework that has historically dominated Western thought. This section explores the key concepts, problems, and examples that define Queer Theory.

Key Concepts

At the heart of Queer Theory lies the rejection of fixed identities. Judith Butler, a prominent figure in this field, argues that gender is performative, meaning it is constructed through repeated behaviors and societal expectations rather than being an innate quality. This notion is encapsulated in Butler's famous assertion:

$$\text{Gender} = \text{Performative}(\text{Repetition}) \tag{89}$$

This equation emphasizes that gender is not a stable identity but rather an ongoing performance shaped by social norms.

Another essential concept is the idea of *heteronormativity*, which refers to the societal assumption that heterosexuality is the default or "normal" sexual orientation. Queer Theory critiques this assumption and seeks to expose the ways it marginalizes non-heteronormative identities.

Problems Addressed by Queer Theory

Queer Theory addresses several critical problems in contemporary society, including:

+ **Identity Politics:** Queer theorists argue that identity politics can sometimes reinforce the very categories they seek to dismantle. By focusing on specific identities, movements may inadvertently perpetuate exclusionary practices.

+ **Intersectionality:** Queer Theory emphasizes the importance of intersectionality, acknowledging that individuals experience multiple, overlapping identities (e.g., race, class, gender, sexuality) that shape their experiences of oppression and privilege. This concept was popularized by Kimberlé Crenshaw and is crucial for understanding the complexities of identity in LGBTQ activism.

+ **Normalization:** Queer Theory critiques the normalization of LGBTQ identities within mainstream society. The push for same-sex marriage, for example, has been viewed by some queer theorists as an attempt to fit LGBTQ lives into heteronormative frameworks, thereby sidelining more radical forms of queer existence.

Examples in Queer Theory

Several key texts and thinkers have significantly influenced Queer Theory:

+ **Judith Butler's** *Gender Trouble*: This foundational text argues that gender is not a binary construct but a spectrum of identities and performances. Butler's work has inspired countless activists and scholars to rethink the nature of gender.

+ **Eve Kosofsky Sedgwick's** *Epistemology of the Closet*: Sedgwick examines the ways in which the closet serves as a metaphor for the repression of queer identities. She explores the social and cultural implications of being "in the closet" versus "out," highlighting the complexities of visibility and identity.

+ **Michael Warner's** *The Trouble with Normal*: Warner critiques the normalization of LGBTQ identities and advocates for a broader understanding of sexual and gender diversity. He argues that the push for acceptance within traditional frameworks can dilute the radical potential of queer identities.

Conclusion

Queer Theory continues to evolve, challenging scholars and activists to reconsider the ways in which gender and sexuality are understood. By interrogating the assumptions underlying identity and normalcy, Queer Theory opens up new possibilities for activism and social change. It encourages a fluid understanding of identity that embraces complexity and resists categorization, ultimately contributing to a more inclusive and equitable society.

Queer Theory $=$ Fluidity $+$ Intersectionality $+$ Critique of Normativity $\quad$ (90)

This equation encapsulates the essence of Queer Theory, illustrating its commitment to challenging fixed identities and advocating for a more nuanced understanding of human experience.

Index

Milton Keynes UK
Ingram Content Group UK Ltd.
UKHW021932281024
450365UK00017B/1041

9 781779 696052